EMPOWERING SME MANAGERS IN PALESTINE

T0304056

Empowering SME Managers in Palestine

FARHAD ANALOUI
University of Bradford, UK

and

MOHAMMED AL-MADHOUN
The Islamic University of Gaza, Palestine

LONDON AND NEW YORK

First published 2006 by Ashgate Publishing

Published 2016 by Routledge
2 Park Square, Milton Park, Abingdon, Oxfordshire OX14 4RN
711 Third Avenue, New York, NY 10017, USA

First issued in paperback 2016

Routledge is an imprint of the Taylor & Francis Group, an informa business

British Library Cataloguing in Publication Data
Analoui, Farhad, 1949-
    Empowering SME managers in Palestine
    1.Small business - Palestine - Management
    I.Title II.Al-Madhoun, Mohammed
    658'.022'095694

Library of Congress Control Number: 2005933815

ISBN 13: 978-1-138-27641-3 (pbk)
ISBN 13: 978-0-7546-4025-7 (hbk)

Contents

List of Figures

List of Tables

Abbreviations

EJ	East Jerusalem
EU	European Union
GCC	Gulf Co-operation Council
GETA	Government Employee Training Act
GS	Gaza Strip
HRD	Human Resource Development
HRM	Human Resource Management
IDP	Individual Development Programme
MD	Management Development
MOPIC	Ministry of Planning and International Co-operation
MT	Management Training
MTD	Management Training and Development
MTP	Management Training and Development Programme
NFID	National Foundation for Investment Development
NGO	Non-Governmental Organisation
NM	Number of Markets
NPE	New Palestinian Entity
OT	Occupied Territories, includes WB and GS
PCBS	Palestinian Central Bureau of Statistics
PDF	Palestine Development Funds
PDP	Palestine Development Plans
PLO	Palestinian Liberation Organization
PNA	Palestinian National Authority
PT	Palestinian Territories
RD	Research and Development
SMEs	Small and Micro Enterprises
SMET	Small and Micro Enterprises Training
SRS	Simple Random Sampling
SWOT	Strength Weakness Opportunity Threat
TD	Training and Development
TNA	Training Needs Assessment
TP	Training Programme
UN	United Nations
UNRWA	United Nations Relief and Work Agency for Palestinian Refugees in the Near East
WB	West Bank
WBG	West Bank and Gaza Strip
WBP	World Bank Publication

Preface

It is now widely recognised that small and micro enterprises are the back bone of an economy, especially where they matter the most; in developing economies and countries. They create employment, wealth and potential for future growth, but more than that in a conflict zone such as Palestine. Because of their micro and small size, SMEs constitute a means for survival, autonomy and maybe even freedom. They act as a means to an end, a way of materialising ambitions of owning, managing and/or running a business. But above all, in an uncertain world of conflict and occupation SMEs are not a choice but a necessity to sustain development. The aid agencies and international donors have realised this and do all they can to promote their development. However, their owner managers or those who manage the business make all the difference between success and failure. Being small has its own draw back. It does not take much to render them vulnerable; a constantly changing environment, ever increasing competition and market forces which are not always easily detectable. To give the managers of SMEs a fighting chance, they need management training to enable them to run their enterprise as a business concern, but this is no easy feat. In Palestine, where owning a business is more than just a means of earning a living, indeed its effective management poses a major challenge. This volume is concerned with this challenge and the dynamics behind the ways of enabling and empowering the owners and managers of these vital economic units. The SMEs in Palestine tell a story which is not too far fetched. Those who manage them have managerial needs similar to their colleagues in other states in the Middle East. The similarities in a cultural context, which are characterised by conflict, uncertainty and a constantly changing socio-economic and political environment, make the findings of this first time study relevant for development of managers in other regions. In reading these pages, it is essential to consider the context in which it is set, the occupied environment where the occupiers pose a threat to the enterprise that managers of similar sized enterprises would never experience in a non conflict zone. Despite the real environmental hazards, those in charge of SMEs go about their business day in and day out, and whenever there is a training opportunity, they take advantage of it and train to become better managers in order to protect their autonomy in the form of a small enterprise.

Farhad Analoui and Mohammed Al-Madhoun

Acknowledgements

The authors wish to acknowledge the contributions of so many who have been either directly or indirectly involved in the presentation of this volume. We would like to thank our families for their support. Also, Dr. Azhdar Karami, from the University of Bangor Business School for his specialised comments and contribution in the field of SMEs and Strategic Management. More so, we would like to thank the owners and managers of the Small and Medium Sized Enterprises who, despite pressures and stresses resulting from working and managing in a 'Conflict Zone', gave their valuable time and attention, and voluntarily took part in this first-time empirical study in Palestine. Last but by no means least, we would like to offer our sincere thanks to Sue Mackrill for undertaking the unenviable task of managing the production of the final camera-ready copy of the work.

Farhad Analoui and Mohammed Al-Madhoun

Chapter One

Small and Micro Enterprises

Introduction

There is no doubt that small and micro enterprises (SMEs) play a crucial economic role, especially in developing countries and economies where low income is the greatest problem and economic growth is at its lowest. In this context the question of heterogeneity is often raised. In this respect, in the SME's universe, it is imperative to recognize that different categories of enterprises tend to offer different contributions to the dual goals of poverty alleviation and economic growth. And as will be explored, the role of management training and all that it entails to develop managers and improve their managerial skills and effectiveness was the central focus of the novel study on which this volume is based.

What are they?

SMEs in their most fundamental forms have been recognised as a major contemporary source of employment and income in a growing number of developing countries and economies. Yet relatively little is known about their characteristics, changing forms, and, more importantly, about the people who manage the daily activities in these enterprises. Arguably, SMEs are the backbone of the economies, especially within the developing world where they account for more than half of the total employment created and over 80 per cent of employment growth in the past decade (Analoui and Karami, 2003). This is why SMEs' much taken for granted contribution, in particular the dynamics of SMEs in the development process, requires serious examination.

Small firms are also claimed to make up the bulk of the total enterprises in all economies in the world (Storey, 1994). It is not therefore difficult to accept the proposition that in the latter half of the last century, the increasingly important roles of small firms and enterprises could not be in any way understated (Bygrave, 1994; Timmons, 1994). Consequently, in recent years there has been a renewed interest in SMEs that has led to an increasing number of studies aimed at examining the various orientations that tend to pre-dominate the settings in which they usually operate.

Definition: A problematic notion

The consensus amongst scholars and policy makers on the usefulness and importance of the SME in a given economy does not preclude the problematic notion associated with its definition. A review of the literature confirms that there is a wide range of definitions emerging from research conducted throughout the world. However, the term 'small', as expected, denotes a relative term and varies from one country to another and worse still, this characteristic may differ from one sector to another even in the same economy. It is very difficult, if not impossible, to make valid comparisons of the importance given to SMEs in various countries, because there are variations in the definitions used (Storey, 1986). Not surprisingly, more than fifty different definitions have been cited in studies conducted in seventy-five countries (Neck, 1977). Some definitions tend to offer more insight into the dynamics and processes involved in their organisation and management.

An example of a useful definition is one that is cited by Bolton (1971) who contends that a small firm can be described as having the following three characteristics:

1. Possessing a relatively small share of its market;
2. Managed by its owners or part-owners in a personalised way, and not through the medium of a formalised management structure;
3. It is independent, in the sense that it does not form part of a larger enterprise. By definition the owner-managers should be free from outside control in taking their principal decisions.

Other studies have shown more concern for quantitative criteria purely for practical purposes; thus adopting some statistical limits in defining SMEs. Arguably, these yardsticks are often set on the low side. For example, Bolton in 1971 posed three criteria: the number of employees, turnover, and the number of vehicles used. The employment criterion used has two upper limits: for manufacturing 200 employees, and for construction and mining 25 employees. In another study by Curran (1986) the definition of 'small' adopted is that of firms employing fewer than 50 people and with an annual turnover of less than £3m. However, since the early 1970s most researchers concerned with small firms in manufacturing have adopted either the '100 or less' criterion or a number lower still to define small firms. These descriptions accord with most definitions used by various relevant professional bodies concerned with small enterprises in the Republic of Ireland. Often the best decided criteria are based on the limitations of SMEs as their common characteristics. This is best exemplified by Carson and Cromie (1989) who suggest that the small firm is actually characterised by three types of limitations – their impact (on markets), finance, and their physical resources.

SMEs' contributions to development

Indeed, there is no one right way to undertake an entrepreneurial approach to the issue of development. There are certainly lots of wrong ways of providing assistance to bring about assumed development that may not really help. Equally, there are seemingly right approaches to providing assistance that is useful but is very expensive. Therefore it appears that there is no one approach that can be identified, let alone generalised or sustained. This lack gets in the way of development that could provide assistance to more people (Liedholm and Mead, 1999).

SMEs are continuing to play an increasing role in the development of western economies (Hill and Wright, 2001). The question is, would they play a similar role in the developing countries and economies of the twenty first century? Indeed, are these small enterprises worthy of study? To answer this question, Liedholm and Mead (1999) optimistically state that SMEs have the potential to contribute in a number of important ways to the development process. Among the most significant of these are the following:

1. Contribution to household income and welfare;
2. Contribution to self-confidence and empowerment of the individual;
3. Contribution to social change, political stability, and democracy;
4. Contribution to distribution or developmental objectives;
5. Contributions in the area of demographic change.

In recent years, approximately 40 per cent of the increased number of workers in the labor force in developing countries have found work in SMEs. On the other hand, the closure rates of SMEs in developing countries are between 9 and 10 per cent per year (Liedholm and Parker, 1989).

From the above debate, it can be deduced that SMEs, despite their variations in forms, size and nature, offer valid and important contributions to the process of development. Of course, they face different needs, and require different ways of being helped. The design of effective policies and programs for their assistance and growth, therefore, must be built on an understanding of their complexity.

Jovanovic (1982) assumes that entrepreneurs have different managerial abilities, yet entrepreneurs are unsure about these abilities when a new business is established. Entrepreneurs gradually 'learn' about their abilities by engaging in the rough and tumble of the business world and observing how well they perform. Pakes and Ericson (1987) have extended this to allow managerial ability itself to be augmented through human capital formulation. Unfortunately, neither Jovanovic nor Pakes and Ericson indicate what the key determinants of this managerial ability might be or how other important variables might affect firm dynamics.

In reality, when asked about the principal problems that constrain their development, entrepreneurs in all countries focus on three main areas:

1. Markets for the products they sell;
2. Access to input required for making these products;
3. Finance.

The relative emphasis placed on these three variables varies from country to country and naturally tends to change from one subgroup to another within a given economy. Never the less, these three indicators have been consistently identified and reported as the most important problem areas SMEs are faced with (Liedholm and Mead, 1999). For example, in Jordan, a study has identified four major problems, namely managerial incompetence, lack of finance, competition and government regulations. The managerial problems highlighted by entrepreneurs were marketing, accountancy, supervisory skills and consumer behavior (Ashi, 1989).

Other studies

Various empirical works have focused on managerial problems and the most frequently voiced reasons for SME failures. For example, data compiled by Dun and Bradstreet (1987) points to management incompetence, rather than lack of capital, as the predominant cause of SME failure. Burr and Heckman (1979) concur with this view and state that perhaps the most frequent cause of failure is general lack of managerial ability. These statements have been supported by many researchers (Krentzman and Samaras, 1960; Pomeranz and Prestwich, 1962; Anderson, 1970; Broom and Longnecker, 1979; Edmunds, 1979; Solomon, 1982; Dickson, 1983; Ashi, 1987; Hodgetts and Kuratko, 2001).

Dun and Bradstreet (1987) classified primary categories of management weaknesses as follows:

Incompetence

About 43 per cent of the SME owner-managers did not have the basic knowledge and skills to plan, manage and control their operations.

Lack of management experience

Approximately 13 per cent did not have sufficient experience in supervisory job responsibilities to deal with the everyday, on-the-job application of management.

Unbalanced experience

Roughly 23 per cent had either considerable formal education but little or no practical experience, or had extensive job experience but inadequate formal training to give meaning and perspective to their work experience.

Broom and Longnecker (1979) carried out another study, comparing ten firms that failed with ten similar companies that succeeded during the same period of time. The results revealed 18 management weaknesses, which were related to three major areas:

1. Poor financial planning;
2. Poor co-ordination;
3. Poor general administration.

However, it must be also noted that the average small business owner is by nature one who likes to be where the action is. He or she does not like detailed work, including record keeping and analysis, and will avoid it consistently (Dickson, 1983).

Many studies have also been undertaken in the USA, Canada, UK, and Jordan (Bolton, 1971; Kennedy et al, 1979; Dickson, 1983; Kiesner, 1984; Dey and Harrison, 1987; Ashi, 1987) analysing the problem areas and managerial training needs of small businesses. They have related these to four major areas:

Management skills

Including leadership and personal management, human relations, communication, information use, planning, building self-confidence, negotiating contracts and computer techniques.

Financial issues

Including costing and control, budgeting, accounting, bookkeeping, cash flow management, bank relations, capital allocation and tax planning.

Marketing

Including advertising, promotion, pricing, selling, import and export, and marketing research.

Production/operation management

Including production and quality control improvement.

The above findings suggest that those managerial problems and the training needs of SMEs in the USA, Canada, UK, Europe and Jordan are similar, if not identical in nature. This conclusion is supported by the findings of Gray (1989), who discovered that the training needs and the managerial problems of SMEs are the same.

Managerial training for SMEs

SMEs generally are not interested in a recommendation to stop offering credit and switch to management training. Growing business requires expanding knowledge about and mastery of improved production technologies, and a variety of associated management skills (Liedholm and Mead, 1999). In the same vein, vertical commercial linkages between independent enterprises can enable small enterprises to specialise in those functions that they perform best. Effective assistance programs can contribute to the spread of such market-based linkages (Grierson et al, 1997).

On the downside, as in many larger companies, small firm owner-managers usually lack the necessary skills to carry out effective performance reviews and in the short term may perceive such a system as taking up too much time. In the long run, however, the benefits of efficient training needs identification, clarity for employees on what needs to be achieved, and linking productivity to rewards in an objective fashion are ones which this research has shown would be positive, as they have been identified as crucial to survival and growth (MacMahon and Murphy, 1999).

Most Management Training Programmes (MTPs) are designed to increase generic skills and behaviors relevant for managerial effectiveness and advancement (Yukl, 2002, p.371). However, MTPs have generally been proven to provide only limited benefits while operating at high costs. Effective programmes to address the non-financial needs of this group must operate primarily at a systems level (Boomgard et al, 1992). For this upgrading, Liedholm and Mead (1999) suggest two approaches:

1. Concentrate on providing experience for those considering setting up a new business, before they start out on their own, by developing internships or on-the-job training programmes;
2. To the extent that one seeks to assist new start-ups, build on existing experience, both in terms of any training offered and in terms of the selection of particular enterprises to support.

Hence, the starting-point for this book is the reflection on what kind of influence or contribution the MTPs have on the life cycle of SME managers. In this context, abundant literature and study materials demonstrate the positive effect of participating in management training and individual counselling programs on the entrepreneurial and managerial attitudes of SME-managers (Fuller, 1993; Gibb, 1995; Iredale and Cotton, 1995; Atherton and Hannon, 1996). Some contributors even consider post-experience management training (MT) to be an important explanatory element for a higher survival rate and chances for growth (Van Clouse, 1990; Crant, 1996; Rosa et al, 1996). Because training is a form of education in general, over the last two decades institutions of higher learning have experienced an increased demand for courses dealing with entrepreneurship and new venture creation (Schamp and Deschoolmeester, 1998).

In the past, such arguments have often led to a suggestion for the promotion of cooperatives or of business associations. In spite of their obvious appeal, each of these institutional arrangements has had a checkered past in developing countries and economies, mainly because they have often been promoted in a heavy-handed, 'top-down' manner (Liedholm and Mead, 1999).

A number of analysts have argued that these geographical concentrations of enterprises in related activities have provided significant benefits to those who participate in them (Schmitz, 1995; McCortnick and Pedersen, 1996; Van Dijk and Rabellotti, 1997).

While Liedholm and Mead (1999) also recognize the great advantages that some enterprises have derived from such networks, particularly in developed countries (for example, Italy), but also sometimes in developing countries (for example, Brazil and India), they have seen little evidence of the advantages of such networks in their survey results; nor have they found it to be very easy to promote their establishment in new locations in the Third World.

There is often a tendency to think in terms of long-term relationships, providing training and advice over a period of several months or even years. Such long-term, 'hand-holding' programs can be very expensive. They often produce only limited results, and frequently involve problems of long-term dependence on the assistance provider. Cost-effective programs are more likely to be built around offering specific answers to specific problems, with a short turnaround, enabling the assistance agency to provide only the help that is needed, but to a large number of clients (Liedholm and Mead, 1999).

The above arguments point to the SME managers and their need for managerial skills in order to ensure success rather than failure.

Managerial skills and SMEs' effectiveness

The inseparable relationship between 'SMEs' and 'management' theories has meant that management theories evolved and were based round the ways SMEs were viewed (Analoui, 1998, p.3). Effective management is therefore the most essential ingredient for productive performance of the SME, and an important need for its success and long-term survival. Arguably, it constitutes the most important determinant of an SME's success. An effective manager is thus one who achieves results, which is usually phrased in terms of profitability or productivity. It is through the process of effective management that the human efforts are co-ordinated and material resources are put into productive use for the attainment of specific goals and objectives (Mullins, 1993).

Drucker (1954, p.161) clearly indicates this relationship between the business and the manager when he states that managers spend a great deal of time, money and energy on improving the performance of a business. Less time, money and energy would probably be needed to improve the managers' performance in developing the business. Effective performance of the SME is therefore necessary for its success, let alone for its survival, and only management can satisfy this requirement. He argues 'the executive is paid for being effective and he owes effectiveness to the SME for which he works' (Drucker, 1988, p.138). In the same way, Stoner et al (1995, p.9) stress that there is a very important relationship between the SMEs performance and managerial performance. They conclude that success for the SME depends to a large extent on its managers. Thus, the success and survival of any SME may well rest upon how effectively management is carrying out the overall responsibility of attaining stated SME objectives. As Carnall and Maxwell (1988, p.15) aptly state, 'management is about creating and sustaining effectiveness'. It is management's responsibility, first, to be effective in leading a productive work force to achieve the needed result. Drucker asserts:

> Every knowledge worker in a modern organisation is an executive if, by virtue of his position or knowledge, he is responsible for a contribution that materially affects the capacity of the organisation to perform and obtain results (1988, p.5).

Reddin (1970) shares the same viewpoint, and states that effectiveness is the central issue in management. It is a manager's job to be effective. It is his only job. As Bennett and Brodie (1979) note, regardless of what roles a manager takes on, performance is a vital factor, and effectiveness remains a key issue in the success of the SME.

As Drucker (1988, p.15) aptly states, 'increasing effectiveness may well be the only area where we can hope significantly to raise the level of executive performance, achievement, and satisfaction'. Dunnette (1971) also maintains that an effective manager achieves this ultimate objective by identification, assimilation and utilisation of the resources that may be available to him to ensure that they are put to their optimum use for the long-term prosperity of the SME.

According to Drucker, effectiveness is also crucial for a person's self-development, and at the same time is the true development of that person. He holds that:

> The development of the executive's effectiveness will challenge the directions, goals and purposes of the organisation and will also raise the egos of its people from preoccupation with problems to vision of the opportunity, from concern with weakness to exploitation of strengths (Drucker, 1988, p.141).

Reddin (1974) seemingly shares the same views, and goes on to say that effective management is necessary for the utilisation of scarce resources on a worldwide basis. At the level of the individual, managerial effectiveness appears to be of importance; effective managers, knowing they are effective, are more likely to achieve job satisfaction and some degree of self-actualisation, with benefits to themselves and to their SMEs.

Effectiveness is about good management. Effectiveness, to a large extent, is about managing people well, and it is the tool of the executives and their access to achievement and performance. Indeed, the research on the subject indicates that managers spend between 70 and 80 per cent of their working time talking in various kinds of meetings with superiors, subordinates, colleagues and people outside the SME (Stewart, 1967). To increase a manager's effectiveness, a manager must be motivated towards increasing his effectiveness, and must be prepared to recognise and accept the need for 'change in attitude, knowledge and skills' (Lewis and Kelly, 1989, p.22). To be an effective executive, one needs to acquire competencies in the work one does, which in other words means to acquire competencies in managing self, managing people and managing the task in hand (Kakabadse et al, 1987).

Through the management process, efforts of members of the SME are co-ordinated, directed and guided towards the achievement of SME goals. Management, therefore, is considered to be the cornerstone of SME effectiveness, and is concerned with arrangements for the carrying out of SME processes and the execution of work (Mullins, 1993).

Morse and Weiss (1955) found that amongst occupational groups, none viewed achievement and accomplishment as more important to their motivation than the management group. Although there is evidence that 'achievement needs' may be different with respect to cultural differences (McClelland, 1961). However, the similarities in 'motivational needs' of managers across various countries are considerable (Haire et al, 1966).

SMEs and management training development in Palestine

In Arab countries and states, as in other developing economies, management and development training efforts have received increasing attention but unfortunately these programs often have lead to poor results and failed to contribute to the effectiveness of the managers involved (Mintzberg, 1975; Analoui, 1999). Most training specialists and managers in the Arab states describe training effectiveness in their countries as being generally 'low' (Al-Ali and Taylor, 1997, p.4).

Accordingly, the Palestinian Development Plan (PDP) (1998-2000) received financial support and aimed at the effective development of human resources for three years (MOPIC, 1997, p.7). As a result, many training programmes were established, which not surprisingly, were almost always of the off-the-job type. Al-Madhoun and Analoui (2002) refer to many training programmes in the Palestinian Territories (PT), conducted after the peace agreement, as 'trying to solve managerial weaknesses'. These include programmes offered by government, international development agencies and Non-Governmental Organisations (NGOs).

However, a number of problems facing the training process in Palestine have emerged. For example, in 1997, the Centre of Palestine Research and Studies (CPR) investigated the training and development needs of the Palestinian National Authority. The report concluded that 75 per cent of Palestinian managers suggested that more aid from international agencies ought to be allocated to activities related to more effective human resource development (HRD). The differences between the needs on the part of the managers for training and the weak results from the training (transfer), indicates the problematic nature of the training programmes themselves (Analoui, 1993; 1999). It is also argued that the problem is not about availability of funds; rather the suitability of methods of management training used and not adequately specifying the target groups and the need for their training (Shaba, 1998; Dajany, 1999). The training courses generally lack practical components and their impact is not systematically evaluated.

An empirical study in Palestine

Unfortunately, the studies concerned with the role of MTPs for the development of small business managers and their relative level of managerial efficiency, based on data derived from Palestinian census, are of limited value (Al-Madhoun, 1997; UNRWA, 1998; Safi, 1998). For this reason a first time study was attempted to generate primary data by applying a cross-sectional data collection method, using survey questionnaires (Ackroyd and Hughes, 1992; Churchill, 1995).

A survey questionnaire consisting of 26 questions (variables) was designed and used in this study. The questions were constructed and designed to elicit data specific only to managerial skills developed by attending MT courses. The researchers specified these questions after consideration of the subjects of the courses that were offered to small business managers during a five-year period (1995–2000). Despite the difficulties involved it was decided to involve all the small business managers (n=447), from five different areas, who attended the management training courses during the specified period.

It is important to note that although the interviewer-administered method is known for being highly time consuming and expensive in so far as research resources are concerned, a decision was made to adopt this approach to collecting data to ensure the highest rate of response, as well as allowing for clarification of possible ambiguities related to the questions asked (Churchill, 1995). Despite adopting the above strategy, primary analysis indicated that only 106 (23.6 per cent) of the whole population were fully involved in the survey. However, by adopting triangulation as our main method of enquiry, the data generated through interviews arguably provided a greater insight into the ways managers viewed their work, development and the courses attended than any other single method form of research.

Plan of the book

This book focuses on the management skill areas that research has identified as being the most important to the development of the SMEs' managers and their business as a result. The discussions in this volume revolve around the concept of effective management of SMEs. They are organised sequentially in seven separate but interrelated chapters.

After briefly introducing the field and its importance for small enterprises, the remaining part of this chapter deals with the concept of SMEs, their managers and the perceived need for managerial skills and its impact on their effectiveness. The task of defining SMEs was attempted by using theoretical backgrounds and practical examples. The relevance of the forgone discussion for the SMEs in Palestine and their importance to the Palestine economy is then briefly discussed.

Chapter Two is concerned with the management, managers, and managerial skills, models for managerial skills and management training and development. It sets the scene for the remaining chapters by exploring the benefits and limitations of managing SMEs in conflict zones such as Palestine. The intention is to show the crucial role of the SMEs in conflict zones. The structure and organisation of the discussions in this book clearly reinforces this point.

In Chapter Three, general issues related to managing SMEs in the Middle East's conflict zones will be discussed. The main part of the debate will be dedicated to developing management skills for SMEs in Palestine.

The issue of managing SMEs in Palestine is discussed in detail in Chapter Four. Here the focus will be first on SME managers' characteristics and attributes, then on the management training programmes and, finally, on the results of training for developing SME managers.

Management of a successful business goes about implementing their plans strategically. They also develop the management skills of their managers. For these reasons, Chapter Five will focus on the latter issues by identifying the clusters of managerial skills, measuring them and ultimately testing the relation between the managerial skills and SMEs' development.

Weaknesses facing the SMEs in conflict zones are also the main obstacles to the challenge of developing SMEs. These weaknesses have been divided into four different types in Chapter Six. These will include those identified in conflict zone situations, management training programmes, trainers' weaknesses, and managers in charge of SMEs.

Finally, in Chapter Seven, it will be contended that in the global competitive market small firms play a decisive role in the economy and can provide successful enterprises for their owners, managers or shareholders. A summary of the foregone discussion will have its emphasis on managing SMEs in a conflict zone with special reference to Palestine and the relation between managerial skills and SME managers, their similarities and concerns for obstacles and weaknesses. Finally, a strategy for implementing successful management training and development will be offered to planners and policy makers in order to survive this and the next decades. It is believed that it is imperative for owner/managers and the top management team to begin to think strategically. It is only in this way that a competitive advantage for SMEs can be successfully secured.

We make no apology for including a section on data management. As we produce this book we find that its references become out of date and any practising manager needs to be up to date.

Summary

This chapter has addressed the conceptual framework of the first time empirical study that was carried out recently in Palestine and explained the influences that have formed the basis for producing this volume. The discussions commenced with the basic definitions for SMEs, and their contributions to development. Based on the work of contemporary writers in management it was argued that for businesses to be successful they must support managers with relevant and appropriate managerial skills and knowledge. SME managers should not be excluded. These managers play critical roles in their businesses success and thus also in their improvement, development and the ways in which they deal with the obstacles and difficulties in their way.

Chapter Two

Managerial Issues: An Overview

Introduction

Business managers play a critical role in the development of the conflict zones. Establishing good practice amongst practitioners therefore is the most proactive way for business development and success in such volatile areas. For this reason, managers need to develop appropriate and relevant managerial skills and competencies that necessitate skill training. Such training constitutes a form of long-term investment for the managers and their enterprises.

Many studies during the last decades have tried to answer questions related to the roles of managers towards successful business development. Here an in depth review of the most important milestones in the literature concerned with managers, their roles and their needs for managerial skills will be attempted.

Management and managers

The purpose of management is to achieve results (Lewis and Kelly, 1989, p.6). Arguably, managerial knowledge and skills to some degree form a necessity for everyone; whether a president of a country, the owner of a small business, or a student. Today management principles have been thoroughly researched, discovered and by and large established. Therefore it is essential for all business managers to become familiar with the processes involved and their underlying philosophies, value structures, beliefs, and, most importantly, the dominant assumptions which have been made by scholars, theorists, developers, trainers, and practitioners at different points in time (Analoui, 1998).

Management forms a generic concept that, like many other concepts in social sciences, has been the subject of different interpretations. Sheldon (1965, p.35) asserts that 'management is the natural outcome of human association'. Bedeian (1989, p.6) defines management as a process of 'achieving desired results through efficient utilization of human and material resources'. In the same way, Armstrong (1994, p.16) views management as 'deciding what to do and then getting it done through the effective use of resources', a definition which emphasises the view that people are the most important resource available to managers.

Koontz and O'Donnell (1980, p.8) view management as a behaviour, and acknowledge that it knows 'how to accomplish desired concrete results'. Accordingly, it has been argued by some that management ought to be considered a practice rather than a science. It is not knowledge, but performance. Thus, leaders ought to base their practice on both knowledge and responsibility.

The systems approach to management maintains that it is impossible to specify a single way of managing that works best in all situations. The systems approach views enterprises as procuring and transforming inputs (people, materials, money, and information) into outputs that are subsequently discharged into their surrounding environment in the form of goods and services. This cycle is continually repeated as the goods and services provided by an enterprise are exchanged for the energy (feedback) necessary to secure further required inputs. Thus, an enterprise can survive only if it is capable of producing some output that can be exchanged for the resources necessary to obtain new inputs and also to maintain it in an operating order (Bedeian, 1989, pp.66-67).

Management process

Since the late nineteenth century, it has been common practice to define management as the process of planning, organising, leading, and controlling. A process which is known as a systematic method of handling activities (Stoner et al, 1995, p.10). It is not surprising if management is often viewed as a process of interrelated functions which are performed to achieve the organisational objectives. Analoui (1997, p.14) comments on the works of many theorists who contributed to the development of management process and the debate concerning the functions of management as a whole. He concludes that:

1. There is no consensus amongst theorists and writers on management about the exact functions that managers should perform;
2. Functions are not precisely defined nor agreed upon;
3. Most attempts to list the functions of management have been based on personal experience rather than empirical work.

Accordingly, the owner/manager of a small business is held responsible for all aspects of its operation; he is an employee responsible for orders' inventory, he obtains bank loans, and he is a decision maker. In an large enterprise, it is difficult for the manager to do all that alone, so he will have to rely on the use of the management process, which collectively refers to the five functions of management: making a plan, organising the work, staffing and human resource management, leading and interpersonal influence, and controlling (Bedeian, 1989, p.7). In the same way, Koontz and O'Donnell (1980, p.67) believe that it is both realistic for managers, and helpful to those understanding management, to utilise those same functions of managers: planning, organising, staffing, leading, and controlling.

The systems approach is often viewed as a management process, and this approach, that later became known as the process approach, has been developed based on the traditions of the classical management school originated by Fayol's ideas. Fayol's classification of the functions of management established the foundation for what is now referred to as the classic functions of management. He contended, 'to manage is to forecast and plan, to organise, to command, to coordinate and to control' (1949, p.6). Accordingly, management functions, as he suggests, can be carried out through forecasting and planning, organising, commanding, coordinating and controlling. In a rapidly changing world, however, managers have reason to infuse their planning, organising, leading, and controlling expertise with vision, ethical analysis, responsiveness towards cultural diversity, and a new understanding of the very idea of work and workplace (Stoner et al, 1995, p.24). The proponents of the classical school of thought in management aimed to describe management functions as being independent of each other. These are:

Planning

Armstrong (1994, p.17) defines planning as 'deciding on a course of action to achieve a desired result and focusing attention on objectives and standards and the programmes required to achieve the objectives'. In the same way, Bedeian (1989, p.8) and Stoner et al (1995, p.11) view planning as 'the process of establishing goals, objectives and a suitable course of action for their achieving those goals'. They add that this function embraces elements of planning and strategy, enterprise objectives, and decision-making. Koontz and O' Donnell (1980, p.156) on the other hand described planning as 'deciding in advance what to do, how to do it, when to do it, and who is to do it'.

Organising

According to Bedeian it is 'the process of dividing work among groups and individuals, and co-ordination of their activities for the purpose of accomplishing enterprise objectives. Organising also involves establishing managerial authority' (1989, p.8). This function embraces elements of organising, job design, and organisational change. Armstrong (1994, p.17) also refers to organising as 'setting up and staffing the most appropriate organisation to achieve the aim'.

Staffing and human resource management

The managerial function of staffing involves effective recruitment selection, placement, appraisal and development of people to occupy their roles in the organisation structure (Koontz and O'Donnell, 1980, p.514). As Bedeian (1989, p.9) states, the process should ensure 'that employees are selected, developed, and rewarded for accomplishing enterprise objectives'. He adds that this function should be to develop human resources, organise labour, and manage a successful career.

Leading and interpersonal influence

Management and leadership are often thought of as the same thing. Although it is true that the most effective managers will almost certainly be effective leaders, and that leading is an essential function of managers, there is more to managing than just leading (Koontz and O'Donnell, 1980, p.610). Stoner et al define leading as 'the process of directing and influencing the task-related activities of group members or an entire organization' (1995, p.12). This function will motivate human behaviour, effective leadership, work group behaviour, and effective communication (Bedeian, 1989, p.9).

Controlling

The managerial function of controlling is the measurement and correction of the performance of activities of subordinates in order to make sure that enterprise objectives and the plans devised to attain them are being accomplished (Koontz and O'Donnell, 1980, p.721). To Stoner et al controlling is 'the process of ensuring that actual activities conform to planned activities' (1995, p.12). Similarly, Armstrong (1994, p.17) has viewed controlling as 'measuring and monitoring the progress of work in relation to the plan and taking corrective action when required'. It is argued that this function includes elements of controlling and the management information system (Bedeian, 1989).

    During the last century, other classifications of management functions were proposed. Gulick and Urwick (1937) introduced the POSDCORB to denote the initials of management functions, that is, planning, organising, staffing, directing, coordinating, reporting, and budgeting. Appley (1965) too also included planning, executing and controlling in his analysis of managerial work. On the other hand, Drucker (1974) and Kakabadse et al (1987) suggested other management functions: motivation, communication, measurement, and the development of people, including the managers themselves. Drucker (1974) mentioned in his study the notion that effective management not only requires the development of people, but the development of the manager's own skills and performance as well.

    On the other hand, motivating, as Armstrong (1994, p.17) poses, is 'exercising leadership to motivate people to work together smoothly and to the best of their ability as part of a team'. As for the absence of motivators, Analoui contends that, 'it is the bureaucratic and traditional managerial approach in operation, with emphasis on the task at the expense of people which is largely to be blamed' (1999, p.387). Kakabadse et al (1987) presented a schematic model of Fayol's wheel of managerial activities, in which a distinction is made between 'people' and 'task' or work-related aspects of managerial work.

Managers

The world of work is largely composed of individuals, groups and teams working closely together. Managers are in a position to design structures for these people to meet their goals. A manager will be able to increase effectiveness by understanding the management system and management functions. Therefore, a manager is one who directs the activities of other people and undertakes the responsibility for achieving certain objectives through their efforts. Basically, a manager has been defined as someone who is responsible for the work of other people. Analoui (1997, p.26) defines a manager as 'one who recognises the need to understand the job content for what it really is and then uses the resources available to him or her to support such operation'. Managers are needed to 'maximise the utilisation of resources in the most scientific and efficient ways' (Analoui, 1998, p.3). In the same vein, Kakabadse et al (1987, p.30) define managers as '[those who] get things done through others'. But Mintzberg (1973) denotes that because of the complexities involved, it has not been easy to determine what defines a manager and what really constitutes a manager's job. However, managers are universal in all types of businesses and are the most important resources for their success.

Businesses begin with people who are purposefully working together in teams in order to achieve common goals, and the person who is responsible for the work of each team – whatever the title – is called a manager (Rowntree, 1989). Managers are key people in any business, and businesses are social systems in which people are working together to achieve a common purpose (Kakabadse, 1983). Businesses give managers the authority to make sure that other persons contribute their work activities to the business purpose. Without businesses, there would be no need for managers. In other words, businesses are not only the work setting for managers, but, more importantly, they lay down the institutional foundation for managerial tasks and responsibilities. But again, without managers and management, businesses do not perform, let alone survive and be effective (Drucker, 1974). Stoner et al mentioned that managers are therefore professionals who practise the function of management; they are responsible for the overall management of an organisation (1995, p.17). They ought to help a business to achieve a high level of performance through the utilisation of its human and material resources.

In pursuit of this idea, Mintzberg (1973, p.4) contends that a manager is considered a specialist because 'the job of managing involves specific roles and skills'. He adds that a manager is a generalist because he is a focal point in the general flow of information in the handling of general disturbances. The perception of the individual managers of their own and their colleagues' effectiveness is also related to the skills and abilities attributed to the effective manager (Analoui, 1999, p.387).

What does a manager do?

Henri Fayol's (1841-1925), the father of modern management, systematic analysis of organisations and management activities led to the most prevalent view of the manager's job, which later became known as the 'functional approach' in management studies (Bedeian, 1989, p.48). It is stressed that managers have to perform certain functions in the business to get things done by others. In thinking about the problems of a manager, he concluded that all activities that occur in a business undertaking could be divided into six essential groups:

1. Technical (production, manufacturing and adaptation);
2. Commercial (buying, selling and exchange);
3. Financial (finding and using capital);
4. Security (protection of property and persons);
5. Accounting (stocktaking, balance sheet, costing and statistics);
6. Managerial (planning, organising, commanding, co-ordinating and controlling).

Fayol (1949, p.3) held that these six groups of activities are always present in any undertaking – simple or complex, big or small business. He added that the manager would be able to practise the above activities with effectiveness by understanding how managerial activities at different levels relate to one another. Drucker talks about five basic ingredients or operations in the work of the manager: sets objectives, organises, motivates and communicates, measures, and finally, develops people including himself (Drucker, 1974, p.400). While the specific job title used to identify managers at the three levels varies among enterprises, general labels such as vice-president and supervisor help in determining the content of different managerial positions.

At the end, the manager's function is the process of management, the major managerial activities that will serve as the foundation for the discussion. Szilagyi (1981, p.6) suggests that a simplified form of the manager's job will consist of five activities which each will lead to another to form a cyclical set of activities (Figure 2.1).

Deciding what to do (Developing framework for performance)

⇩

Deciding how to do it (Establishing order function and design)

⇩

Directing performance (People in organisation)

⇩

Evaluating performance (Control, evaluating and feedback)

⇩

Deciding what should be changed (Changes in goals, plans, design, motivation, and control system)

Figure 2.1   Managers' job in simplified form

Managerial pyramid

There are differences among managers' jobs in most enterprises but there are three distinct but overlapping levels of management, each requiring a different managerial emphasis: first line, middle, and top management (Bedeian, 1989).

First-line management

Managers responsible for directly managing operating (non-managerial) employees and resources. This is basically management's first line of contact with employees.

Middle management

Managers occupying roles positioned above first-line management and below top management.

Top management

Managers who determine the form of an enterprise and define its overall character, mission, and direction (Bedeian, 1989, pp.13-14), with the top managers being responsible for all the functions in an organisational unit (Stoner et al, 1995, p.24).

The manager of a small business is responsible for all aspects of its operation, however, although individualised work patterns still exist in many developing countries, relatively few people continue with this pattern (Bedeian, 1989, p.6).

Manager's success

Bedeian (1989, p.20) argues that when it comes to management success, there are many factors involved, including the individually-defined and institutionally-defined criteria. Managers can also be successful by their own criterion, but less successful by their employers'. A manager can be successful in reaching some objectives, and less successful in reaching others. Regarding what factors determine managerial success, to perform effectively managers must possess abilities appropriate to their assigned jobs, be motivated to achieve, and have a clear understanding of their assigned roles (Bedeian, 1989, p.20).

He discusses the factors involved in managerial success. First he talks about the personal factors. The relationship amongst them is simply expressed as:

Performance = Ability * Motivation * Role clarity

Hard work is included under motivation, and it is believed that most successful managers do work hard: 'the typical top manager works 55 to 65 hours a week'. The match between personal factors (performance) and job factors, which are the work requirements of a particular task, also influences managerial success. Interpersonal factors are also important. These relate to evaluation by a superior, and peer co-operation. The last factor, 'luck', is almost never mentioned in relation to management success. In addition to the personal factors, the impact of job factors and interpersonal factors, as well as luck, must also be considered.

Managing can be a rewarding, challenging, and fulfilling career. To be successful, managers must have the requisite abilities, a motivation to achieve, and a willingness to meet the role demands of an ever-evolving world. Kotter's (1982) study involved 15 successful general managers in a broad range of industries. He found that most of the managers' time was spent in interaction with people other than their direct subordinates and bosses. The nature of the contacts was found to be network building, which was more concerned with other requirements of managers than the manager's training and development needs. Kotter found that general managers covered a wide range of topics in their short disjointed conversations with others and asked questions, and rarely gave orders in a traditional sense. He asserts that:

> The basic personality themes that one finds in a group of successful general managers relate to power, achievement, ambition, emotional stability, optimism, intelligence, analytical ability, intuition and a personable style (Kotter, 1982, p.6).

In conclusion, Kotter considers successful managers as competent people who implement policies, objectives and activities through a diverse number of individual and group managers. The leading is largely by trial and error, and lacks guidance or structure. For a manager's development there are four ways (opportunities) to develop a manager's own experience: action of other managers, talking with other managers, reading, and attending courses (Lewis and Kelly, 1989, p.20). On the other hand, they add that, for manager's development, the manager must accept responsibility, be aware of his development needs, establish his objectives, identify his opportunities, and monitor and review progress (ibid, p.21).

Managerial roles

What are the roles of managers? Will a manager who understands the discipline of management still be effective? A person who knows only the skills and techniques, without understanding the fundamentals of management surely is not a manager; he is '...at best, a technician. A manager does not require a big title, a big office, and other outward symbols of rank; rather he requires competence and performance of a high order. Management is a practice rather than a science' (Drucker, 1974, p.17).

Lewis and Kelly stress that managers can increase their effectiveness through gaining insights into the roles they are required to perform. If roles are not clearly defined, managers are uncertain about:

1. What they are required to do;
2. Boundaries of responsibility;
3. Relationships with others;
4. Need to develop appropriate skills (1989, p.6).

They also propose three issues:

1. What they actually do in relation to what they should be doing;
2. The extent to which their roles are changing;
3. Their needs for further training and development.

Managers have to perform diverse activities and adopt different roles within the context of their everyday jobs. Managers have to achieve objectives, often not set by them, and have to achieve those objectives through the management of work and the management of people. 'Although, historically, emphasis has been placed on the controlling, planning, and co-ordination skills, it is actually the people skills that decide between a good and poor manager' (Kakabadse et al, 1987, p.30). The traditional perspective, not surprisingly, did not place emphasis on people, and therefore paid more attention to task, at the expense of people and their development (Analoui, 1998, p.3). Lewis and Kelly suppose eleven roles of the manager, which include: group leader, liaison, information sharing, information seeking, spokesman, innovator, delegator, disturbance handler, negotiator, performance appraiser, and trainer (1989, p.7).

Mintzberg's (1973, p.25) reviews of five chief executives daily activities has been the most influential of all studies and has served as a landmark in studies of managerial behaviour. His theory of the work content of managers offers an alternative view of the job of managing. He highlights how managers spend their time and perform their work. He made an extensive survey of existing research on this subject and integrated those findings with the results of the ideas in his own study of the five chief executives.

The conclusion reached was simple: managerial work in practice is not systematic and planned, and that there are all the indications that the procedures of scientific analysis have not yet been successfully applied in programming the ambiguous work of managers. Meaning that manager's work still remains the domain of art rather than science (Mintzberg, 1973). He asserts that:

> It was clear in my study of chief executives that almost nothing senior managers do is programmed, that is, formally recorded as a series of steps to be carried out in a systematic sequence (Mintzberg, 1973, p.51).

He (ibid, p.51) offers a list of thirteen propositions about managerial work characteristics, which are summarised (Labbaf, 1996) into four general points:

1. Brevity, variety and discontinuity characterise managerial activities, and managers are strongly oriented to action and dislike reflective activities;
2. Managerial work has a number of regular duties involved, including ritual and ceremony, negotiations and the processing of information, both within and between organisations;
3. Managers strongly favour personal communication by talking, rather than documents and the written media, and as a result spend a considerable time the telephone and in meetings;
4. Managers do not have a formal programme upon which to base their behaviour, but rely on judgement and intuition, and the process of decision-making used is not clearly observable (Mintzberg, 1973, p.51).

Mintzberg (1973, p.59) and Kakabadse et al (1987, p.19) refer to the characteristics with a set of ten different roles that managers must be prepared to perform in order to fulfil their work responsibilities in the organisation (Figure 2.2).

Interpersonal Roles	Informational Roles	Decisional Roles
1. Figurehead	4. Monitor	7. Entrepreneur
2. Leader	5. Disseminator	8. Disturbance handler
3. Liaison	6. Spokesman	9. Resource allocator
		10. Negotiator

Figure 2.2   Managerial roles

Source: Adapted from Kakabadse et al (1987, p.19)

Formal authority and status

Bedeian (1989, p.15) and Analoui (1997, p.24) elaborate on the three sets of roles of managers:

Interpersonal roles

The three interpersonal roles (figurehead, leader, and liaison) derive from the formal authority and status of top management. First and foremost, top-managers are figureheads. The top manager's leadership role entails influencing the activities of subordinates. In their liaison role, top managers interact with peers, as well as individuals in other enterprises, to gain favours and knowledge. Most of a manager's time is spent interacting (through oral and written communications, with a performance for the former) with other persons inside and outside the work unit (Mintzberg, 1973, p.56). He discusses this aspect of managerial activities which causes managers at all levels to be involved in the three interpersonal roles. The manager's involvement in the interpersonal roles in turn places him or her in a unique informational position that gives rise to the three informational roles (Mintzberg, 1973, pp.56-58).

Informational roles

The easy access to information and the special status and authority are attributed by interpersonal roles. A major part of any manager's job is information processing, that is, managers can spend up to 50 per cent of their time giving and receiving information (Mintzberg, 1973, p.56).

Table 2.1   Ten roles of top management

	Role	Description of Roles	Activities Undertaken
Interpersonal Roles	*Figurehead*	Symbolic representative in social and legal matters.	Welcomes dignitaries; signs official documents.
	Leader	Influences hiring, training, and motivating of subordinates.	All activities involving subordinates.
	Liaison	Interacts with peers and other individuals in different enterprises to gain favours and knowledge.	Processes mail, telephone calls; confers with clients.
Informational Roles	*Monitor*	Receives and collects information necessary to deal with in-house events and environmental occurrences.	Attends professional meetings and trade shows; reads industry periodicals and newsletters.
	Disseminator	Transmits information internally to peers, subordinates and superiors.	Staff meeting; internal reports and memos.
	Spokesperson	Transmits information externally into enterprise's environment.	Press conferences; public interviews; speeches to external groups; political lobbying.
Decisional Roles	*Entrepreneur*	Initiates changes to improve enterprise performance.	Develops new products, original sales promotions, and novel pay schemes.
	Disturbance Handler	Deals with unforeseen events or crises.	Resolves subordinate conflicts; responds to disgruntled suppliers.
	Resource Allocator	Decides how an enterprise will expend its resources.	Distributes manpower, money, materials, and information.
	Negotiator	Bargains with individuals, representatives of other enterprises.	Negotiates labour-management contracts; settles shipping rates; deals with wholesalers; mediates consumer claims.

Source: Adapted from Bedeian (1989, p.18)

Decisional roles

Mintzberg (1973) adds that interpersonal roles provide four decisional roles for a manager to take an active part in. The most crucial roles are in fact said to be associated with decision-making. Managers by definition are decision makers (Analoui, 1997, p.25), and they ultimately use information to make decisions that solve problems and/or take advantage of opportunities (Mintzberg, 1973, p.56). Mintzberg (1973, p.58) stresses that the ten roles cannot be isolated and should be considered as a system of managerial work behaviour.

Analoui (1997, p.26) is concerned with beyond-roles and self-management; he mentions in his study of 15 managers that most of a manager's time was spent in interaction with people other than their direct subordinates and bosses. On the other hand, he argues that self-management is one of the most unrehearsed subjects. He, like Mintzberg (1973), mentions that there is considerable similarity in the behaviour of managers at all levels.

Bedeian (1989, p.18) summarises the three sets of roles as shown in Table 2.1. Casey's (1976) work with South-east Asian countries shows the work content of managers is similar, in that 70 per cent of management time is spent in talking with other people and paperwork.

Lau et al (1980, p.519) concluded that the work content of public sector executives corresponds to Mintzberg's managerial role descriptions, and that the major roles are remarkably similar in both sectors. On the other hand, most managers cannot possess the complete system view of the business's problems and cannot be aware of all interpersonal and inter-group relations and related training needs (Kubr and Prokopenko, 1989, p.53).

Manager's effectiveness

To be effective, a manager needs a balance of technical, social and conceptual knowledge and skills acquired through a blend of education and experience. There is, therefore, a continual need for training and development of managerial talents. An effective manager is one who is:

> Able to diagnose people and situations, understanding basic behavioural concepts why he and other people behave as they do. And translating these principles and techniques into the practical skills of managing his job and the people with whom he works in order to achieve his managerial goals (Kakabadse, 1983, p.7).

Managerial effectiveness is a complex, multi-faceted organisational phenomenon. 'The "awareness" shown and the required abilities and competencies alone cannot sufficiently explain the nature of managerial effectiveness' (Analoui, 1999, p.386). Drucker argues that effectiveness is essentially concerned with the achievement of results (1974, p.45). For him, 'effectiveness is the foundation of success'. Reddin (1970) supports the idea and asserts effectiveness is the extent to which the manager achieves the output requirements of the job, by what he achieves rather than what he does. Reddin (ibid, p.7) has produced a model of managerial effectiveness, which takes into account a set of three interrelated factors: behaviour, task, and circumstances. He clarifies the concept of apparent effectiveness when he states that, 'it is difficult if not impossible to judge managerial effectiveness by observation of behaviour alone. The behaviour must be evaluated in terms of whether or not it is appropriate to the output requirements of the job'.

The work of Campbell et al (1970), in which three key concepts of person, process, and product are conceptualised to incorporate the determinants of effective managerial behaviour and performance, has developed a model of managerial behaviour. Based on this model, a manager's effectiveness is influenced by different sets of potential factors relating to personal characteristics, organisational results, and organisational environment. This model is essentially based on the answers provided to three groups of questions:

1. What sorts of persons are effective managers?
2. What is the process of effective managing?
3. What is the product of effective management?

Accordingly, Campbell et al (1970, p.12) assert:

> Effective executive behaviour is a function of complex interactions between individual or personal characteristics. The demands and expectations placed upon persons by the physical, administrative, and social environments of their organisation; and the nature of the feedback, incentives, and reward systems developed by organisational policies and practices.

Whatever the emphasis may be, it is important to know that efforts aimed at measuring managerial effectiveness can be objective only if they are based on some tangible aspects of behaviour which lead to the accomplishment of organisational objectives (Campbell et al, 1970; Porter et al, 1975).

Stewart (1976) also views managerial effectiveness as a dual function of individual characteristics and organisational variables. The three components of Stewart's analytical framework are 'demands', 'constraints', and 'choices', for the understanding of the patterns of managerial effectiveness. Based on this model, a manager's behaviour can be analysed in terms of these three sets of determinants.

1. Demands are what must be done in terms of job requirements;
2. Constraints are those limiting organisational and environmental factors that affect behaviour;
3. Choices are what a manager can do and achieve within the context of the above forces.

A definition put forward by Bennett and Brodie (1979, p.14) signifies effectiveness as 'the relationship between performance and task objectives, between achievement assessed against goals and purposes'. This perspective not only elaborates on the content variables and environmental factors, but also takes into account the relationships involved. Managerial effectiveness is therefore viewed in terms of both psychological and organisational concepts. Burgoyne (1976) supports this view, and believes that effectiveness is important, because it is the key factor to the success of our organisations and to the achievement of our social goals. In this respect, the role of managers has been considerably more significant in the overall success of their businesses and the development of their nations. This has meant greater responsibility and demand on their part to increase their managerial effectiveness (Analoui et al, 2000).

Manager's skills

What skills besides style and flexibility will an effective manager have? He must know how to read a situation, and the skill to change the situation if it needs to be changed, and an ability to use high or low task or relationships orientation (Reddin, 1970, p.14).

Skills such as delegation, being a good planner, organising ability, good human relations and leadership skills were indicating that, as expected, senior managers are more in need of 'interpersonal' and 'analytical' skills rather than 'informational' and 'decisional', as has been described in the available literature (Analoui, 1999, p.369).

Mintzberg (1973) even predicted that the next revolution in management education would be the training of managers through skill development. His vision of the future trend of management development was indeed precise, considering that skill-based education was one of the major issues in management research in the 1980s (Porter, 1983). It still persisted in the 1990s, and with an increasing support and repertoire, it may well be the major issue in years to come (Bigelow, 1991).

Mintzberg concluded that the management school gives students MBA and MPA degrees; it does not in fact teach managers how to manage. He said that, 'just as the medical student must learn diagnosis, and the engineering student must learn design, so also must the student of management learn leadership, negotiation, disturbance handling, and other managerial skills' (1973, pp.187-188). He goes further to assert that one-way to determine what skills managers need is to analyse their roles.

Management is tasks. Management is a discipline. But management is also people. Every achievement of management is the achievement of a manager. Every failure is the failure of a manager (Drucker, 1979, p.14).

Which means that it is expected of them to get the right things done first. For developing of the manager's skills, Dickinson (2000) states three theories that, used together, go some way to explain how and why managers develop their skills. First, there has to be the motivation to want to develop, and it is widely acknowledged that there are many factors that increase or decrease an individual's motivation. Second, it is noted that individuals' ability to learn from an experience and critically reflect on the experience enhances their knowledge base and increases performance and confidence, while, third, the way in which people develop is often a progression through specific phases, each phase requiring different handling by 'developers'. This theory-practice interface suggest that 'development' can be brought about by an aggregate of factors such as 'training/support', 'relevant experience', 'time to reflect', and 'feedback' based on sustained 'motivation'.

Management development

A question which needs to be answered is why management development (MD)? Why not management education? Or management training (MT)? Education is usually reserved for that type of learning that takes place in a structured, formal, institutional framework, such as a university or college. It must be remembered that management training has in the past referred to vocational-oriented education, or hands-on skill development, where skills are developed through practice which is guided by formal structured means. But MD may include one or both of these (Woodall and Winstanley, 1998, p.9). MD demands an investment in the long-term potential of the total organisation, which may depress the immediate results of development in the short-term. Operating management will only make the necessary sacrifices of time and money if top management make it clear that they give a high priority to MD, and are prepared to assess the performance of management in this area, as well as through the budget, and if they take a personal interest in MD programmes (Kreiken, 1975, p.12). MD has become an increasingly complex task, and MD is used essentially as an indication of a complex process of raising managerial ability in order to improve the effectiveness of management action (Al-Madhoun, 2002). If top management would only show active support of the programme, it would be a certain success (House, 1967, p.10). Kreiken when discussing the top management role in MD argues that there are three sides to MD:

Development of people

Top management can fulfil this responsibility in three ways. First, by creating the climate, structure and relevant procedures that foster the development of people for management functions. Second, appraising the present and future management talents periodically, both in quantity and in quality. Third, by organising internal and/or external programmes.

Development of management process

Functions of management, such as planning, selection, duration, organisation, and controlling need to be developed.

Self-development

Objectives in this context are more important than methods. It means the provision of the right intellectual environment and resources.

MD is a process of acquiring knowledge and skills in order to improve current or future managerial performance. The aim of MD should be to increase work group and organisational effectiveness, which, in turn, is a function of the interaction between the characteristics of the organisation, that is, environment and people (Woodall and Winstanley, 1998, p.4). MD should be of strategic importance and must be used as a competitive weapon for continued organisational survival and success (Hussey, 1988).

MD has been defined in a myriad of different ways. The Training Services Agency (1977) defines MD as 'an attempt to improve managerial effectiveness through a planned and deliberate learning process' (Woodall and Winstanley, 1998, p.4). MD is the planned process of ensuring through an appropriate learning environment and experiences the continuous supply and retention of effective managers at all levels to meet the requirement of an organisation and enhance its strategic capability (Harrison, 1995). Similarly, Bettignies (1975, p.4) defines MD as an 'attempt to improve managerial effectiveness through a planned and deliberate learning process'. House (1967, p.105) refers to MD as 'any planned effort to improve current or future managers' performance by imparting information, conditioning attitudes, or increasing skills'. Schein (1988, p.9) sees MD as a 'learning process of acquiring a certain body of knowledge, skills in implementing this knowledge, and the attitudes and values that define how and when and for what ends the knowledge and skills are to be used'. Cole (1988) stresses that MD is a systematic process by which an organisation can meet its current and future needs for effective managers. Therefore, MD can be considered as being related to businesses' objectives and how to increase demand for better managerial performance. Pedler et al (2001) suggest six points need to be considered for MD objectives:

1. Cognitive: knowledge;
2. Affective: attitudes and feelings;
3. Psychomotor: mainly manual skills;
4. Interpersonal: person-to-person skills, blending specific cognitive, affective, and psychomotor skills in face-to-face interactions;
5. Self-knowledge: personal growth and an expanded awareness of one's strengths and weaknesses;
6. Knowledge retention.

Morris (1975, p.35) considers MD as 'the systematic improvement of managerial effectiveness within the organisation, assessed by its contribution to organisational effectiveness'. According to Steers (1977), MD seeks effectiveness as the final result of change, which is expected to take place in individual performance. More precisely, Woodall and Winstanley (1998, p.5) discuss the MD as purpose, processes and prerequisites.

Purpose

Primarily oriented towards developing individuals in ways which are complementary with the organisation and its objectives, and appropriate for meeting the individual's own career and development needs.

Processes

Provide opportunities for individuals to develop cognitively in their understanding of management and behaviourally in their managerial skills and competencies.

Prerequisites

A positive attitude towards learning; a willingness to develop and change in the learner; capability of the facilitator (or developer) and support from the organisation (Woodall and Winstanley, 1998, p.5).

More over, Woodall and Winstanley (1998, p.10) contend that there is a relation between *business* needs, organisational needs, and individual needs. They are described as roles for MD (see Figure 2.3).

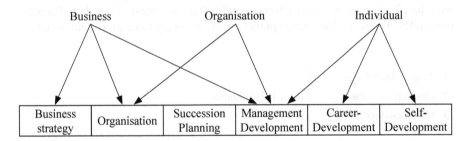

Figure 2.3   MD in the context of organisational and self-development needs

Source: Adapted from Woodall and Winstanley (1998, p.10)

Needs

MD programmes are, therefore, designed to increase managerial effectiveness by providing the working managers with the additional knowledge and skills needed. In the same way, Analoui (1997) states that MD programmes always aim at changing three basic elements: knowledge, attitudes and skills.

MT concentrates on all difficult processes that are related to developing, improving, teaching and raising managers' standards of skills and abilities to achieve complicated and interrelated tasks and jobs which are surrounded by a big net of relationships and expectations. MD focuses on the factual practice of a profession, related to a manager's daily tasks and activities, and whose standard of performance must be adequate for the accomplishment of required results (Taylor, 1966). He states the complementary aspects of the same process, and it is difficult to imagine any training which does not have some educational effect, and vice versa; in short, some of each exists in both. A complementary relationship exists between MT and MD.

Mumford (1994, p.4) discusses the three aspects of effectiveness in MD as follows:

1. A contingent definition of effective managerial behaviour;
2. A development process which emphasises activities in which managers are required to be effective, rather than emphasising the knowledge necessary for action;
3. The identification of a learning process, which is effective for the individual or group rather than being economical and convenient for tutors and trainers.

House (1967) suggests the objectives of MD efforts can best be described as a desired change in the areas of knowledge, attitudes and skills, and job performance at a point after the training is completed. House (1967, p.11) reviews 200 studies found to be meeting the minimum requirements; approximately 135 dealt not only with the effect of development efforts on individuals or organisations, but also with the conditions under which development efforts are likely to be successful or not.

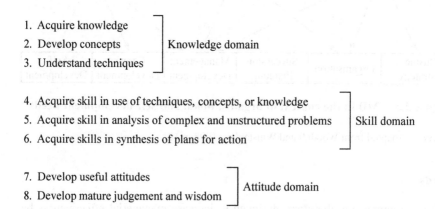

Figure 2.4   Range of possible management development objectives

Source: Adapted from Dooley and Skinner (1977, p.283)

Dooley and Skinner (1977) have also developed a comprehensive framework for better understanding of MD objectives. The framework (Figure 2.4), which is based on three learning domains, establishes eight MD objectives that are useful in guiding MD efforts.

Kerrigan and Luke (1987) have added three additional MT objectives to the above list: transfer of learning, capacity building, and inspiration for continued learning. It is suggested that 'a key function of strategic management development is to provide managers with access to knowledge and relationship networks that can help them become life-long learners and to cope with the issues of their continually changing agendas' (Kolb et al, 1984).

Vineall (1994, pp.31-32) stressed that planning for MD is a series of regular tasks which highlight the shape of the present situation and point to potential problem areas and contribute to good decisions about actual people and their careers. But how useful it is will depend on the use made of it – it will give no automatic answer.

To be effective, a development plan must take into account the many factors present in the manager's environment (House, 1967, p.19). In changing by MD on the job, the manager works within the previously established management practices. The policies of top management, the practice of his immediate boss, and the behaviour of job associates constitute the most influential aspect of the environment. The changed job performance of individual managers will result in improved organisational performance when it is co-ordinated with that of others in the development programme towards specified organisational goals (House, 1967, pp.14-15).

Training and development

The accurate identification of the training needs of an organisation is crucial to its success and development. Training and Development (TD) is a subsystem of the organisation and has its inputs from the organisation and outputs to the organisation. Priorities of training needs must be related to organisational goals (Bramley, 1991, p.9). What are the differences between training and development? Phillips (1985) asserts that MD concentrates on an organisation and the future of its activities so it can develop and change in order to survive. For Labbaf (1996, p.57), training is thought of as formal classroom learning activities, while development is thought of as all learning experiences, both on and off the job, including formal classroom training. However, development refers to teaching managers the skills needed for both present and future jobs. Therefore, organisations in USA spend nearly $100 billion each year on training (Daft and Marcic, 2001, p.305).

Time and again, commitment to TD among the ranks of management seems low (Scherer, 1978). Scherer also further argues that it is the responsibility of all management levels throughout the organisation to accept responsibility not only for their own development but also for the development of their subordinates. In this regard, Scherer (1978, p.3) contends:

The fact is that the training staff are not responsible for developing people. It is the management of the organisation that is responsible for promoting better performance and for stimulating career growth in individuals. The function of the trainers is not to relieve management of that responsibility, but to assist them in accomplishing it.

TPs seek to maintain and improve current job performance, while MTPs are designed to impart skills needed in future jobs. The need of training may be determined through performance appraisal, job requirements, organisational analysis, and human resource surveys. T&D methods can be classified as on-the-job or off the job. Coaching is the most important formal on-the-job development method. Other development methods include job rotation and classroom teaching. Both training and development should be reinforced in the work situation (Stoner et al, 1995, p.405).

Bramley (1991, p.36) states the purpose of training is to improve the performance of individuals, and thus increase the effectiveness of the organisation. He adds that there are three questions, which should be posed:

1. What changes are expected to result from this programme in terms of individual performance levels?
2. How are these changes linked to organisational effectiveness?
3. How do these changes relate to overall corporate objectives?

More recently, corporate strategy, corporate culture, and top management commitment to MTD are viewed as the most influential factors affecting TD function/programmes (Brown and Read, 1984; Hussey, 1988; Latham, 1988; Mol and Vermeulen, 1988). Therefore, these latter factors are the focus of the following sections.

Training

A manager has to acquire relevant managerial skills. Management training will enable the managers to deal with different aspects of their business more effectively. It is believed that training is important and is needed to enhance the manager's personal and managerial skills. The training is to be designed for and used to meet the training requirements of the operatives or that of the management (Analoui, 1996, p.59).

What follows here will highlight some of the key points for the training concepts such as training objectives, training systems, training methods, training progress, and the ways to evaluate the training programmes. Then, attention will be paid to management training.

The process of training is defined in different ways by different authors. A typical British definition is offered by the Department of Employment Glossary of Training Terms (1971), 'The systematic development of the attitude/knowledge/skills/behaviour pattern required by an individual to perform adequately a given task or job' (Bramley, 1991, p.xiv). A typical American definition is very different from the above. For example, according to Hinrichs (1976) training is 'Any organisationally initiated procedures which are intended to foster learning among organisational members in a direction contributing to organisational effectiveness' (Bramley, 1991, p.xiv). The US Government Employee Training Act (GETA) defines training as:

> The process of providing for and making available to an employee, and placing or enrolling such an employee in a planned, and co-ordinated programme, course, curriculum, subject system, or routine of instruction or education, in scientific, professional, technical, mechanical, trade, clerical, fiscal, administrative, or other fields which are or will be directly related to the performance (Fraser et al, 1978, p.685).

Bedeian (1989, p.306) comments that training is 'the process of developing skills, knowledge, and abilities so as to improve present and future performance'. To Analoui (1993, p.3) training means 'learning to do something'.

Robinson (1985, p.12) perceives training as 'any instructional or experiential means, to develop a person's behaviour pattern, in the areas of knowledge, skills or attitude, in order to achieve a desired standard or level of performance'. Interestingly, Kerrigan and Luke (1987, p.152) place stress on more behavioural and attitude related change. They suggest training is a way of 'altering an individual's behavior by changing knowledge level, attitudes and skills levels, for the ultimate purpose of creating desirable consequences for the individual's organization'. Hussey (1985) has argued that top management should review training objectives, especially for MD, whenever a major change in strategic emphasis is planned. Hussey argued for a shift in thinking regarding the purpose of training. For him, training should not be for the sole purpose of improvement of the individual with the hope that it will benefit the organisation; training should be originally for the benefit of the firm, knowing that this in turn will benefit the individual.

According to Kerrigan and Luke (1987, p.152), the most cited objectives for general training efforts are:

1. Knowledge acquisition;
2. Change attitudes;
3. Problem solving skills;
4. Interpersonal skills;
5. Participant acceptance.

Aims of training

There are still business managers who view training and development as unable to promote or develop the strategic aims of the business. However, businesses with a more positive view believe training is an investment that will pay off in the long term. They understand that it may be difficult to calculate the return on investment, but believe the tangible and intangible benefits of training will more than justify the cost (Worth, 1998).

In these regards, Robinson (1985) postulates the unification of training objectives, policies and strategies with the business plans of the organisation if the TD is to be truly seen as an effective process. This point of view raises several questions including 'How can TD and corporate managers' work together to improve organisational objectives?' and 'Why have so few managers, and in particular top managers, availed themselves of MTD programmes?' Hence, these questions and other related issues would be the focus of this part of the literature review. Warren (1969, p.7) stresses that a training sub-system's value is its ability to bring about required behaviour change in terms of skills, knowledge, and attitudes, not the number of programmes it runs, or its ability to utilise the newest technical advances in the field of education. Therefore, it is the line manager's responsibility to work in harmony with the TD personnel to bring about the desired results.

Training should be a continuous process of helping managers and employees to be more effective in their present and future work. The training is more important for the managers. There should be deliberate provision to understand and practise the training – on the job, or in the classroom. The purpose of training is to help the individual manager to reach his or her maximum potential as quickly as possible.

However, training is likely to be dependent on a manager's individual perspective. For a business, a TP may aim to give managers and employees the knowledge and skills and motivation to ensure the ability to perform a specific task that is required of them in the workplace.

A manager, on the other hand, is likely to view training from the point of view of maximising the returns from the skills' acquisition, either in financial terms or as net advantages of a more general kind, such as job satisfaction or ease of work. The amount of interplay between the varied interests will be expressed in an organisation's approach to training in its training philosophy. The training philosophy of businesses expresses the degree of importance they attach to training. Some take the view that managers will find out what is required on the job by simply 'getting on with it' and learning from trial and error. Some simply assume, for example, that the department manager should ensure training to the required level (Worth, 1998).

However, a belief in the value of training must be supported by a positive and realistic philosophy of how training contributes to organisational success. Armstrong (1994) described such a philosophy as being built around the following:

1. Training must be strategic in nature and a long-term view ought to be taken of the skills, knowledge and levels of competence required by employees. This approach regards training as an integral part of the strategic management of the organisation, with continual evaluation of training needs.
2. Training must be relevant to the specific needs of the organisation and not 'training for training's sake'.
3. Training should be problem-based, in that it should be designed to fill the gap between what people can do and what they need to be able to do, both now and in the future.

4. Training should be action-oriented and enable trainees to make things happen immediately. The objectives of the training event should be described in terms of what trainees will be able to do, and what they will have achieved after training.

5. Training should be directly related to performance requirements. It should be designed to fulfil the specific needs of the situation.

6. Training is not something that is provided to people by an organisation at the start of their career or at occasional points in their career. It is a continual process with less emphasis on formal instruction and an increased requirement for trainees to be responsible for their own learning.

Training methods

Basically, selection of the methods of training will, by and large, depend on the type of job and its skills requirements (Hodgetts and Kuratko, 2001, p.322). Therefore, choosing a method for a training programme depends on the nature of the operation. Furthermore, Analoui (1993, p.60) contends that there is no single correct way with management training. He further adds two major problems in devising a comprehensive scheme for the classification of the MTD methods currently in use:

1. There is as much variety in the nature of the managerial jobs in industry as there is in the roles which managers' play when doing their job;

2. Difficulty is one which is inherent in the hierarchy used to describe different managerial jobs.

There are numerous training methods available to managers and trainers for presenting information and transmitting skills. Mumford (1994) identifies around 300 MD techniques. Wexley and Latham (1991) differentiate between on-site training methods (for example, orientation, on the job training, mentoring, coaching, and job rotation), and off-site training methods (for example, lecture, audio-visual techniques, teleconferencing, corporate classroom). Analoui (1993, pp.72-75) discusses management-training methods in some length and see them as having two sides. Firstly, in-house-type methods, such as those which place the trainee to work closely with someone who is already experienced in the job; place the trainee in someone else's position to do his/her job; and place the trainee in charge of his/her own development. Secondly, outside-type methods, such as lectures, seminars, workshops, conferences, and participation in management games and role-play.

Laird (1978, pp.127-160) suggests that there are 31 methods for training; lecture, reading, demonstration, field trips, note-taking, programmed instruction, discussion, panel discussion, open forum discussion, question and answer sessions, performance try-out, brainstorming, action mazes, case studies, jigsaws, in-baskets, incident process, team tasks, buzz groups, agenda-setting, fishbowls, role plays, reverse role plays, doubling role plays, rotation role plays, simulations, games, clinics, critical incident, training groups, hot role plays, and OD data-gathering.

Alternatively, Christiananta (1987, p.89) specifies that there are training methods for MD development such as self-management, coaching, understudy, position rotation, multiple management, role-playing, simulation, case study, and special courses. But Analoui (1993, p.60) simply calls training either on or off the job type. He mentions that operative training has traditionally been used as an on the job method, whereas in the field of MD he has observed that increasingly employers buy into off the job courses which are offered by an assortment of business and management centres as the solution to the ineffectiveness of individual managers.

The following will discuss briefly four methods often used in training:

Lecture technique The lecture is a teaching method used by most training institutions. Lee (1991), in his survey of most frequently used instructional methods, reported that the lecture was used by 85 per cent of the organisations surveyed. Another survey by (Caeeol et al, 1972) revealed that the lecture method was very poorly regarded for achieving training objectives.

Some criticisms can be traced to the deficiencies in the traditional lecture method. It is a one-way flow of communication from trainer to trainees. The lecture is felt to be deficient for teaching job-related skills that can be transferred from the learning situation to the actual work situation, the lecture ignores differences among trainees' abilities, interests, background, and personalities, and lecture as a method of changing action, that is for the objective of training, is found to be ineffective (Lynton and Pareck, 1967).

It is worth noting at this point that Burke and Day (1986) have integrated the findings from 70 different managerial training research studies. They examined the effectiveness of seven different training methods, and they found that each of the lecturing approaches was effective in improving on the job behaviour as perceived by the trainees themselves, peers, and superiors.

Case study Including cases in the training content is one of many attempts to introduce more real life simulations into the classroom and training programmes. The case study is widely accepted as a method for improving analytical and problem-solving skills. In use, the case study will usually have a description of a problem situation which is given to each trainee, a small group of trainees will discuss and propose solutions, and there are no right or wrong answers (Wexley and Latham, 1991). The trainees must have the opportunity to ascertain the relation between the given case study and their jobs (Pigors and Pigors, 1987).

Role-play Playing roles is a very flexible training method which is frequently used in MD for teaching personnel skills such as interviewing, handling grievances, human relations, leadership styles and their impact on others, and effective communication (Wexley and Latham, 1991). Role-playing is useful because it encourages changes in attitudes and enables trainees to actually learn by doing (Lee, 1991). Kubr and

Prokopenko (1989, p.145) stress that role-playing is related to 'learning through doing; imitating; observation; feedback and analysis'. Role-play is usually used with other training methods such as lecture and group discussion. There are other methods frequently used for training managers, such as case study, which are very similar (Analoui, 1993, p.70).

Business games The purpose of business games is to increase an understanding of specific organisational problems, the relationship between the sector and the environment, the process of company policy and decision making, and participants' training needs or areas for performance improvement (Kubr and Prokopenko, 1989, p.146). Business games are a training technique in which participants are asked to play the management game themselves as a team. This approach to training is currently enjoying a great deal of popularity in both MTD programmes and business school courses (Wexley and Latham, 1991). In this approach, a good deal of information is given about a hypothetical model and about external factors affecting it, in which participants assume various roles as managers of the operations involved. In most games, participants as a team follow a sequence of steps in dealing with problems, make certain decisions, and receive feedback, which reflects the action taken by the opposite team (Kubr and Prokopenko, 1989).

Many Arab researchers (for example, Durra and El-Sabbagh, 1990; Atiyyah, 1993; Al-Rasheed, 1994; Abu-Doleh, 1996) have argued that training methods in the Arab countries are of a conventional nature (mainly lectures), and do not involve the trainees in a dynamic learning process. According to the observations made by the researchers, in the West Bank and Gaza Strip (WBG) the trainers have developed themselves by participation in courses for the training of trainers. These courses are organised by TPs that are interested in developing the training in Palestine, such as the United Nations, MA'AN, and Development Resource Centre. They use different training techniques, such as games, groups, case study, fieldwork, and so on. Management skills and development are usually placed at the top of the list of general types of training for most industries (Lee, 1991).

Managerial skills

Katz (1974, p.94) regarded skill as an 'ability which can be developed and which is manifested in performance, not merely in potential, the ability to translate knowledge into practice'. Many studies (Livingston, 1971; Mintzberg, 1973; Katz, 1974; Albanese, 1989; Lewis and Kelly, 1989; Analoui, 1993; Armstrong, 1994; Whetten and Cameron, 1995; Daft and Marcic, 2001; Yukl, 2002) have proposed myriad management skills required by all managers, which they believe are directly related to the managers' success.

A manager's job is complex and multidimensional and requires a range of skills. Although some management theorists propose a long list of skills, the necessary skills for managing an organisation or a business can be summarised in three categories: conceptual, human, and technical (Daft and Marcic, 2001). Analoui (1993) incorporated managerial skills in three broad and often interrelated categories that are essential for the successful performance of managers:

1. Analytical and self-related skills;
2. People-related skills;
3. Task-related skills.

He proposes that there is a direct relationship between the levels of the skills and the effectiveness of the managers.

Conceptual in nature, the analytical and self-related skills become most important as managers progress to higher positions. Managers, therefore, become increasingly reliant on their abilities to think strategically, and to develop an overview of the business; this means strategic planning and commitment to the realisation of SME objectives. At this level, conceptual skills become the most important of all for successful performance (Katz, 1974). They may include personal skills and personal development, change management, clear and creative thinking, continuous improvement, crisis management, objective setting, performance management, report writing, time management, presentation skills, planning and SME, delegation and control, resource-allocation skills, problem-finding skills, information gathering and problem analysis, decision-making and problem-solving skills, and developing a natural management style.

People-related skills or human (social) skills are argued to be essential for managing people at work. These people-related skills or human skills relate to the interpersonal abilities that one must have to influence people and affect action. Human skills also involve the ability to delegate, and develop subordinates and staff, and are crucial to executives and senior managers. People-related skills are important and require a broad range, which may include communication, motivation, team building and team management, negotiation, consulting, developing people, co-ordinating, leadership and SME skills, and conflict management.

According to Analoui (1993), task-related skills are those which enable managers to manage the work in hand effectively by determining objectives, forecasting, planning, and organising the tasks involved. These may include a range of managerial skills and knowledge, which are specific to the nature of the task performed by them.

Models of skill training in management

Managers play a critical role for business development yet themselves are in need of all three categories of the skills. However, a factor which has been observed to have influence on the preparation of training programmes is the managers' positions in the authority hierarchy of the organisation (Katz, 1955; Mann, 1965; Boyatzis, 1982; Jacobs and Jaques, 1987; Mumford and Connelly, 1991; Mumford et al,

2000). During the last three decades of the 20th century, many theories have talked about different models for MT skills, such as Livingston (1971), Mintzberg (1973), Katz (1974), Boyatzis (1982), Lewis and Kelly (1989), Armstrong (1994), Whetten and Cameron (1995), Analoui (1997), Pedler et al (2001), and Yukl (2002). These different theories have introduced specific models for manager development. These models describe different knowledge and skills for the effective performance of managers. The approach for improving managerial skills for managers throughout MT will be represented by three of the models (Katz, 1974; Analoui, 1997; Yukl, 2002).

Katz's Model (1974)

Katz (1974, p.94) was mostly concerned with the skills that managers needed to do their jobs effectively and defined skill as an 'ability which can be developed and which is manifested in performance, not merely in potential, the ability to translate knowledge into practice'. He proposed a taxonomy of managerial skills for improving managerial work, which was largely based on his experience in working with and studying managers. Many writers such as Wexley and Yukl (1977), Szilagyi (1981), Schermerhom (1984), Albert (1986), Kupr and Prokopenko (1989), Mullins (1993), and Stoner et al (1995), stress that Katz's MTD model of managerial skills is well recognised throughout the literature, and is incorporated in most textbooks on management and organisational behaviour.

It is argued that managers at different levels need different types of skills. Lower-level managers need technical skills more than higher-level managers, who rely more on conceptual skills. Managers at all levels need human skills (Stoner et al, 1995, p.24). Kubr and Prokopenko (1989) talk about three basic managerial skills for the three levels of managers, which Katz called Technical, Human (Social), and Conceptual (Figure 2.5).

Categories of skills	Conceptual	Human	Technical
Level required:	High	Medium	Low
Top Management			
Level required:	Medium	High	Low
Middle Management			
Level required:	Low	Medium	High
		Supervisory Management	

Figure 2.5   Katz' categories of varying required categories of managerial skills

Source: Adapted from Kupr and Prokopenko (1989, p.28)

Kupr and Prokopenko (1989, p.27) aptly remind us that the medium-to-large typical business organisations normally show three basic echelons of the management hierarchy: lower, middle and top management. The number of echelons grows with the size and can reach 4-7 levels in a large business; in a small enterprise, all functions may be concentrated in the hands of one sole person – the owner/manager. Therefore, the scope of competence and the nature of training needs are different at each echelon of the hierarchy and may differ from one business to another depending on the size and nature of the enterprise. Katz (1974, p.102) argues that:

> Managers at all levels require some competence in each of the three skills. A clear idea of these skills and of ways to measure a manager's competence in each category still appears to me to be a most effective tool for top management, not only in understanding executive behaviour, but also in the selection, training and promotion of managers at all levels.

He refers to these skills for managers as follows:

Technical skills These skills are primarily used by lower level managers who are involved with the application of specialised knowledge in the process of producing the goods and services. These skills become relatively less important and more dependent at the top manager levels.

The technical aspects of a manager's job are required by managers who are most concerned with the activities relating to the mission of the business. It is important to be able to follow a production process. Technical skills 'appear to be the easiest to acquire through educational and training activities' (Kupr and Prokopenko, 1989, p.28).

Human (social or people) skills These skills form the ability to select, work with, understand, motivate and lead other people individually or in groups, and work effectively in co-operation with other people. People management skills are important, and require a broad range of communication, motivation, team building and organisation skills, but the importance of organisational, co-ordination and conceptual skills at the middle management level is greater than at a lower level of management. At the top management level, the critical human skills include leadership, understanding environmental trends, constraints and opportunities, conceptualisation, organisation, co-operation, negotiation and public relations (Kupr and Prokopenko, 1989, p.27).

The managers are skilled in understanding what others really mean by their own behaviour (Katz, 1974). Human skills relate to the interpersonal abilities that one must have to influence people and affect action. Thus, they emerge as a spirit of trust, enthusiasm, and genuine involvement in interpersonal relationships. Human skills also involve the ability to delegate and develop subordinates and staff. It is the ability to appraise effectively, and to guide and control the behaviour of subordinates towards better quality performance. Human skills are the key component of effective communication and negotiation.

Human skills are thought to be important for every level of management and remain fairly constant across the levels. However, Katz (1974) believes that they are more important at the lower level of management. However, this does not mean that top management should not be concerned with human skills; on the contrary, human skills are crucial to executives and senior managers. These skills are divided into two subdivisions: leadership ability between the manager's and other units, and leadership ability between the manager's own units.

Conceptual skills Conceptual skills draw heavily on one's mental capacity to recognise problems and opportunities in a given situation. These are the mental ability to integrate and coordinate the organisation's interests and activities. It is the executive's ability to see the business as a whole, to understand how the different parts fit together and depend on each other, and to realise how a change in one part can affect other parts, and subsequently result in changes to the whole business.

To conceptualise the interrelated pattern of relationships among the skills so that the most effective possible course of action can be taken is in the best interest of the organisation (Szilagyi, 1981). For Katz (1974), conceptual skills can be equated with what he terms the 'general management point of view'. This unique point of view, according to Cunnington (1985), involves thinking in terms of the following:

1. Relative emphases and priorities among conflicting objectives and criteria;
2. Relative tendencies and probabilities; rough correlation and patterns among elements.

It is argued that conceptual skills become most important as managers progress to higher positions. Senior managers, therefore, become increasingly reliant on their abilities to think strategically, and to develop an overview of the business, which means strategic planning and commitment to the realisation of organisational objectives. At this level, conceptual skills become the most important of all for successful performance. Conceptual skills extend to visualising the relationship of the individual business to the industry, to the community, and the political as well as social, and economic forces of the nation as a whole (Katz, 1974).

Analoui's model (1997)

Analoui (1997) has introduced three-dimensional areas of concerns for the TD of managers. This model is a descriptive attempt and is primarily concerned with what managers actually do, and what their real TD needs are. His framework (see Figure 2.6) incorporates three distinct categories of managerial skills necessary for the successful performance of managers in an organisation.

For instance, most managers at the beginning of their career tend to show concern for specific (task-related) aspects of managerial activities, and how to cope with its demands, constraints and challenges. Analoui's model works on the principle that, in both theory and practice, as managers move from junior towards more senior and executive positions, they develop concerns that reflect their required categories of skills, namely 'analytical and self-related, people-related, and task-related skills' (p.77).

Consequently, managers become increasingly aware of their micro internal and macro external environments related to each of these areas of concern. It is expected that managers' awareness go beyond their own individual work environment towards the wider environmental context. Hence, middle managers at this developmental stage of their managerial concerns are typically concerned with, and are aware of the business activities, and as they take up even more senior management and executive positions, they are more likely to develop further awareness of aspects of their own self, people and tasks which are beyond the conventional boundaries of the business. These concerns may even extend to national and international activities related to the people and cognitive concerns of their work.

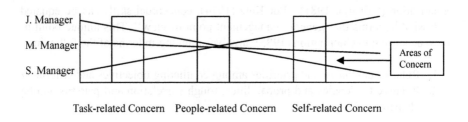

Task-related Concern   People-related Concern   Self-related Concern

Figure 2.6   Managers' areas of concern

Source: Adapted from Analoui (1997, p.31)

Yukl's model (2002)

Yukl (2002) argues that Skills priorities at different levels of management are related to the differing role requirements at each level. Moreover, to be successful, a leader also needs to have considerable ability. Thus, three general categories of skills relevant to managers are conceptual, interpersonal, and technical skills. Figure 2.7 shows the relative importance of the three broad skill categories to leadership effectiveness for low-level managers, middle-level managers, and top executive. Managerial level affects not only the relevance of the three broad categories of skills described earlier in Katz's model (i.e., conceptual, interpersonal, technical), but also related to the relative importance of specific types of skills within each category.

The relative priority of the three types of skills probably depends on the specific skills within each broad category which also depends on the situation. Some skills such as persuasiveness, analytical ability, speaking ability, and memory for details will help a manager to be successful in any situation, whereas some other skills are not easily transferred to different types of position. Relevant competencies identified in more recent research include emotional intelligence, social intelligence, and the ability to learn and adapt to change.

In the recent past, scholars, educators and practitioners of management have shown much concern for the learning and acquisition of managerial knowledge as apart from the development of management skills (Livingston, 1971; Filley, 1979; Peters and Waterman, 1982; Hayes, 1983).

Nowadays, attention has turned to the improvement of managerial skills as the most appropriate means of achieving MTD objectives (Livingston, 1971; Katz, 1974; Drucker, 1974; and Boyatzis, 1982; Analoui and Hosseini, 2001).

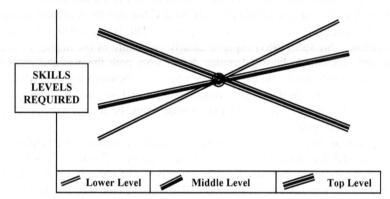

Figure 2.7   Levels of management and required levels of skills

Source: Adapted from Yukl (2002, p.199)

The effectiveness of managerial behaviour is thus considered to be both a function of knowledge and of skills. In addition to analytical skills, it is argued that managers, in particular senior managers, require skills for managing themselves, other people, and tasks (Kakabadse et al, 1987).   For example, Katz (1974) developed a MD model, which incorporated the above basic categories of skills: technical, human, and conceptual. Katz's (1974) commentary on his original article written some 20 years earlier contends:

> I now realise more fully that managers at all levels require some competence in each of the three skills. A clear idea of these skills and of ways to measure a manager's competence in each category still appears to me to be a most effective tool for top management, not only in understanding executive behaviour, but also in the selection, training and promotion of managers at all levels (p.102).

His work provides some support for the argument that the hierarchical level in which managers function tends to influence their need for the three broad categories of technical, human, and conceptual skills. He further contends that in practice these skills are so closely interrelated that it is difficult to determine where one ends and another begins. Moreover, although all three sets of skills are important, they vary in relative importance at different managerial positions. Technical skill is said to be seen as more important by those who function at lower levels of the managerial hierarchy, whereas human skills are thought to be essential at all levels. For top management, however, conceptual skills become increasingly important.

Katz's (1974) model, however, did not address a set of very important skills – analytical and self-development – which are now believed to be highly influential in terms of achieving managerial effectiveness (Stewart, 1963; Margerison, 1984, 1985; and Analoui, 1990). Thus, little seems to have been established about the importance of the aspect of self-management and the relevant managerial skills and abilities and their exact contribution to the effectiveness of senior managers.

Managerial tasks and responsibilities may be divided into three primary areas; managing self, managing others, and managing work. This is referred to as 'aspects of management'. Stewart (1963) explains clearly the nature of the manager's job based on some commonly known features drawn from both theories and proven facts. She makes a distinction in the manager's functions between deciding what to do and arranging for it to be done. She favours a simple and practical definition, and broadly defines the manager's job as 'deciding what should be done and then getting other people to do it' (p.65).

She explains in detail how these two tasks, which are actually overlapping in practice, demand different sets of capabilities from managers. The first task demands that the manager should be capable of setting objectives, planning, decision-making, and organising the work in the organisation. The second task requires the ability to motivate, communicate, measure, and control as well as develop other people. Clearly the emphasis here is placed both on 'managing the work' and on 'managing the people'.

The importance of self-management has only recently been brought to our attention as a major part of managerial behaviour (Luthans and Davis, 1979; Manz and Sims, 1980; Margerison, 1984; Jones and Woodcock, 1985). As Luthans and Davis (1979) have observed, the aspect of self-management is perhaps the most overlooked area in the field of management. They view self-management as a basic prerequisite for increased managerial effectiveness. They claim that 'behavioural self-management may be the important missing link – the first step in the inductive chain – for increased managerial effectiveness' (p.43). Based on this premise, it is claimed that behavioural self-management is the missing link for improved managerial performance.

In an effort to provide a holistic picture of what really constitutes effective managerial behaviour, Jones and Woodcock (1985) state that managing self is the core of managerial effectiveness. Accordingly, they assert that self-management sets a ceiling for managerial effectiveness.

Managers who look after themselves have more energy available for directing the work of others. On the other hand, managers who feel stressed, who do not direct their own career development and create situations for their own advancement, waste a lot of time and energy that might otherwise be available for organisational tasks (p.43).

To be effective, therefore, implies that managers must first ensure their self-development as a continuous process through personal and professional growth, and then the acquisition of sufficient related managerial skills for managing tasks and people. Each aspect of management, therefore, demands a different set of demonstrable skills from effective managers at all levels. It is for this reason that managerial skills are classified into three basic, albeit overlapping, categories: analytical and self-related, people-related, and task-related skills which all need to be incorporated in a model of management training and development. A model originally developed by Analoui (1989 and 1993) is based on the above theoretical premise.

It is interesting to see that most available literature considers senior managers as a homogeneous group, especially with respect to their MTD needs. Thus, no significant attempts have been made to classify senior managers by their seniority or to examine how the occupants of each category perceive the importance of their required skills, or how the need for skills may vary in accordance with the different demands and constraints experienced by a top management team (Analoui et al, 2000).

Management training and development (MTD)

In addition, Porter and McKibbin (1988) and Rosti and Shipper (1998) have asserted that training in managerial skills is lacking. Management training aims at effective, direct and rapid development of specific useful skills, and concentrates on preparing individuals for effective performance in defined positions. MT programmes can be carried out either inside or outside the organisation. Management Training is part of Human Resource Management (HRM). What is the responsibility of the HRM to a manager? What kinds of job and what skills are stressed for Human Resource Development (HRD)?

Bedeian (1989, p.288) states HRM should specify employment planning, performance appraisal, recruitment, training, selection, compensation, orientation, and discipline. He defines HRM as 'the process of assuring that competent employees are selected, developed, and rewarded for achieving enterprise objectives'. The task of training others is not an easy assignment, especially for those individuals involved.

The degree of importance of MT depends on the management system used in the business, and depends on the organisation as well. The inseparable relationship between organisations and management theories has meant that management theories evolved and were based around the ways organisations were viewed (Analoui, 1998, p.3). The existing literature on management education and training reveals a widely recognised need for managerial skill development as the most appropriate approach to MTD and business school education (Livingston, 1971; Mintzberg, 1973, 1975;

Waters, 1980; Boyatzis, 1982; Peters and Waterman, 1982; Porter, 1983; Powers, 1983; Waters et al, 1983; Behrman and Levin, 1984; Whetten and Cameron, 1984; Hopelain, 1985; Mol and Vermeulen, 1988; Kuber and Prokopenko, 1989; Davis, 1990; Analoui, 1993, 1997; MacMahon and Murphy, 1999; Analoui and Husseini, 2001; Al-Madhoun and Analoui, 2002).

Since the nature of training for non-managerial employees differs from that for people in managerial and executive positions, it is desirable to differentiate between employee training and management development. Much of employee training is job or task-centred rather than career-focused, and it is supplementary to the basic job and skill training obtained from other institutions, such as public and technical schools. On the other hand, MT includes the processes by which managers and executives acquire not only skills and competencies in their present jobs, but also capacities for future managerial tasks involving complex intangibles, such as conceptual thought and powers of analysis and decision making (McFarland, 1968, pp.291-293).

Hussey (1988, p.69), in his study of the general practice and approach to management training in the UK, concluded that MT should be for the improvement of the individual, because this will benefit the firm. Training should be for the benefit of the firm, but will also benefit the individual. This change of emphasis is more than a play on words. Mumford (1991, 1994) argues that one major problem of MD is the fact that it has been separated from the reality of managerial behaviour, as well as the perceptions and understanding of managers themselves. Livingston (1971) said that there was no direct relationship between performance in business school or training programmes and successful performance in management jobs. He claimed that 'men who get to the top in management have developed skills that are not taught in formal management education programmes and may be difficult for many highly educated men to learn on the job'.

Wall (1963) maintained that the effectiveness of this method is increased if the training goals are set for each job assignment and a coaching manager provides instruction and feedback. Koontz and O'Donnell (1955) also hold that if rotation provides for 'assistant to' or 'acting' in managerial positions, the trainee can get actual job experience in administrative and supervisory skills with some of the risk removed.

An underlying theme that emerged from the training literature over the past decade is that training must be linked to an organisation's strategy if it is to be viewed by higher management as effective (Latham, 1988). Ensuring that the training plan is constructed in the same context and the same process as the business plan should do this. More recently, the current approach to defining training needs is based on a thorough analysis of the training provider's mission. From this mission-based analysis, training objectives are derived. There are some key words here that warrant attention. First, MT as part of management development should be considered as a continuous process as well as an integral part of management work, and to be successful, it should provide and maintain a balance between the changing needs and nature of individuals, jobs and corporation (Temporal, 1990). In this regard, Temporal goes further to say that MD is wasting its time and making futile investment unless it is strategically focused. Bearing this point in mind, Mitchell (1993) stated clearly the necessity to establish the link between organisational strategy and executive TD.

From Mol and Vermeulen (1988, p.22), the message is that 'two-thirds of the factors that are essential to the success of a management development programme depend on the management of the organisation, and more specifically, top management, rather than on the trainers'. In this regard, House (1967) has postulated that top management commitment is probably the most critical requirement for the success of any development effort. He stresses two fundamental requirements for a development programme to achieve its goal. Top management a) must participate actively in the process of establishing the programme, and b) ought to accept the responsibility for creating an environment conducive to development (House, 1967, p.60).

To sum up, numerous research projects and studies conducted on MTD in different industries and in different countries have centred on the commitment of top managers (senior management) as a prerequisite for successful training programmes. Examples of this research include Jones and Woodcock (1985), Collins (1990), Conant (1991), Long (1991), Sinclair and Collins (1992), Delatte and Baits (1993), and Mitchell (1993).

The aim is to delineate the motives for MTD. Peel (1984), quoted in Gordon (1987, p.4), has provided survey data on what companies perceive their MTD objectives to be. Peel lists these as follows:

1. To improve manager's/company performance;
2. To develop the manager to meet company requirements;
3. To improve specific knowledge and skills;
4. To increase job satisfaction;
5. To up-date in new techniques;
6. To broaden experience/provide appreciation of other functions.

Time and again, the nature of the responsibility for training and how it is exercised varies with the level of management, the culture or sub-culture, and size of the corporation. In this regard, Kenney and Reid (1986, p.35) maintain that top management have four major responsibilities towards the training function as follows:

1. They bear much of the burden for creating and sustaining a positive attitude towards human resource development through their organisation;
2. They determine the organisation's policies for TD and ensure that they are supported with the necessary resources;
3. To a greater extent than they often realise, top management, by their personal involvement in training and by taking a consistent interest in training decisions and interventions, provide the environmental energy which gives the training function much of its corporate vitality.

The quality of an organisation's MTD is critically dependent on the personal commitment of its top management.

In the field of MTD, management trainers and educators play an important part in achieving the required development objectives and the range of competencies, knowledge and skills which are necessary to meet effectively the training needs of those trainee managers for whose training they are held responsible. Both management trainers and their institutions ought to be prepared to cope with the constant change in what is demanded of them, should they be interested in the survival and future development of their institution in the competitive environment in which they operate.

Recently, the trainers who deal with managers from developing countries are, therefore, required to acquire a variety of forms of knowledge and managerial skills to be able to carry out their jobs effectively. Recent studies in the field of MT (Analoui, 1990) further indicated that there is also the need for self and career development on the part of managers which must be considered. This desire on the part of managers for discovery of their own potential adds another important item to the list of MD needs which management trainers and educators normally face. Managers have indicated that the satisfaction of their desire for self-development will also function as a motivator for further learning and, consequently, the development of the organisation as a whole (Analoui, 1990).

In short, management trainers and educators, in order to do their job effectively, have to perform a multitude of roles. The difficulty lies in finding a single statement as to what the role of training specialists should be. Indeed, the part that trainers play in the process of training is by no means standard – there is a multiplicity of roles they can take on (Analoui, 1990). It is therefore not surprising to see that the search on the part of management educators and trainers for the most effective ways to train and develop managers and officials has gathered such a pace.

Analoui (1994) outlines five areas of expertise and competence for trainers involved in the effective training of managers and officials:

1. Up-to-date knowledge and skills of technical (task-related) and social (people-related) aspects of managerial theories, practices and methods of training for on and off-the-job training situations.
2. Adequate knowledge about the trainees' learning capabilities, style and attitudes, as well as knowledge of the use of relevant learning aids.
3. Sufficient knowledge of trainees' tasks, roles, organisational culture and socio-economic, political and cultural environment.
4. Knowledge of the trainees' unique cultural background and the influence, which political, socio-economic and educational factors will have on their organization and the trainees themselves. (This aspect of knowledge required on the part of the trainer may be extended to the relationship between the trainees' organisation and the international agencies whose support is needed to implement the changes required by the trainees.)

5. Awareness of the issues, which affect the quantity and the quality of the learnt material to be transferred to the trainees' organisation.

In brief, the reader should be reminded that environmental, social, and organisational factors, all have their influences on TD functions/ programmes, let alone the effectiveness of training. We take the stand to understand the mechanism of the MTD functions within the organisation itself, therefore the above discussion was limited only to the organisational factors affecting TD.

Management training systems

There is no one single system for training (Goldstein, 1980). Goldstein added that the Training Agency has defined the system as the process of 'identifying inputs, outputs, components and sub-systems, and then seeking to identify the contribution that training can make to improving the operation by enhancing the contribution of the human components as opposed to machinery and operational procedures'. The system approach is next applied to the training design, where the components are learning strategies and people, and the objectives are in terms of learning. Finally, the systems approach is applied to the interaction between training and the operation to produce a feedback, which can be used to improve subsequent training (Abu-Doleh, 1996, pp.2-11).

Warren (1969) stresses the fact that the training must be considered as a sub-system within the organisation. For him, 'what makes a training sub-system valuable is its ability to bring about required behaviour change in terms of skills, knowledge, and attitudes, not the number of programmes it runs or its ability to utilise the newest technical advances in the field of education' (p.7).

Therefore, it is the line manager's responsibility to work in harmony with the T&D personnel to bring about the desired results. Wexley and Latham (1991) include such contributing factors as the company financial position, organisation strategy, structure, technology, management attitudes, and legal aspects of training and development.

Thus MTD is based on a systematic process. Kubr and Prokopenko (1989), however, take one further step and suggest a global model of the MD cycle. They have developed a five-stage model to describe the system approach to the MTD cycle. This model is made up of five sequential activities. These are:

Needs assessment

This comes at the beginning of any systematic approach to MTD. The needs assessment is very important to understanding the gap between the needs and the results.

Objectives setting

The information obtained from the needs assessment is used to construct the training programme and training methods. Abu-Doleh (1996, p.15) poses that objectives should be tailored to the people who will take the training course. Without such stated training objectives, evaluation of training results becomes impressionistic, and it will be impossible to assess accurately the overall effectiveness of training (Kubr and Prokopenko, 1989). McDonald also expresses a similar view: 'Without a stated plan of activity or with merely a vague statement of intention, training of participants and organisation resources can lack co-ordination and a common direction' (1989, p.63).

Programme design

The training plan described above is useful to the programme designer and to the compatibility between TP and managerial and organisational needs. As Analoui (1993, p.59) emphasises, the TP should be designed for and used to meet the training requirements of the operatives or the management.

   However, the content of MTPs should focus in particular on the real issues and problems those managers have to deal with. Therefore, as designers or as managers of the programme design, T&D specialists need knowledge, experience, and the value system of learning/training methods (Laird, 1978). Abu-Doleh (1996, p.16) argues that the investigations of on-site and off-site MT methods are crucial at this stage to ensure not only the cost/benefit analysis of the training programme but also to ensure its content validity.

Programme implementation

It is important to implement the MTP in accordance with the programme design. However, those who are responsible for delivering the programme should be qualified and experienced in solving managerial problems (Abu-Doleh, 1996, pp.2-16). Davis stresses that the goals of MTD and the methods of implementation need to be considered together (1990, p.58). He points out eight approaches to delivering a MTP: internal training specialists; the manager's boss; the individual manager; senior management; external trainers and educators; internal promotions; rotations; transfers and special assignment; external recruitment; and external consultants. Davis further argues that the strengths and weaknesses of different approaches to delivery need careful analysis before a commitment to particular methods of TD is adopted, since there is no best approach to MTD.

Evaluation and follow-up

Only through evaluation can one gauge a TP success. The most common reason for evaluation is to determine if the effectiveness of future programmes can be improved (Laird, 1978, p.254).

The evaluation process attempts to measure the costs and the benefits of a complete training system rather than merely the achievement of its laid-down objectives. The training needs analysis and objectives setting are prerequisites to programme evaluation (Abu-Doleh, 1996). Hamblin (1974) refers to evaluation as 'any attempt to obtain information (feedback) on the effects of a training programme and to assess the value of the training in the light of that information'. For him, training evaluation is one part of a long-term systematic process in order to maintain and develop an effective TP. Kirkpatrick (1979, p.78) stresses that the evaluation of a TP in terms of results is progressing at a very slow rate, where the objectives of a TP may be as specific as the reduction of accidents, the reduction of grievances, and the reduction of costs. More recently, Goldstein (1986) considers that in evaluating the TP, content validity (TP design should reflect the domains of the trainees' knowledge, skills, and abilities) by itself is not enough to guarantee the trainees' ability to transfer what they were taught back to their job-related setting. On the other hand, it is more difficult to evaluate training simulations. Also, the simulations are more cost-effective in training for skills and attitude changes than in training for knowledge (Latham, 1988).

MT evaluation could be one of the most neglected stages in any MT process. The thrust of effective evaluation is to make responsible judgements about the important question of how you do a TD. Interestingly, American business spends US $30 billion on TD programmes, and less than 10 per cent of that expenditure is evaluated for value-adding impact (Fitzenz, 1988). The Manpower Services Commission published a Glossary of Training Terms (1981), which distinguishes between the meanings of the terms internal and external validation.

Internal validation is a series of tests and assessments designed to ascertain whether a TP has achieved the behavioural objectives specified. External validation is a series of tests and assessments and is designed to ascertain whether the behavioural objectives of the internally valid TP were realistically based on an accurate initial identification of training needs in relation to the criteria of effectiveness adopted by the organisation (Terms, 1981). Krein and Weldon say that there are four levels of evaluation of the TP:

1. How participants reacted to the programme;
2. What participants learned from the programme;
3. Whether what was learned is being applied on the job;
4. Whether that application is achieving results (1994, p.63).

Laird (1978, pp.256-266) argues that there are three ways for evaluation: by measuring contribution to goals, by achievement of training objectives, and by perceptions. By contribution to goals, he stresses that to establish success or failure in this dimension, the evaluation must be based on quantitative data. Quantitative data immediately suggest baselines: 'How many defective units did the organisation suffer from before the programme? After the programme?'.

In general, quantitative analysis is rarely done in organisations to ensure that training is effective (Stephen et al, 1988; Carnevale and Schultz, 1990; Church, 1997; Rosti and Shipper, 1998).

Kirkpatrick's (1994) now classic model of four levels of training evaluation is probably still the most robust and widely used both in research into training effectiveness and in HRD practice:

Level 1: What is the initial *reaction* of participants to the training?
Level 2: What have participants actually *learnt* from the training?
Level 3: Are participants *behaving* differently as a result of the training?
Level 4: Has the training of these participants had the desired *result* in the workplace?

This has been derived and adapted from Kirkpatrick's original and numerous subsequent sources. You may want to compare it with others, including Warr et al's (1970) CIRO (context, input, reaction, and outcome) approach. This has tended to be used more widely in Europe. A succinct explanation can be found in Phillips (1991, p.41). Further applications can be found in Bramley (1996), Barrington and Reid (1997), and Wilson (1999).

The most common way that training has been evaluated, when it is done, is through the reaction of the participants to the training (Brown, 1980; Dunn and Thomas, 1985). This assumes that if the participants like the training, it must be effective. Such evaluations provide little substantive information regarding the value of the training. Obviously, a more rigorous assessment of the effectiveness of the training is needed (Brown, 1980; Dunn and Thomas, 1985; Carnevale and Schultz, 1990; Rosti and Shipper, 1998; Analoui and Hosseini, 2001; Burke and Collins, 2001; Al-Madhoun, 2002).

Therefore, training evaluation should include transfer validity. As recently as the early 1970s, people were taught how to train others by trial-and-error methods. Basically, they were thrown into a room of people and told to train them. Needless to say, the use of this approach often produced mixed results (Ellis, 1989, p.136). Kirkpatrick (1976) suggests that there are four levels requiring assessment when analysing the effectiveness of a MTD programme. He identifies those four levels as reaction, learning, behaviour, and results.

Emotional reaction/response

This is designed to answer the question of whether the participants like the TP or not. This is usually related to the trainees' attitudes towards a particular programme, including content of training, methods of training, trainer competence, facilities, length and pace of training, accommodation, learning acquisition, and so on.

Learning

This is typically an end-of-course evaluation to measure the knowledge, skill and behaviour gained through the TD intervention.

Behaviour change

It was noted earlier that measuring reaction and learning could be accomplished at or near the end of the TP. On the other hand, behaviour change refers to any changes in skills, knowledge, and attitude brought about by the TD programme.

Results

It is important to measure the results of training in terms of organisational or group performance. Results might include a change in turnover, improvement in communication systems, increase in quantity and quality of units produced, and so on. For Mol and Vermeulen (1988, p.22), the message is that 'two-thirds of the factors that are essential to the success of a management development program depend on the management of the organisation, and more specifically, top management, rather than on the trainers'. In this regard, House (1967) has postulated that top management commitment is probably the most critical requirement for the success of any development effort. For him, if a development effort is to succeed, top management must meet two fundamental requirements: 'active participation in the establishment of the development program and acceptance of responsibility for providing an environment conducive to development' (House, 1967, p.60).

In brief, environmental and social factors, the business, and the manager, all have their influences on MTD programmes for effectiveness of MT. This study of MTD is for managers and businesses, therefore the above discussion was limited only to the manager and business factors affecting MTD.

Summary

This chapter addresses different managerial issues. At the start, the chapter discussed the basic definition for management, managers, and the role of MTD for business success.

Many authors consider that for businesses to be successful they must support managers by managerial skills and knowledge. Managers, in particular senior managers, play critical roles in business success. So managers need to improve their managerial skills, for developing these skills they need to attend MTPs.

From the survey of MTD characteristics in general, there are many different results from MTD in businesses; in particular, some of these results come from the managerial abilities and skills of the managers.

MTD plays an important role in the developing countries. This importance can be shown on the side of income generation.

In brief, the reader should be reminded that management is an important determinant of the businesses development. The main functions of MTPs ought to include enabling managers to practise an effective role. These concerns for increasing the knowledge and skills of managers in Palestine has led to a decade of MTPs being implemented by various national and international donor agencies. Their effectiveness and their impact on the SMEs business has been the subject of first time study, and its results will be discussed in following chapters.

Chapter Three

Management Training and Development in the Middle East

Introduction

Small and Micro Enterprises (SMEs) in Palestine

During the last decades of the twentieth century, SMEs began to occupy an important position thus playing a significant role in the global economy. In Palestine, SMEs have played a critical role in the building of a strong and independent economy (UNRWA, 1998, p.4). There are 22,495 businesses in the GS (PCBS, 1999), 91 per cent of which is comprised of the SMEs sector (20,470). These have only one to four employees, while 83 per cent of the businesses were reported to have sole proprietorships (PCBS, 1996, p.70). In the same vein, the International Labour Organisation reports that 97 per cent of the Palestinian businesses are micro- and small, with fewer than ten workers, although the majority of the businesses are family businesses. Male ownership still prevails since less than 10 per cent of the total businesses are owned by women (PCBS, 1996, p.80).

In Palestine, the prevalence of the SME is basically due to the Israeli occupation, which since 1967 employed specific measures to restrict the development of the Palestinian economy and compel the OT to be dependent on the Israeli economy (Naser, 1999).

The owners and managers of SMEs are experienced and have survived turbulent market conditions, but they suffer from administrative and managerial skill and competency weakness. Most SMEs have been initiated on family capital by ex-Palestinian labourers of Israeli firms with few, if any, management skills (Abu Eljedian, 1996). To solve this problem, TPs organised training courses to develop the managerial skills for the owners and managers of these micro and small enterprises. This cadre of owners, owner/managers and managers have been the primary target group for the above training programmes.

Safi (1998, pp.4-5) argues that there are many obstacles which faced the training for the SMEs in the GS. For example, there are no training modules or manuals which might be considered as reference materials by trainers, and in general, few trainers use the modern training methods. The characteristics of the target group (prospective trainees) are not always analysed well; trainers who are contracted to deliver training for potential owner/managers are usually lecturers in business colleges, but they do not possess adequate background knowledge about the SMEs in the GS.

In this context, we argue that management training for business development needs to be identified as a priority area. Those managing SME programmes should be assisted and encouraged in acquiring basic management skills at the start-up, followed at later stages by more comprehensive MTPs, which are appropriate to running a growing concern (Salman, 1997, p.294).

Budget for the PDP (MOPIC, 1997, p.136) emphasises the SME development programme needs, during three years, (1998-2000) to be as much as $5 million. The problem, however, is not funding alone. Indeed, in so far as funding is concerned, many countries have shown a willingness to support the SMEs in Palestine with aid, consultants and training.

Lending to SMEs

Despite their recent decline, lending NGOs still have an important role to play in the WBG financial system. Unlike other NGOs, such as those involved in health and education, lending NGOs serve a function that has not been assumed by the PNA. Lending NGOs extend loans to SMEs that lack collateral and credit history and which, therefore, are not of interest to commercial banks. If small enterprises are to become sustainable, they must find ways to become less dependent on subsidies. To do so, lending NGOs may have to eliminate most of their interest subsidies, as some have already done. They also may have to find ways to minimise default risk without relying entirely on collateral. One achievable option is to make use of the group risk-sharing method, which was pioneered by UNRWA and Save the Children. The UNRWA's Solidarity Group Lending Programme, offering working capital loans to women micro-enterprise owners, has consistently had 100 per cent repayment rates since its inception in 1994. Managerial and technical assistance is provided to small borrowers, especially to those likely to suffer from market discrimination (Diwan and Shaban, 1998, p.27).

Hamed (1998) believes that there is still a need for lending NGOs, since the banks are not interested in small loans or credit to individuals without security. The experience of the Third World supports this conclusion and shows that if provision of credit from these organisations is halted, credit will still continue, but in secret and at high interest rates. Hamed argues that legislation by the Palestinian Monetary Authority to forbid money changers from receiving deposits is a positive step to encourage investment in the financial sector. However, legislation to prevent credit from money changers is unjustified economically, since money-changers lend money from their own capital. Hamed recommends that the relationship between the formal and informal sector should be strengthened. The two sectors already complement one another to a certain extent. For example, merchants who sell their goods on credit borrowed from banks and lend it on through the selling process. Hamed suggests a separation between the two types of NGOs involved in the lending. The first type are those NGOs that provide credit without interest and carry the responsibility to grant loans as a form of assistance to certain sectors of society. The second type give credit with interest, since external funding is not permanent and the interest would be the principal means to cover running costs. The importance of these organisations lies in their ability to provide credit to individuals who are unable to obtain a bank loan due to the obstacles discussed above.

Most of the SME owners in the WBG use irregular loans granted to friends and neighbours based on their emergent needs. Hamed's study shows that 7.1 per cent of the population, aged 18 years old and over, put their money with friends and relatives rather than in banks. At the same time, it is concluded that 70 per cent of loans in the WBG take place through money-changers, and this highlights their importance to the financial sector and the Palestinian economy as a whole.

Kanan (1998, p.32) discusses investment in the WB and GS, arguing that during 1993-1997 the size of deposits of the commercial banks increased from $500 million to $1.9 billion. The banks opened for lending to SMEs; at the same time, some aid from donors went to the local banks for lending to the SMEs.

In his study, Hamed (1998) investigates the role of the informal financial sector and lending NGOs in the WBG. The study considers the scope and extent of coverage of informal finance and the relevance of this sector after 1993 with the growth of the formal financial sector. The informal sector plays a substantial role in the WBG. Correspondingly, the new study (Qudeh, 1999) from the Palestinian Planning Centre emphasises that the size of the lending from the banks to businesses during the last three years was around $130 million ($44 million per year). At the same time, the lending from the lending programmes was about $115 million ($39.38 million per year).

The above study also points to the obstacles facing the lending programmes, such as money collection, lack of co-operation between lending programmes, lending programmes missed, lending policies with legal weaknesses, sectors that need development not specified because they work without an investment development plan. Also, Kanan (1998) adds to the list of the obstacles facing lending agencies the important fact that the SMEs need more experience of establishing and maintaining relationships with the banks, because the owners of SMEs have been without a banking system for 25 years.

After the peace process (1993) there were more than 25 lending and training programmes opened for development of the SMEs in the GS (UNRWA, 1998). These programmes are different and have different target groups and objectives. A number of them offer small-scale loans for women (Salman, 1997).

Al-Madhoun and Analoui (2002) discuss four kinds of programmes that support SMEs.

First, 'lending and training programmes', which develop the SMEs through lending and training, most of the programmes in the GS are engaged in both activities. These programmes include international organisations, such as UNRWA's development and planning department, and micro-enterprise lending programme (UNRWA, 1998, p.5), and NGOs, such as the Women's Affairs Centre. At the same time, both the international organisations and the NGOs are almost all financed by donors.

Secondly, 'the SME training programmes' that develop the Human Resources in managerial and technical skills. Some of these programmes are managed directly by international organisations, such as the Italian Association for Women in Development. The other programmes are managed by the NGOs, such as the Palestinian Institution for Professional Training, and the National Foundation for Development and Investment.

Thirdly, 'the lending organisations programmes', which have been developing SMEs during the lending period. There are many banks in the GS, such as the Palestinian Commercial Bank, also institutions such as the Micro-enterprise Project started in 1998 with a budget of $20 million from the World Bank, International Finance Centre, and from the three participating banks. The Project finances the SMEs in the WBG through the banking system (World Bank, 1998, p.10). Other international organisations too, such as the Palestinian Development Fund (PDF), a privately owned, non-profit development agency have been established and help by promoting the sound growth of the Palestinian SMEs. Through the provision of medium-term loans and associated financial aid, 80 per cent of PDF projects are funded by the European Union (Alrisala al Uropia, 1996, p.4), and NGOs, such as the Palestinian Development Institution, the biggest programme for lending (Qudeh, 1999), with $45 million from the European Union to aid the SMEs in WB and GS through this programme (European Union Report, 1996, p.10). Qudeh (1999) argues that the lending institutions have spent $39.38 million per year as a loan. On the other hand, the banks have spent $43-44 million annually. The MAS (1998) discussion concludes that the gap between the needs and the offers is $118 million if the minimum expected is $200 million.

The studies about the lending institutions and their roles for development mention many problems with which the lending institutions are faced. These include cases where some of the businesses can not repay the loan, a lack of co-operation between institutions, a lack of clear plans and policies, the evaluation of the managers of SMEs by the lending institutions, missing statistical data about the businesses, institutions not studying the real loan needs, lack of managerial experience of the lending institutions, lack of follow-up for the businesses which have loans, and the problems concerning the business of changing money from the US $ and the Shekel (Al-Qady, 1997; Qudeh, 1999).

Fourth, 'the organisations that help to develop SMEs through information and consultation', thus enabling them to compete in local, regional and world markets (Alrisala al Uropia, 1997, p.4). There are four kinds: governmental organisations, such as investment departments; private sector offices for studies; consultants such as Master and Palcon; and the NGO programmes, such as the Development Resource Centre.

The World Bank and MAS (1997) conclude that long-term SME development is directly associated with their need to finance themselves. Having said that, NGOs and banks also need to follow a new policy and a direction that does not ask SMEs for a high percentage for fixed yearly interest, and does not ask SME owners for high liability, which means high risk. Also, they should advise the SME to start as a sharing group and follow shareholding company strategies, and be advised to use the money from the retirement fund for new investment.

Finally, it could be argued that there is an urgent need for a strategy with emphasis on development of SMEs in the PT. It is hoped empirical studies help to provide the necessary information, knowledge and guidelines to enable the researcher to draw a more comprehensive framework of analysis for future development.

Management and development for SMEs in the Middle East

It is aptly argued that basically, in the developing countries, 'managers should be trained to play the roles of developer, change agent, innovator and creator, resource optimiser, and manager of differences and conflicts, as well as entrepreneur. The management training effort in the developing countries must strive to build up its own national identity' (Bharadwaj, 1975, p.160). However, it is imperative to consider the development of the managers in a specific context namely the developing world. It is in this domain that the realities of managing tasks, people and self take a particular significance. Bussom et al, (1984) draw major lessons from the study of the developing countries. They argue that inter-organisational context and inter-organisational dynamics can have a great impact on large-scale MD programmes in developing countries. The impact of culture on individual, managerial and organisational behavior is seen as being significant.

Bharadwaj (1975, p.160) also refers to the problems faced and difficulties encountered by MTD in the developing countries. He argues that, in most developing countries, there seems to be hardly any systematic approach towards training needs assessment (sometimes called training needs assessment – TNA) at the national level, organisation level, or individual level. Often, even the existing facilities for MD are not fully utilised. Evaluation of the effectiveness of MD activities is universally difficult. These findings, as we have already pointed out, are not unique to a specific part of the world. Indeed, many examples of these mal or non-existent practices have been observed in the Middle East.

Leaving the twentieth century behind, it is not possible to chart the future of MTD in the Arab world. The Arab world runs from the Atlantic Ocean in the West, to Iran in the East, and to the Mediterranean Sea and Turkey in the North. There are 200 million Arabs in 22 Arab countries, and 90 per cent of them are Muslims. Religion and language are two important elements of culture (El-Hifnawi, 1997, p.206). The studies concerning MTD in the Arab world are not sufficient (Al-Falah, 1987; Abu-Doleh, 1996). Although this volume is dedicated to the practices of MTD in Palestine, it also attempts to compare the results with other studies conducted in other Arab countries. Interestingly, Roy's (1977) study of management education and training in the Arab world has shown that the days of exporting western training packages to other developing countries which have their own cultural values are definitely over. Al-Ali and Taylor (1997) describe MTD in the Arab world, after independence, by saying that Arab countries had to face a number of problems, such as lack of manpower, lack of well educated and trained management, and lack of professional and skilled management staff. They highlight other problems: non-existence of a comprehensive, well-integrated national plan for administrative development, lack of co-ordination among agencies, lack of proper commitment among management, and a shortage of experienced personnel, trainers and consultants who take responsibility for smooth administrative development.

Many difficulties and obstacles face the Arab countries; to tackle these, many efforts have already been made, such as the establishment of public institutes for administrative studies, government support, and funding and facilitating a number of research projects which have been conducted by specialists. Despite these efforts, there remains very little research about MD.

Al-Faleh (1987, p.20) explored the phenomenon of cultural influences on Arab MD in Jordan, and made the following observations about the nature of Arab management:

1. Within an organisation, status, position and seniority significantly outweigh ability and performance. Organisations are centrally controlled with a low level of delegation. The authoritarian management style is predominant.
2. Decision-making is constantly pushed upwards in the organisation. Management is reactive and crisis-oriented. An atmosphere of low-trust and political gamesmanship characterise organisations, and this, together with closed information systems and low levels of disclosure by organisation members, is regarded as natural and acceptable.
3. Arab managers run their organisations as family units and often assume a paternalistic role in them. They value loyalty over efficiency. Punctuality and time constraints are of much less concern than in Western cultures. Managers rely upon family and friendship ties for getting things done within an organisation and in society in general.
4. Managers' behaviour is greatly influenced by cultural values and historical background. Writers and scholars of management often quote the above characteristics when they describe management in any Arab country (Muna, 1980; Shaikh, 1988).

These characteristics led Al-Faleh (1987) to question the effectiveness of development programmes for Arab managers, which attempt to transfer Western management training techniques to Arab countries that have a different cultural environment.

Al-Faleh, in his study of the cultural influences on Arab management development, reported that 'a country's culture has a great influence on the individual and managerial climate, on organisational behaviour, and ultimately on the types of management development programmes offered' (1987, p.19). Furthermore, Al-Faleh argues that culture has its roots in a long history of traditions, in religion, and in past and present philosophical, political or economic ideology. Moreover, we believe that it is the senior management's responsibility to lead the necessary changes in corporate culture, so that changes are accepted and enacted by other middle managers, or symbolic managers.

One of the current problems for managers in the Arab countries is that MD programmes offered by local institutes are translated from foreign sources and are not written with Arab managers in mind. Trainers are often heard explaining about textbooks, exercises, and cases having little relevance to the managers' positions. Most films used in training are imported (Deal and Kennedy, 1982; Al-Bahussain, 2000).

In the case of the PTs, the managers expressed the view that they believed that they did not need more managerial skills. They justified this by declaring that they have already acquired technical skills whilst working with big companies in Israel. At the same time, they did not and could not differentiate between the technical and managerial skills (Al-Madhoun, 2002). Inevitably, the question posed is: should the designers of MD programmes adapt their programmes to suit the culture of the business or should they aim at changing that culture? In either case, it is the management's responsibility to improve organisational effectiveness through creating an appropriate culture. This, of course, requires investing continuous effort and courage to look at the possibility of trying to change the corporate culture, or at least to re-assess it. In this regard, House (1967) and Analoui (2002) have indicated clearly that management commitment is probably the most critical requirement for the success of any development effort. For them, if a MD programme is to achieve results, it should not conflict with existing corporate culture, strategic objectives, policies, and management practices.

It is generally agreed that the classical definition of the management process and system is a convenient way of viewing management. However, the concepts of management introduce the functions of management to identify the management skills and knowledge, which are supposedly required to perform those functions effectively. Several researchers have, therefore, considered management definitions, system, and functions as a basis and may be the first important stage to understand the roles managers are likely to play. The next part of this review will be devoted to managers and their roles.

Managerial roles and training

Roy (1977), in his study of management education and training in the Arab world, reported that a shortage of able and appropriately educated and trained managers has been, and continues to be a major problem for many Arab countries. With regard to cultural influence on MTPs in the Arab world, he questions the adoption of Western standardised TP by Arab organisations. He therefore calls for the development of teaching material relevant to the Arabian culture.

Furthermore, many other Arab writers have echoed Roy's view, such as Al-Faleh (1987) and Atiyyah (1993, p.3). Atiyyah recognises the fact that 'the shortage of qualified managers presents a major obstacle to the development of less advanced countries'. He further argues that the future of MD in Arab countries largely depends on developments in their political, economic, socio-cultural and organisational systems. Writers such as Chanaiz (1978), Badaway (1980), Muna (1980), Ali and Al-Shakis (1985), and Kaynak and Yucett (1986) report that organisational characteristics and management practices are strongly influenced by the indigenous culture. Accordingly, Arab culture plays a significant role in influencing managerial attitudes in adoption of policies for MTD. In asserting that the corporate culture is one influence upon MTPs, and getting the right culture is essential, others should not be ignored. McDonald (1989) stresses 'programme trainer competence, learning styles, means of processing, and content are all relevant in determining the success of a programme' (p.63).

In addition to corporate culture influence, other writers (such as El-Fathaly and Chackerian, 1983; Al-Tayeb, 1984; Atiyyah, 1992; Abu-Doleh, 1996; Al-Ali, 1999; Al-Bahseen, 2000; and Al-Athri and Zairi, 2002) suggest that the low effectiveness of training in Arab countries stems from many factors, such as management protective attitudes among Arab managers, the absence of clear training policies, the shortage of competent trainers, and inadequate facilities.

As for continuity and sustainability of the programmes, Abdalla and Al-Homoud (1995) in their survey found that some 93 per cent of the training programmes used did not have built into them specific follow-up procedures for evaluating their effectiveness. Because of this, no data were available regarding the benefits of the programme, nor was any meaningful information available as to what type of training programmes were needed in the future. Thus, the conclusion reached is that in most organisations, training was viewed as a 'stand alone' process with no ties or links to other parts of the total development system, such as selection procedures, performance appraisal and reward systems. More importantly, most organisations lacked a formal MTD system. In the words of Abu-Doleh (1996), MTD programmes were still carried out on a piecemeal basis rather than as a long-term policy. Therefore, most of the managers were found to hold a negative attitude towards the usefulness of MTD programmes. Below, specific studies from Arab countries will be considered specifically in relation to the application of the MTD programmes.

Egypt

Egypt is the border country to the Gaza Strip (GS), which for twenty years (1948-1967) remained under Egyptian control.

In a study of 100 Egyptian managers, Bussom et al (1984) concludes that:

1. Status, position, and seniority significantly outweigh ability and performance in the organisation.
2. Organisations are centrally controlled and demand obedience to formal authority.
3. The autocratic management style is predominant.
4. Managers are reluctant to make decisions and tend to pass the buck.
5. Organisation members are motivated by evaluation and power rather than by performance or achievement.

MTPs in the Arab world attempt to adopt the Western model of MTP or methods used in a dramatically different cultural orientation. Accordingly, the authors stated that there is a need to tailor MTPs to fit their corporation's specific cultural needs. In support of this argument, Murrell (1984) also states that Western training and management ideas are flooding into Egypt and, as they enter, they are affected and modified by the country and its centuries-old culture. For him, transferring Western training programmes to other developing countries, which have their own unique culture, should be undertaken with the utmost care, if these programmes are to be viewed as important by the trainees of those countries. In this context, Murrell (1984) states that Egypt, as well as most of the developing countries, are experiencing rapid changes and a transitional society. In these countries, old values, attitudes, managerial practices, and peoples' expectations are gradually changing. Therefore, Murrell questions how TD activities can keep pace with these changes, on the one hand, and how they can help the country manage its transitions, on the other.

Jordan

Jordan is the nearest country to the West Bank (WB), the second part of the land under the control of the Palestinian National Authority (PNA). The WB and GS joined together after the peace agreement established the new Palestinian entity. The WB was controlled directly from Jordan for more than twenty years.

Little is known about MTD in Jordan. With few studies available, there are not sufficient data available to chart the future of MTD in that country. Interestingly, most of these studies seem to focus heavily on the public rather than the private sector (Abu-Doleh, 1996).

Durra (1991), in his study of the assessment of training needs within the context of administrative reform in the Jordanian public sector, found that the staff of administrative development and training units (ADTUS) were not qualified enough to perform their duties in general and to assess training needs in particular, and arguably more effort should be exerted to select better qualified ADTUS officers.

Accordingly, Durra suggests that MT in Jordan should be addressed by further empirical research. Al-Faleh (1987) studied the cultural influence on Arab MD, and found lack of commitment to MD on the part of many enterprises and their senior managers.

The content and methodology of the existing TPs in Jordan does not reflect the actual needs of the Jordanian companies. Thus, without such an adjustment to the cultural situation, MTD can never be achieved. Al-Faleh argues that the government must take more responsibility for enhancing MD in both the public and private sectors. Al-Faleh (1987) also explored promotion and morale in business firms in Jordan, and found that 55 per cent of the respondents expressed dissatisfaction with policies used by their firms. Favouritism rather than merit assessment was seen as a criterion to promote employees.

Persian Gulf

Qatar is one member of the Gulf Co-operation Council (GCC). Other GCC Countries are Saudi Arabia, Kuwait, Bahrain, Oman, and the United Arab Emirates. These countries, located around the Persian Gulf, are homogeneous, and have similar cultures. Also, they are oil-producing countries. Muna and Bank (1993, p.470) studied 177 managers representing the six GCC countries. The main findings were:

1. No significant difference and/or relationship between nationality and explanation for managerial success. Most managers perceived a good education, training opportunities and career development as important factors that contributed to their success.
2. Gulf companies are rarely engaged in real training evaluation.
3. The use of annual performance appraisal forms and/or requests from line departments were the major sources of training requirements.
4. Three times as many Arab managers have university degrees as British managers.
5. Organisations spend three times as much money and time on their management.

There are two examples from GCC countries, Qatar and Kuwait. Firstly, we are concerned with Qatar's MTD experience; Muna (1987) reported that early in 1982 he had participated in the setting-up of the Qatari development training systems for the petroleum companies. His main findings indicated that implementation of the individual development programme (IDP) as a tool to bridge the gap between job requirements and existing capabilities of the individual has generally been successful. The IDP involved counselling Qatar national employees on their possible career paths, and what they must do to achieve promotion to senior management levels, usually occupied by expatriates from western oil companies.

By 1987, Muna indicated, over 135 IDPs had been prepared. Some of them were failures and others did exceptionally well. The IDP training plan was successful in targeting a number of Qataris towards departmental manager positions.

The success of the IDP efforts encouraged the Minister of Finance and Petroleum to request the National Petroleum Corporation to submit a five-year training development plan.

Al-Ali and Taylor (1997) considered MTD in the State of Kuwait, which is a typical small, oil-rich Gulf state with a small population. Kuwait started its administrative development in the 1950s and has continued since. Now more than 90 per cent of the country's economy is in the domain of the governmental sector, and hence managed by bureaucracy and autocracy. Kuwait has therefore recently adopted a policy of administrative development. Kuwait is one of the Arab countries which faces a shortage of qualified human resources in general, and managers in particular. This has been made clear in the proposed national five-year plan (1995/1996-1999/2000), which emphasises the preparation and development of the national workforce. On the other hand, it is urged that MTD must be applied systematically to cope with government strategy towards implementing privatisation. However, these processes may face some obstacles in their implementation, which might slow them down or prevent them from achieving their goals, such as bureaucratic inflation, malfunction and inefficient current MTD practices. Other obstacles include lack of investment in TD programmes.

The researchers conclude that the obstacles to administrative development in Kuwait are economic, political and social ones. In addition, the organisations did not pay enough attention to MD, and there is a strong tendency to use expatriate consultants for this purpose.

Al-Ali and Taylor (1997) found that Kuwait has two types of organisation. First there are the ministries, and second are those business organisations which are owned by the government. Their aims are to make the organisations more efficient in conducting their activities, and by reducing costs, including utilising human resources more effectively. In Kuwait, people perceive the government's position as a way of distributing the national fortune and not for career development. This affects the perception of TD.

In some governmental organisations, training policies are neither clear nor written, and are built upon informal policy. On the other hand, some organisations do have training policies and plans. Consequently, this leads to the absence of clear policy and vision. The future vision is not clear, due to managers' overemphasis on routine working practices and on concentrating on solving the current deficiencies of employees' performance in getting the job done.

Al-Ali and Taylor (1997) discuss the private sector in Kuwait as being small and underdeveloped. In private and joint venture organisations, the management picture is different, with a style of management with more freedom in the way decisions are made, their procedures and policies, and the leadership style. Some of these organisations take T&D more seriously. Some organisations are working in an environment where the government has less effect on their managerial functions, including TD activities.

Some Kuwaiti organisations have one-person training units, while others may have more professional staff. Some organisations have an HRD strategy that consists of localisation policy and TD. There is no link at all between training and the organisation's policies and strategies.

The researchers talk about the managers' attitude and awareness towards training as another crucial point facing T&D in these organisations. The attitude among managers indicates, in most circumstances, frustration and disillusionment with the TD function. In general, two types of attitudes exist among line managers, which affect their mutual understanding and co-operation with training managers. There are those who are convinced of the importance of training for their ultimate success, whilst others lack seriousness and commitment. The researchers found that the efforts towards TD are facing some obstacles that deter them from achieving their goals.

The government and private joint venture organisations have varying attitudes and acceptance levels of western management style and concepts, due to the difference of culture. While private joint venture organisations are more open and willing to change, government organisations are less likely to accept the new management concepts and approaches. Any transfer of western ideas and practices to the Arab countries needs to be adapted to the local culture.

Summary

Almost all countries in the Middle East need to make greater efforts towards investing more in establishing sound effective TD activities. These efforts ought to be based on a modern management philosophy which sees the links between the training system, promotion, incentives and career development according to established criteria and not a rigid system of participants' selection, rather a systematic process of assessment of training needs and evaluations, and a flexible budget. Line managers should be made aware of the importance of training for their ultimate achievements and for organisational goals. Top management support should be committed to TD activities, including the involvement in assessing training plans and policies. Organisational culture, based on commitment, competency and performance should be created and maintained so that ultimately the proposed policies for more effective development at organisational and individual levels can be realistically translated into action.

It is not usual to conclude that all countries, regardless of their socio-economic and cultural conditions, require a high level of TD programmes. In more specific terms, the scant literature available strongly suggests that there is an acute lack of MTD programmes in Arab countries such as Egypt, Jordan, Kuwait, Saudi Arabia and Qatar and those that do exist are unfortunately only paid lip service by the present traditional management.

Chapter Four

SMEs in Palestine

Introduction

The economy of Palestine is small, poorly developed, and highly dependent on Israel; at the same time, the land is limited, Israel controls 80-85 per cent of the Palestinian water, and there is large-scale unemployment. Faced with this situation, SMEs have come to play a critical role in the PT economy.

Donors, the Palestinian Authority (PNA) and the United Nation Refugee Work Agency (UNRWA) have recognised that many of the managers suffer from managerial weaknesses, and training is one of the long-term keys to promote the development of SMEs to alleviate the problem of persistent unemployment in Palestine.

To support the peace agreement, the international community promised to support the Palestinian economy. Part of this aid has been to spend funds on SME development, and establishing MTPs. These programmes aim to encourage the economic development of the PT, through supporting small business education and entrepreneurship training.

These programmes suffered from various problems, such as a lack of professional trainers and the majority of the SME managers did not attend the TP courses. Not surprisingly, some of these programmes missed funding. Therefore, some TPs were not implemented during the last two years of the programme. Still, managers of SMEs suffer from various managerial weaknesses and problems.

This study explores the effects, if any, of the management training programmes for business development provided to meet the needs of the managers of SMEs. It also provides a description of the current situation in Palestine, especially the managerial situation for the SMEs and the Training Programmes in Palestine.

This chapter will explore the SME managers' backgrounds, bearing in mind these different categories of managers having different reasons for attending MT courses. Then, the management training programmes for SMEs in Palestine will be investigated in some detail. Using the results of the study, an analysis of the managers, the training attempts, theory contribution and effects on businesses in PT and other related issues will be addressed.

Background

It is not an exaggeration to note that the twentieth century has been 'the bloodiest […] in history' (Wusten, 1993, p.65). For Palestine, this century has been marked by a prolonged conflict, by dispossession and displacement, and by war and military occupation (MOPIC, 1998).

The West Bank (WB) and the Gaza Strip (GS) are parts of Palestine which were entrusted to Britain by mandate of the League of Nations in 1922. In 1948, the Israelis occupied Palestine except the WB, including East Jerusalem (EJ) and the GS, and established Israel. After the occupation, the GS came under Egyptian control and the WB became part of Jordan until the 1967 Arab-Israeli war. After the war, Israel occupied the WB and the GS (WBG).

The occupation of the WBG continued from that time until the peace treaty between Israel and the PLO in 1993, which led to the Oslo agreement and the Paris economic protocol in April 1994. As a result, the Palestinian Territory (PT) was established in the GS and Jericho in the first stage and includes the GS and most of the WB cities in the final stage.

The WBG has a combined area of about 6000 sq. km. The population of the WBG is 2,601,669 (Palestinian Central Bureau of Statistics, PCBS, 1999), while another 3.3 million refugees are living in neighbouring Arab States (UN, 1997).

The Gaza Strip is the name given to the strip of land on the Egyptian-Palestinian border, occupied by Israel during the 1967 Arab-Israeli war. It is located on the eastern shore of the Mediterranean Sea. Measuring only 360 sq. km in area, in 1993 the GS was home to about 830,000 people (Roy, 1995). The population of the GS increased to 1,001,569 Palestinians in 1997 (PCBS, 1999). The Palestinian population of the GS has control of only 60 per cent of the area (Daibes and Barghouthi, 1996, p.13). More than 746,000 of the Palestinians are registered as refugees (UNRWA, 1998, p.1). The annual population growth rate in GS is 4 per cent per year, one of the highest in the developing world (Roy, 1995, p.15). A high number of Palestinian refugees fled to the GS during the 1948 Arab-Israeli war. The high growth of its population and the returnees after the 1992 Gulf war and the 1993 peace treaty make the GS one of the most densely populated areas in the world. The population of the GS is predominantly young, 59.2 per cent of the population is under the age of 15 (Mosawady, 1999, p.5).

For 52 years, UNRWA has figured significantly in the lives of the Palestinian refugees living in the WBG. In the GS, UNRWA's departments are playing key roles in the WBG areas of youth and women, environmental health, economic development, and income generation. Largely as a consequence of the policies in force in the WBG for more than two decades, the productive capacity of its economy is limited, its institutions stunted, and its human resources underdeveloped (UNRWA, 1998, p.3).

The role of UNRWA has been changing since the peace agreement. UNRWA has been called upon to implement social welfare and infrastructure projects in support of the peace process, to include development projects valued at over $100 million; UNRWA has implemented projects in the GS (UNRWA, 1998, p.2). In the same way, the UN, in partnership with the Palestinian Authority (PNA) and the international donor community, has made a concerted effort to advance socio-economic development in the WBG (UN, 1998, p.1).

Palestinians suffer from poverty, and the families living in poverty amount to 20 per cent. This figure is 33 per cent in GS, which means that one family in three is living in poverty. The poor are not able to pay for their basic needs such as food, clothes, housing, medicine, learning, and public transportation. The poverty measurement for a family of six persons is $765 per year per person. The measurement of destitution for the families in the PT is an income of less than $47 per month (Alquds Alarabi, 2000; Has, 2000). Compared with other Arab countries, it is a very high percentage; for example, Algeria has 1.15 per cent, Morocco and Jordan 5.7 per cent, and Tunisia 13 per cent (Has, 2000). Globally, poverty has been commonly defined as a lack of minimum income or resources to meet basic needs, or 'an inability to maintain a minimal standard of living' (MOPIC, 1998). With strong assets but equally burdensome liabilities, the Palestinian economy is on a knife's edge between take-off and collapse.

The sustainability of donors' assistance will also depend on the evolving relations between donors, the PNA and the private sector. A crucial issue is how to support investment projects to ensure sustained growth and poverty alleviation without relying solely on the public sector. The challenge will be to assist and encourage the private sector to undertake projects with donors offering complementary finance, political risk guarantees or insurance. Likewise, more attention should be given to building capacity within the PNA to ensure a capable entity with the means to foster and complement private sector-driven growth (Diwan and Shaban, 1998, pp.34-35).

However, there is a grave need for the establishment of a framework to organise the development of Palestine and to formulate a strategic Palestinian Plan to move from emergency relief projects to sustainable development. Such programmes must consider that the international community and the donor countries will not continue their donations for ever, therefore building the national economy must be given particular attention.

Many studies have discussed and listed these obstacles and constraints (for example, Spector, 1978; Sadler, 1984; Bahiri, 1987; Okasha & Zarifa, 1992; Iftaimeh, 1993; Abu-Eljedian, 1996; ASIR, 1996; Abu-Zarifa, 1997; DRC, 1997; Rajab, 1997; UNIDO, 1997; Migdad et al, 1998). Some of them classified the obstacles into Israeli and internal obstacles. Abu-Zarifa (1997) argued that after the establishment of the PNA there was no essential change to all of these obstacles and the majority were still the same as before.

It is not only the Israeli obstacles that face the private sector in the PT, as internal obstacles also exist. For example, lack of finance, lack of demand, high local competition, low income and poverty, and the absence of effective laws that support industry in the PT. This has led to the reduction of private investment by up to 50 per cent in the last few years (Abdol Shafi, 1998).

However, the private sector in Palestine is still traditionally based on micro and small-size firms. Economic growth potential in Palestine lies with the Palestinian private sector. Small-scale, single owners and family enterprises dominate the business sector. The private sector is very important in general and has special importance in the GS, despite the modest share of the private sector there. This is due to the lack of land and water and the different obstacles facing the private sector in the GS. The private sector has been accustomed to profiting under difficult circumstances during the occupation, using its size as a source of flexibility in favourable market conditions (Palnet, 1999).

Small and Micro Enterprises (SMEs) in Palestine

During the last decades of the twentieth century, SMEs have come to occupy an important part of the global economy. Thus, they play a critical role in building a strong and independent economy in the PT (UNRWA, 1998, p.4). There are 22,495 businesses in the GS (PCBS, 1999); 91 per cent of them are SMEs (20,470) with between one to four employees, while 83 per cent of the businesses were sole proprietorships (PCBS, 1996, p.70). In the same way, the International Labour Organisation reports that 97 per cent of the Palestinian businesses are micro- and small, with fewer than ten workers, although the majority of the businesses are family businesses. The fact that SMEs are so prevalent is due basically to the Israeli occupation, which since 1967 employed measures to restrict the development of the Palestinian economy and compel the OT to be dependent on the Israeli economy (Naser, 1999). Another important statistic is that women own fewer than 10 per cent of the businesses (PCBS, 1996, p.80).

The owners and managers of SME have experienced and have survived turbulent market conditions, but they suffer from administrative and managerial weakness. SMEs were initiated on family capital by ex-Palestinian labourers of Israeli firms and most of them have few management skills (Abu Eljedian, 1996). To remedy this problem, the TPs organise management-training courses to develop the managerial skills for the owners and managers. These managers are the primary target group of the training programmes.

Safi (1998, pp.4-5) argues that there are many obstacles in the path of training for the SME in the GS. For example, there are no training modules or manuals, which might be considered as references for training; in general, few trainers use the modern training methods. The characteristics of the target group are not analysed well, trainers who are contracted to deliver training for potential owner/managers are usually lecturers in business colleges, but they do not have enough background knowledge about the SMEs in the GS.

Management training for business development needs to be identified as a priority area. Those running SMEs should be assisted and encouraged to acquire basic management skills at start-up, followed at later stages by more comprehensive MT appropriate to running a growing concern (Salman, 1997, p.294).

The budget for the PDP (MOPIC, 1997, p.136) the SME development programme needs during three years (1998-2000) is estimated as $5 million. Many countries are willing to support the SME with aid, consultants and training.

Lending to SMEs

Despite their recent decline, lending NGOs still have an important role to play in the WBG financial system. Unlike other NGOs, such as those involved in health and education, lending NGOs serve a function that has not been assumed by the PNA. Lending NGOs extend loans to SMEs that lack collateral and credit history and which, therefore, are not of interest to commercial banks. If small enterprises are to become sustainable, they must find ways to become less dependent on subsidies. To do so, lending NGOs may have to eliminate most of their interest subsidies, as some have already done. They also may have to find ways to minimise default risk without relying entirely on collateral. One achievable option is to make use of the group risk-sharing method, which was pioneered by UNRWA and Save the Children. The UNRWA's Solidarity Group Lending Programme, offers working capital loans to women micro-enterprise owners and has consistently had 100 per cent repayment rates since its inception in 1994. Managerial and technical assistance is provided to small borrowers, especially to those likely to suffer from market discrimination (Diwan and Shaban, 1998, p.27).

Hamed (1998) believes that there is still a need for lending NGOs, since the banks are not interested in small loans or credit to individuals without security. The experience of the Third World supports this conclusion and shows that if credit from these organisations is prohibited, credit still continues, but in secret and at high interest rates. Hamed argues that legislation by the Palestinian Monetary Authority to forbid moneychangers from receiving deposits is a positive step to encourage investment in the financial sector. However, legislation to prevent credit from moneychangers is unjustified economically, since moneychangers lend money from their own capital. Hamed recommends that the relationship between the formal and informal sector be strengthened. The two sectors already complement each other to a certain extent. For example, merchants who sell their goods on credit borrow money from banks and lend it on through the selling process.

It is also suggested that a separation must be made between the two types of lending NGOs. The first type are NGOs that give credit without interest and carry the responsibility to grant loans as a form of assistance to certain sectors of society. The second type give credit with interest, since external funding is not permanent and the interest would be the principal means to cover running costs. The importance of these organisations lies in their ability to provide credit to individuals who are unable to obtain a bank loan due to the obstacles discussed above.

Most of the owners of SMEs in the WBG use irregular loans granted to friends and neighbours based on need. Hamed's study shows that 7.1 per cent of the population aged 18 years old and over put their money with friends and relatives rather than in banks. At the same time, Hamed concluded that 70 per cent of loans in the WBG take place through moneychangers, and this highlights their importance to the financial sector and the Palestinian economy as a whole.

Kanan (1998, p.32) discusses investment in the WB and GS, arguing that during 1993-1997 the size of deposits of the commercial banks increased from $500 million to $1.9 billion. The banks opened for lending to SMEs; at the same time, some aid from donors went to the local banks for lending to the SMEs.

A study of the role of the informal financial sector and lending NGOs in the WBG and their scope and extent of coverage of informal finance and the relevance of this sector after 1993 revealed the signs of growth in the formal financial sector. The informal sector plays a substantial role in the WBG. Correspondingly, the study (Qudeh, 1999) from the Palestinian Planning Centre emphasises that the size of the lending from the banks to businesses during the last three years was $130 million ($44 million per year). At the same time, the lending from the lending programmes was about $115 million ($39.38 million per year).

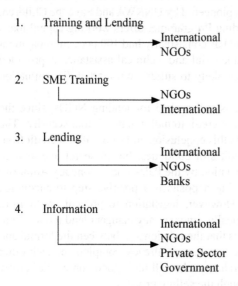

1.   Training and Lending
                                International
                                NGOs

2.   SME Training
                                NGOs
                                International

3.   Lending
                                International
                                NGOs
                                Banks

4.   Information
                                International
                                NGOs
                                Private Sector
                                Government

Figure 4.1   Kinds of programmes to support SMEs

Source: Adapted from Al-Madhoun and Analoui (2003)

This study also points to the obstacles facing the lending programmes, such as debt collection, lack of co-operation between lending programmes, weak policies, law and regulations for lending programmes. These programmes do not specify precisely which sectors need development simply because they lack proper investment plan. Also Kanan (1998) draws attention to yet another obstacle, claiming that the SMEs need more experience of working relationships with lending programmes and banks – unfortunately, the owners of SMEs have missed out on having a banking system for the last 25 years.

After the peace process (1993) there were more than 25 lending and training programmes opened for the development of the SMEs in the GS (UNRWA, 1998).

These programmes are different and have different target groups and objectives. A number of them offer small-scale loans for women (Salman, 1997).

Al-Madhoun and Analoui (2002) discuss four kinds of programmes that support SMEs (see Figure 4.1).

Training and lending programmes These programmes develop the SMEs through lending and training. Most of the programmes in the GS do both. These programmes include international organisations, such as UNRWA's development and planning department, the micro-enterprise lending programme (UNRWA, 1998, p.5), and NGOs, such as the Women's Affairs Centre. At the same time, both the internationals and the NGOs are almost all financed by donors.

SME training programme These programmes aim to develop the Human Resources in managerial and technical skills. Some of these programmes are managed directly by international organisations, such as the Italian Association for Women in Development. The other programmes are managed by the NGOs, such as the Palestinian Institution for Professional Training, and the National Institution for Development and Investment.

The lending organisations programmes These programmes are concerned with the development of the SMEs during the lending period. There are many banks in the GS, such as the Palestinian Commercial Bank, also some institutions such as the Micro-enterprise Project started in 1998 with a budget of $20 million from the World Bank and the International Finance Centre. The Micro-enterprise Project finances the SMEs in the WBG through the banking system (World Bank, 1998, p.10).

International organisations too, such as the Palestinian Development Fund (PDF), a privately owned, non-profit development agency, established to promote the sound growth of the Palestinian SMEs also helps. Through the provision of medium-term loans and associated financial aid, 80 per cent of PDF projects are funded by the European Union (Alrisala al Uropia, 1996, p.4), and NGOs, such as the Palestinian Development Institution, the biggest programme for lending, (Qudeh, 1999), with $45 million from the European Union to aid the SMEs in WB and GS through this programme (European Union Report, 1996, p.10). Qudeh (1999) argues that the lending institutions have spent $39.38 million per year as a loan. On the other hand, the banks have spent $43-44 million. It is concluded that the gap between what is needed and what is being offered is $118 million, if as expected, the amount available will be $200 million (MAS, 1998).

The studies about the lending institutions and their roles for development, have mentioned many problems that face the lending institutions, such as some of the businesses not being able to repay the loan, a lack of co-operation between institutions, no clear plans and policies, the evaluation of the managers of SMEs by the lending institutions, missing statistical data about the businesses, institutions did not study the real loan needs, lack of managerial experience of the lending institutions, lack of follow-up for the businesses which have loans, and the problem the businesses have in changing money from the US$ and the Shekel (Al-Qady, 1997; Qudeh, 1999).

Information (consultation)   These include organisations that provide SMEs with information and consultation in order to enable them to compete in local, regional and world markets (Alrisala al Uropia, 1997, p.4).   There are four kinds: governmental organisations, such as investment departments; private sector offices for studies; consultants such as Master and Palcon; and the NGO programmes, such as the Development Resource Centre.

The World Bank and MAS (1997) conclude that in the long run, the SME needs to finance itself.   On the other hand, NGOs and banks need to follow a new policy that does not ask for a high percentage for fixed yearly interest and does not ask SME owners for high liability, which means high risk.   Also, they advise the SME to start as a sharing group and follow shareholding company strategies, and to use the money from the retirement fund for new investment.   Meanwhile the NGOs prefer to control this investment by themselves without government intervention.   Finally, it could be argued that there is a great need for a strategy for development in the PT. It is hoped that the research will help to gain the necessary knowledge to enable the researcher to draw a framework of development.

Management training development (MTD) for SMEs in Palestine

In recent years, MTD in the developed countries has gained a rightful place in organisation activities.   It has become a separate function that contributes to the development of the human resource, and to prepare the organisation for change and development (Abu-Doleh, 1996, pp.1-2).

In the Arab countries, the MD efforts, by and large, have been found to be ineffective and inadequate.   Most training specialists and managers describe training effectiveness in these countries as generally low (Al-Ali and Taylor, 1997, p.4).

The conference for development strategy in Palestine in September (MOBIC, 1995) recommended that HRD concentrate on training as a means to enable Palestine to meet its future development needs through the establishment of research and training centres for managerial and technical skills.

In the Palestinian Development Plan (PDP) (1998-2000), HRD is the second largest programme area (UN, 1998).   During three years, it will be financed 24.41 per cent from the general budget (Shath, 1998, p.11).   The PDP (MOPIC, 1997, p.22) argues that this will assist the effective development of HRM.   The aim of this assistance is to support the PNA and to finance the building of the economy and society in both the WB and GS (MOPIC, 1997, p.7).

HRD is also considered to be important, due to its emphasis on the individual as the target for development.   Priority is given to programmes and projects that increase the involvement of the private sector (MOPIC, 1997, p.27).

In the same way, UNRWA (1998) assistance to the private sector aims to promote sustainable economic development by contributing to the development of the institutional and HR capacities of the public and private sectors.

The Centre of Palestine Research and Studies (1997) assessed the aid from donors (1997), and the results of a questionnaire emphasised HRD needs in the PT. 75 per cent of responses emphasised that training and HRD are rated as aid priorities. Also, 34 per cent of the sample believes that the impact of aid on training and HRD is positive. The difference in results between the need for training and the weak results from the training means there are some problems faced by the TP.

Regarding HRD, there is a lack of professionals who are able to plan, implement and evaluate the PNA development policies, leaving the responsibilities to unskilled people and the old guard of the PLO. Moreover, the Israeli restrictions during the last thirty years have had a negative impact on HRD. It could be argued that the Palestinian who has lived in different communities with a different system and structure will affect the Palestinian experience negatively. However, Zahlan (1997, p.142) has another point of view that:

> They have lived and worked in many countries and this could enhance their culture. Diversity could enhance creativity. From the Israeli view, regarding the Israeli-Arabs, currently, very few Israeli-Arabs are part of the growing MD market. Many educated Arabs are not recruited by Israeli corporations for 'security' reasons, (whether justified or not). Consequently, they find positions in the public educational system, which enable them to be promoted to managerial jobs within that system. An alternative avenue for managerial progress is through entrepreneurial activities. The Israeli free-enterprise market system enables willing Arabs to start their own businesses and be a part of the success-failure rates. Some have managed to develop commercially successful ventures, mainly in construction and commerce (Reichel, 1996, p.31).

Al-Madhoun and Analoui (2003) categorise TPs in the GS, after the peace agreement, that try to solve the managerial weaknesses as follows:

Governmental TPs

1. Training department in ministries: there are departments for training in almost all the ministries in the PNA. Usually, the departments are responsible for the training of the governmental employees (training on-the-job).
2. The National Centre for Public Administration. The Palestine Human Development Profile (1996, 1997, pp.88-89) emphasises the strategy for Palestinian development. This stresses the development of local Human Resources (HR). However, the PNA had established the National Centre for Public Administration in October 1995. The problem with this programme is that only 23 per cent of participants in different training courses at the National Centre have transferred the knowledge, the skills and the information learnt back to their departments.

3. The technical and professional training organisations, such as the Institution for Technical Training in the Labour Ministry, aim to develop the skills of the labour force.

International TPs

1. International TPs for the private sector aim to develop the managerial and technical skills for SMEs. There are many programmes, such as the German Palestinian Programme.
2. International TPs for the public sector. The British Council finances this. The difference between this programme and the public sector programme is that the international TP for the public sector is managed directly by the donor countries, for example, the TP for Health Ministry Development in the PNA is managed by the British Council.

Non-governmental organisations (NGOs) TPs

1. For the private sector, which aims to develop two sides of businesses, the managerial and the technical skills, e.g. the Development Resource Centre (DRC).
2. For the Palestinian people, that aim to improve the skills of Palestinian people; the donors also finance it.
3. For students and labour, such as Community Service and Continuing Education at the Islamic University in the GS.

In general, the NGOs and the governmental programmes are almost completely financed by donors. Safi (1998) describes the needs of the target group in terms of developing their necessary traits as entrepreneurs who can then play a role as business managers in developing the economy in GS. He used Strengths, Weaknesses, Opportunities and Threats (SWOT) analysis to identify specific factors related to the characteristics of the target group (see Figure 4.2).

As shown, SWOT analysis can provide a basis for analysis of the training needs of the SME managers, based on which an appropriate programme can be designed, taking into account all the relevant features. It is hoped that as a result, managers' attitudes can be altered, modified and even changed.

The most important obstacle against HRD in Palestine is the lack of MTD. The percentage of Palestinians trained by the training institutions in WBG in 1984 was just 3 per cent, in comparison with Jordan where it was 35 per cent, and in Israel it was 70 per cent. The reason for this obstacle is that Israeli (occupation) policy did not allow for providing licence to the training institutions. The PT faced the managerial weakness that, during 23 years under Israeli occupation, the Palestinian people did not have the opportunity to practise any serious managerial roles, especially in top management positions. Thus, the PNA has allocated more financial resources to this area hoping to solve this problem by training. There are many TPs established in the PT, almost all of which use off-the-job training. However, as aptly argued by Analoui 'there are no correct ways of managing organisations to be provided with MT' (1993, p.60).

Strengths	Weaknesses
• Skilled • Hard working • Network of relations in same sector • Highly motivated • Opportunistic • Independent • Easy access to suppliers • Enterprising values • Personal responsibility • Commitment • Ambitious • Have savings • Communicative	• Lack of management skills • Hesitation • Not decision-makers • Poor at planning • Lack of awareness of business • Services providers • Lack of ability to access funds • Risk-averse
Opportunities	**Threats**
• To be a partner in business • To get a loan and establish a business • To negotiate with ex-employer to have mutually beneficial business	• Unacceptability of failure (difficult in the culture) • Fear of losing savings or inability to pay off the loan

Figure 4.2   SWOT analysis to identify characteristics of managers

Source: Adapted from Safi (1998, p.13)

Safi (1998) reports that the business of training in GS is faced with several obstacles such as no training modules or manuals available, the target group has not been well analyzed and few trainers use modern training methods simply because they do not have enough background knowledge about small businesses, and they lack familiarity with the variety of new training techniques. Shaban (1998) when commenting on TPs in Palestine suggests that the problem is not the adequacy of the aid, rather whether or not the TP is managed properly. He argues that there are many problems facing the TP. For example, the TP do not specify the alternative solutions to the target groups, they do not use good practices, the TP do not evaluate the training impacts, and the TP do not know their specific training needs.

In the same vein, Salman (1997) discusses the MT problems in relation to women; virtually none of the women had participated in any training courses in business management, and their present skills had been developed through a process of trial and error. She believes that women who have businesses suffer from lack of some basic management skills in production, marketing and finance. She suggests that those women running small businesses should be assisted and encouraged in acquiring basic management skills at start-up, followed at later stages by more comprehensive MT appropriate to running a growing concern (pp.293-298). Finally, she poses several questions:

1. How training subjects are chosen?
2. Who makes the choice?
3. Is there an overall plan?
4. Who oversees the training sessions conducted in Palestine?

To face these problems, the Palestinian Economic Council for Development and Rebuilding is prepared for a national training conference to discuss the best ways to achieve quality results from the training (Dajany, 1999).

The TAMI Institution conducted a survey of women in the GS who took loans to start businesses. The published results (Alquds, 1997) show that 20 per cent had work experience, 40 per cent had never worked before and 40 per cent had worked in an unrelated field. Moreover, 90 per cent of the businesses were in agriculture; women chose these projects in order to have members of the family also share in their work.

The business weaknesses associated with running the projects can be summed up as follows:

1. Time management (31 per cent);
2. Marketing (34 per cent);
3. Dealing with customers (42 per cent);
4. Planning (50 per cent);
5. Costing (65 per cent);
6. Accounting (75 per cent);
7. Growth issues (85 per cent).

Management training programmes (MTPs) for SMEs

The training and rehabilitation of the Palestinian work force is one of the main goals of the Palestinian National Authority. The Ministries of Labour and Education are responsible for vocational training and education. There are ten industrial secondary schools in the WB, and thirteen vocational training centres run by the Ministry of Labour: nine in the WB and four in the GS. In addition, there are four other vocational training centres in Palestine: three in the WB and one in the GS. The Ministry of Labour has launched a campaign to actively encourage registration in vocational training centres. This will further equip the labour force with the necessary skills to respond to the demands of the Palestinian and regional markets (Palnet, 2000).

Al-Madhoun (1997), Al-Nearab (1997) and Mehesen (1997) discuss the system that these TPs follow. The first stage for a new course is to discuss the alternatives by studying the needs through meetings, questionnaires, statistical information, and from the historical training in the same field and the same programme. At the same time, TP managers study the technical experience and the facilities for the course, and ensure its funding.

The second stage deals specifically with more details for the course, such as the title, the co-ordinator, the objectives, the place, signing the contract, the contents, the budget, the participants and identifying the standard evaluation.

The third stage starts the training itself and follows the results. The final stage assesses the impact of the training by using daily evaluation and evaluation at the end of the course by questionnaire and open discussion. Some TPs included visiting the businesses for evaluation of the training.

Funding of the training programmes

The financial income for the training programmes is the major important point that gives the TPs in Palestine continuity. The finance from donors alone will not give the training this continuity. There is also some funding from the local sponsors and from the fees.

Table 4.1 illustrates that the international funding is the major source of funds for the TPs. Basically, these programmes come up with their own strategy plan and operate for as long as the funding lasts. The researchers observation confirmed that some TPs, during the last two years, have been closed down because they lost funding such as the Development Resource Centre and the NFID. MOPIC (1997) concluded that the major difficulty facing the TPs is that they cannot find new sponsors when the old funding finishes.

Table 4.1   TP programmes in Palestine and their sources of funding

Programmes	Local	Private	Labour Ministry	Social Affairs Ministry	Total (%)
Numbers of Programmes	48	6	13	11	78
International	27.1%	16.7%	---	---	17.9%
Local	6.3%	33.3%	---	---	6.4%
Fees	2.1%	16.7%	---	---	2.6%
International and Local	41.7%	---	100%	100%	56.4%
Local and Fees	8.3%	33.3%	---	---	7.7%
International and Fees	8.3%	---	---	---	5.1%
No information	6.2%	---	---	---	3.8%
Total	100%	100%	100%	100%	100%

Source: Adapted from MOPIC (1997, p.35)

Training programmes

There are many TPs for providing management training in GS. The following is a brief outline of some of them.

The SMET Programme is the biggest and oldest TP for SMEs in the GS (UNRWA, 1998). UNRWA recognises that training is one of the key long-term means of promoting the development of SMEs for alleviating the problem of persistent unemployment in the GS. It is generally believed that SMEs will be the engine that drives economic growth in the future.

Small and Micro-Enterprises Training (SMET) programme UNRWA launched its income-generation programme in the GS in June 1991. It started off as a small programme that made capital available to SMEs and, within a relatively short period of time, the programme has developed into the largest SME training and lending programme in the Palestinian areas (Salman, 1997). Over a period of five years, its capital base grew from $100,000 to $10 million. By September 1997, the programme had provided 8,500 loans valued at $15.49 million (UNRWA, 1998, p.4). In addition to the income generation programmes and SME Solidarity Group lending, UNRWA then established in 1995 another new programme: the SMET Programme.

At the end of 1995, a two-year programme development grant from the government of the Federal Republic of Germany enabled UNRWA to introduce a longer-term training programme designed to meet the needs of the owners of SMEs. The introduction of this SMET Programme was the first sustained effort to provide continuous adult-education to the small business community in the GS (UNRWA, 1998, p.6).

The project proposal for the SMET Programme (1998) emphasises that the importance of this programme for the Palestinian economy is that its objective is to contribute to the economic development of the GS, through supporting SME education and entrepreneurship training. There are also other objectives, such as providing a range of business training courses, promoting entrepreneurial awareness and skills, and improving local training capacity by identifying and training a team of trainers. Producing business curricula using local case-study materials, promoting co-operation and co-ordination among institutions, promoting the growth and development of private enterprise, and assisting businesses to improve their management efficiency.

Since SMET was formally established in 1995, it has gained a reputation as an institution providing practical enterprise training based on the needs of the business community.

A team of experienced trainers has been assembled. The programme retains 16 trainers on a regular course basis. The training team includes university lecturers, educators, successful entrepreneurs, and business executives with experience. During the first two years, SMET succeeded in developing 16 course manuals, covering three major topics; Management, Marketing and Finance. In 1998, SMET further improved these manuals with examples from local businesses.

Also during 1998, SMET successfully added more short courses (44) to its programme, some of which were about how to use the computer in business. It also added two new intensive courses, under the slogan 'managing your own business' and 'growing your own business', and also SMET conducted some training courses outside Gaza City (UNRWA, 1998). In future, SMET plans to add to the number of short courses to become 4-6 on a monthly basis, and to conduct further courses outside Gaza City (Safi, 1998). The main target groups are the owners and the managers of small and micro-enterprises, who suffer from managerial weakness; another target group is skilled workers and trades-people, who have launched many new businesses as a result of the lack of employment in Israel. New graduates are a further group.

MA'AN Development Centre   The MA'AN Development Centre is a Palestinian non-profit institution, dedicated to promoting social and economic development in the WBG. The centre was set up in 1989 to lessen Palestinian dependency and build self-reliance by strengthening local skills, especially in the economic sphere. The MA'AN Development Centre works towards sustainable development and concentrates on organisational development and project management. The GS Centre was opened in 1993. It has a board of directors, consisting of 9 members; a director runs the GS branch. Part of its activities is organisational and managerial development (UN, 1998, p.6). Part of the target group is the managerial workers and SME owners. For these activities, MA'AN organised different courses on topics such as HRD, project development, accounting and bookkeeping, financial analysis, writing reports, meeting management, time management, how to start your own business, and quality control. Funds are provided through the international community, and from the income from some activities. The number of participants up to 1997 was 149 from GS and 567 from the WB (MA'AN, 2000).

Development Resource Centre (DRC)   DRC had been dedicated, prior to its closure in 1997, to serving the Palestinian industrial sector. Founded in 1992 and incorporated in New York City and GS as a non-profit organisation, DRC was established with the principal goal of increasing Palestinian self-sufficiency by upgrading the quality, technical capabilities and marketing skills of the manufacturing sector in the WBG. It was one of the biggest programmes working with the businesses through different departments, such as training, technical, project development, marketing, and research, with a small library and database (DRC, 1997, pp.4-6). DRC's activities focused on three main areas:

1. Research on industrial production in WBG;
2. Maintaining a database;
3. Providing technical assistance and training.

DRC had a board of directors, consisting of 11 members and 3 volunteers. Part of its activities were concerned with enterprise development (United Nations, 1998, p.49). The international community usually provided funds. According to the manager of DRC in GS 'during the 1997-99 the main funding came from the European Union. The funds amounted to approximately $1,118,555'. The DRC brought together organisations that focused on the provision of high quality technology and production support services to the Palestinian manufacturing sector.

Palestinian Centre for Micro-Projects' Development The Palestinian Centre for Micro-Projects' Development was founded in January 1995 in Jerusalem. It was initiated by a group of Palestinian national figures in order to contribute to the social and economic development of Palestinian society by supporting and promoting community projects and NGOs. Funds are provided exclusively through the European Commission (EC). The GS branch was opened in September 1995. The Project provides for 1250 SMEs all over the GS at a total amount of $ 331,000 (UN, 1998, p.51).

National Foundation for Investment and Development (NFID) NFID is a non-profit making organisation. It was founded in Jerusalem in 1991, and the GS branch was established in 1994. NFID organises training courses in the technical and administrative fields to contribute to the development of the skills and capacity of trainees. NFID organises vocational management training courses such as management and negotiation skills, strategy planning and project development (UN, 1998, p.76).

Palestinian Association for Vocational Training (PAVT) PAVT is an independent, non-profit organisation specialising in management and technical training. Its main mission is to provide capacity-building programmes as well as other support services to the local community, with special emphasis on disadvantaged groups; women; micro, small and medium enterprises; and private and public institutions. PAVT is the largest training institution in Palestine, with 10 centres. Over the past 6 years, PAVT has been an implementing institution for bilateral and multilateral projects in the above areas, and customised as well as regular training courses. PAVT has different projects, such as vocational training programmes; management and institutional capacity-building programmes; business incubators for micro and small projects, owned and run by women; entrepreneurship development programme for the private sector; and a business centre in the GS industrial park (UN, 1998, p.80).

Centre for Women's Economic Projects OXFAM-QUEBEC This project, supported by the Dutch Government, offers loans to Palestinian women in the WBG in order to improve their position in society and encourage their integration in the economic field. Its Loan Programme for Women makes available loans of $1,000 to $10,000 to women to help them establish or improve their enterprises. It also helps women by providing training services such as administrative training organised by local training institutes (UN, 1998, p.181).

Women's Affairs Training and Research Centre The Women's Affairs Training and Research Centre GS began operating in 1991. Through five ongoing programmes, it provides training for women in a range of non-traditional skills to further their integration into all areas of public events, to raise awareness about women's film festivals, public lectures, workshops on legal rights, plays, exhibitions and regular workshops throughout the GS (UN, 1998, p.210).

Women are the target group. There are different courses for women who start a new business and women SME owners, such as financial analysis; how to start a business; how to manage a business; relations with banks; marketing; business plan; and feasibility studies. Funds are provided from the international community and from other income generating activities. Up to 2,000 women had participated in these courses until 1999 (Women's Affairs, 2000).

The Women's Affairs Centre systematically trains hundreds of women every year in various fields, such as communication, managerial and administrative skills, gender sensitivity and human rights. It constantly puts emphasis on improving the capacity of women working with women's organisations through training specifically designed to meet their needs. Moreover, when resources are available, the WATC does its best to meet the constant demand for training from municipal and governmental employees and from women who are interested in entering the political scene on both the local and national level (WATC, 2000).

Development Centre for Small Businesses The Development Centre was founded in 1997 in Nablous. Supporting the SME is its main target, through information, loans and training. The Development Centre has organised different MT courses such as how to start your business, how to develop your business, accounting, pricing, managerial skills and communication skills. Funds are provided exclusively through the European Commission (EC). The GS branch was opened in 1997 (Al-Hayat Aljadeda, 1997).

Deutsche Gesellschaft fur Technische Zusammenarbeit GmbH (German Technical Co-operation) (GTZ) The GTZ was founded in the WBG in 1997 to support the SMEs, through loans and training for the businesses that had been established during the last three years. The maximum loan offered for one business is $85,000; the loan is organised through the DTA German Bank. At the same time, the programme has organised training courses for the SME managers who receive loans (UNRWA, 1998).

Characteristics and attributes of managers

High unemployment, low income, closure of the Palestinian areas, Israeli control of the borders, and many other obstacles are still facing the private sector in Palestine. Furthermore, Migdad et al (2001) listed other obstacles facing the private sector in the territories: shortage of skilled work-force and entrepreneurs, limited power supply, lack of marketing channels, absence of protection policies for the private sector, and an absence of central authority to institute policy and to promote the private sector and investment in infrastructure. In a study of the WBG, Migdad (1999) found that 34 per cent of the owners were considered to be qualified persons while 69 per cent had completed only the middle school. He considers that there is a problem of training, especially managerial training.

Many studies shed light on the weakness associated with the finance. Most of the firms are financed by owner capital. Okasha and Abu-Zarifa (1992) showed in their study that more than 95 per cent of firms in the GS are financed by owner capital, while only 3.2 per cent get loans from banks. In a study by ASIR in 1986 on the WBG, it was found that none among 684 factories in the sample borrowed any money from banks. In 1997, the Governor of the Palestinian Monetary Authority found that the loans given by banks to the private sector were only 16 per cent of the total deposits in the banking system, which is a very low percentage, if compared with Jordan's 68 per cent and Israel's 80 per cent (Al-Hayat, 1997). Under these conditions, the prospects for development in the WBG are deemed to be very slim.

Gender and age

As shown (see Table 4.2), from the 106 survey responses received, 102 responses passed the criterion of validity. Almost 76.5 per cent (78) of the respondents (managers) are male. The gender factor is not taken seriously in most developing countries, and the result clearly shows that the male figure is still dominant at the managerial level. There may be some minor difference in Palestine as 23.5 per cent (24) were women. This means that there is a good percentage of women who own their businesses and are participating in MTP.

The managers were widely spread between the youngest aged 21 to the oldest aged 55. As expected, the majority of the managers (76.5 per cent) are in the age groups below 40. Most of these are below 30 years of age (47). This category formed 46.1 per cent of all the respondents. The second largest group of respondents were in the age range 31-40 (31), that is, 30.4 per cent of all the managers involved in the study.

The number of managers who are 41-50 years of age is 22 (21.6 per cent of the respondents). But the fewest respondents seem to be located in the age category 51 and above. There are only 2, that is, 2 per cent from this age group. It is interesting to note here that 76.5 per cent of managers are under 40 years' old (mostly, 46.1 per cent between 20 and 30), and the youngest is aged only 21.

Women's age compared with men's suggest that the women tend to participate less in TP as they become older. These results indicate that young women may have a relatively higher level of education. Observations support the claim that most women with businesses may have lost their 'supporter' (husband or relative), either by death or arrest; it could be the case that their partners are unemployed. The above clearly shows that age is not the main factor for being a manager. In this case, employees between 20 and 30 years of age could have already become a manager.

Table 4.2   Age range and gender (throughout)

	Age				
	20-30	31-40	41-50	51+	
Male - No.	33	23	20	2	78
%	32.4%	22.5%	19.6%	2%	76.5%
Female - No.	14	8	2	0	24
%	13.7%	7.8%	2%	0%	23.5%
Total - No.	47	31	22	2	102
%	46.1%	30.4%	21.6%	2%	100%

Source: Data analysis

As shown in Table 4.3, the majority of the managers 60.4 per cent (n = 64) were educated at degree level; a few respondents (10.4 per cent, n = 11) possess technical certificates, and 29.2 per cent (31) obtained school certificates.

The data concerning the area of studies of the managers shows the majority of the participant managers (44, 62 per cent) have specialised in commercial (Management, Accounting, Economics) fields. The study in these fields may have encouraged them to start their own business. The second field of study is science (9, 12.7 per cent), followed by engineering (8, 11.3 per cent). Social sciences came next in ranking (7, 9.9 per cent), before Islamic studies (3, 4.2 per cent).

Table 4.3   Education level and area of study

Education	Frequency	Per cent
School	31	29.2
University	64	60.4
Technical	11	10.4
Total	106	100
Area of study	Frequency	Per cent
Social	7	9.9
Engineering	8	11.3
Commercial	44	62.0
Science	9	12.7
Islamic study	3	4.2
Total	71	100

Source: Data analysis

Age and education (cross-tabulation)

As expected the younger managers who possessed a degree attended MT courses more than those who did not. Furthermore, as shown (see Table 4.4) 31.4 per cent of the managers who had a university degree were 20-30 years of age, as opposed to 9.8 per cent of those who held a school certificate. 12.8 per cent of the managers with a university degree were more than 41 years of age, while 6.9 per cent of this age group held a school certificate.

Table 4.4   Age and education

| | | Education | | |
Age		School	University	Technical	Total
20-30	Count	10	32	5	47
	%	9.8%	31.4%	4.9%	46.1%
31-40	Count	13	16	2	31
	%	12.7%	15.7%	2 %	30.4%
41-50	Count	6	12	4	22
	%	5.9%	11.8%	3.9%	21.6%
Over 50	Count	1	1	0	2
	%	1%	1%	0%	2.0%
Total	Count	30	61	11	102
	%	29.4%	59.8%	10.8%	100%

Source: Data analysis

Gender and education (cross-tabulation)

Table 4.5 shows that 56 (52.8 per cent) of the male managers were holders of a university degree, while 8 (7.5 per cent) of the female managers had a degree.

In comparison, 19 (17.9 per cent) of the male managers and 12 (11.3 per cent) of the female managers had a school certificate.

Table 4.5   Gender and education (cross-tabulation)

		Education			
		School	University	Technical	
Male	Count	19	56	7	82
	%	17.9%	52.8%	6.6%	77.4%
Female	Count	12	8	4	24
	%	11.3%	7.5%	3.8%	22.6%
Total	Count	31	64	11	106
	%	29.2%	60.4%	10.4%	100%

Source: Data analysis

Managers' experience

Many managers are recent graduates, and some have also had a few years of prior work experience in other companies, before starting businesses.

As indicated earlier 60.4 per cent of the managers possess a university degree. Thus, the question posed here is, what skills or expertise are seen as important to these managers? This question will be answered in the following sections.

Learning the business

From 100 valid responses received, almost 41 per cent (41) of the respondents indicated that they had learnt by official ways as opposed to the 35 per cent (35) who learnt the business on-the-job. Finally, 24 per cent (24) of the respondents reported that they learnt the business by trial and error.

Regarding years of work experience, from the 106 completed questionnaires 104 were valid responses. Table 4.6 shows that the 5 (4.8 per cent) SME managers who had less than a year of managerial experience formed the smallest cluster. Managers with from 1 to 5 years of experience constituted 42.3 per cent (44), those with 6 to 10 years 26.9 per cent (28), and those with 11 to 20 years 19.2 per cent (20). A number of the managers, 6.7 per cent (7), had between 21 and 30 years' managerial experience.

The number of years of managerial experience seemed to play a very vital part in determining the success of managers. Nearly 50 per cent of the managers have had less than 5 years' managerial experience. On the other hand, 45 (45.5 per cent) of the managers did not have any managerial experience before establishing their own businesses.

Table 4.6   Years of managerial experience

Years	Frequency	%
<1	5	4.8
1-5	44	42.3
6-10	28	26.9
11-20	20	19.2
21-30	7	6.7
Total	104	100

Source: Data analysis

One observation made is that 3 (3 per cent) of the managers aged between 20 and 30 have less than one-year managerial experience, 31 (31 per cent) have between 1 and 5 years, 10 (10 per cent) between 6 and 10 years, while 1 (1 per cent) has between 11 and 20 years. This is particularly revealing. People often start their own business after gaining sufficient experience from working in other firms. It is usually during their course of employment that they come up with ideas and initiatives for their business.

Once established in their own business they begin to accumulate managerial experience. Moreover, SMEs are likely to suddenly close down for variety of reasons and open up under different names. The smaller the businesses the more likely managers and owners are to experience this turn around. The opportunities available determine, to a large extent, the reason for change of product or services offered or both.

Age and previous managerial experience

Cross-tabulation between years of previous managerial experience and the managers' age are based on 99 valid responses (see Table 4.7). One observation that can be made is that 26 (26.3 per cent) of the managers aged between 20 and 30 had no managerial experience before establishing the business, while 20 (20.2 per cent) had gained experience since then. This often accounts for the high turnover of the businesses during the first 2 years of their establishment.

Similarly, 13.1 per cent of the managers aged between 31 and 40 had no previous managerial experience, while 18.2 per cent reported that they had gained the experience after establishing their business.

Table 4.7   Age and managerial experience before and after establishing business

| | | Managerial Experience | | Total |
		Before	After	
20-30	No.	20	26	46
	%	20.2%	26.3%	46.5%
31-40	No.	18	13	31
	%	18.2%	13.1%	31.3%
41-50	No.	16	5	21
	%	16.2%	5.1%	21.2%
Over 50	No.		1	1
	%		1.0%	1.0%
Total	No.	54	45	99
	%	54.5%	45.5%	100%

Source: Data analysis

The relation between total managerial experience and previous managerial experience for the SME managers is explained by cross-tabulation in Table 4.8. The first observation made is that the managers, who have less than a year of managerial experience in their own business, also do not have any previous managerial experience before establishing it. It is interesting to note that the high percentage of the SME managers who have just 1-5 years of managerial experience (17, 16.8 per cent) had previous managerial experience before establishing the business, while 26 (25.7 per cent) of the managers had none, and the largest proportion of this percentage came from the young managers.

Supervision and number of workers

The respondents were asked 'How many people report to you directly?' and 'How many employees are there in your business?'. The intention was to get a better understanding of the span of a manager's supervision, especially as high-level managers in their businesses, and to understand the structure of businesses in GS by making two different categories, micro with from 1 to 10 workers and small with from 11 to 50 workers. This is important, so as to make a comparison among the different managers' supervision and from different sized business groups. It is interesting to observe that even though they come from almost the same business group, their duties and supervision are somewhat different.

Table 4.8   Total managerial experience and previous experience

Managerial Experience		Previous Experience		Total
Years of Experience	No. and per cent	Yes	No	
0 – 1 year	No.	-	5	5
	%	-	5.0%	5.0%
1-5 years	No.	17	26	43
	%	16.8%	25.7%	42.6%
6-10 years	No.	20	7	27
	%	19.8%	6.9%	26.7%
11-20 years	No.	14	5	19
	%	13.9%	5.0%	18.8%
21-30 years	No.	6	1	7
	%	5.9%	1.0%	6.9%
Total	No.	57	44	101
	%	56.4%	43.6%	100.0%

Source: Data analysis

Span of supervision

Table 4.9 illustrates the distribution of respondents and the number of subordinates directly responsible to them. Analysis of the data shows that 87 from 101 respondents reported that they had a number of subordinates who worked under their direct supervision along the chain of command. The managers' supervision span in this survey is described in five groups. Fourteen managers (13.9 per cent) keep a direct relation with workers. This is not something unusual in a micro business (1-10 workers), especially a family business. Surprisingly, it was found that even 3 per cent from the total 13.9 per cent were managers of the small business (11-50 workers); they too are keeping direct control of all the workers. The analysis of the data shows that 3 per cent of respondents had 21-30 subordinates who worked under their direct supervision, which seems to be a large number, especially since the biggest of the small businesses have no more than 50 workers.

A large number of the managers (46, 45.5 per cent) had from 1 to 5 subordinates who worked under their direct supervision, 38.6 per cent from 45.5 per cent were micro businesses (fewer than 10 employees). Twenty managers (19.8 per cent) had from 6 to 10 subordinates who worked under their direct supervision, 11.9 per cent from 19.8 per cent were micro businesses; it seems to be a high percentage when comparing between the number of subordinates and the number of employees. 18 managers (17.8 per cent) had from 11 to 20 subordinates who worked under their direct supervision; all of them were in small businesses (11-50 employees).

Table 4.9   Supervision span and business size (cross-tabulation)

| Supervision Span | | Business Size | | |
		Micro (1-10)	Small (11-50)	
0	No.	11	3	14
	%	10.9%	3%	13.9%
1-5	No	39	7	46
	%	38.6%	6.9%	45.5%
6-10	No.	12	8	20
	%	11.9%	7.9%	19.8%
11-20	No.		18	18
	%		17.8%	17.8%
21-30	No.		3	3
	%		3.0%	3%
Total	No.	62	39	101
	%	61.4%	38.6%	100%

Source: Data analysis

It was also discovered that more businesses could be classed as micro (62, 61.4 per cent), compared with the number of small businesses (39, 38.6 per cent). Although the difference in numbers between the two is evident, it still reveals and reflects the percentage of micro businesses in GS, which is more than 90 per cent (PSBC, 1999).

Business characteristics and managerial training processes

Business location and MT courses

This section deals with the SME manager respondents who have attended MT courses in the recent past in relation to developing their managerial work by attending such courses. Also, it examines their perceptions about the distribution of participants in MTP courses attended in the different GS sites. The objective of this inquiry was to identify the relation between the location distribution in the different GS sites and the percentage of participants in MTP courses during 1995-2000.

First of all, it should be mentioned that the research followed the geographic declaration by the PNA. A total of 66 (64.7 per cent) of the businesses, the majority, were located in Gaza City, sixteen (15.7 per cent) are in Khanyones, eleven (10.8 per cent) in the Middle GS, six (5.9 per cent) in Rafah, and three (2.9 per cent) in the North GS (see Table 4.10).

Table 4.10   Sites of business and participants in TPs

Site Of Business	SMET	DRC	GTZ	Ma'an	Women	NFID	Agri	Total
Gaza	40	26	20	16	15	17	12	146
Khanyones	13	0	6	3	1	1	4	28
Rafah	6	1	1	3	3	0	3	17
North GS	5	1	1	4	0	1	3	15
Middle GS	8	1	1	1	3	0	0	14
Total	72	29	29	27	22	19	22	220

Source: Data analysis

As shown (see above) SME managers in Gaza City participated in 146 courses from a total of 220 courses. It is interesting to observe that the SMEs were, for the main part, service sector (53.9 per cent). Furthermore, this sector is mainly in Gaza City itself. Although there is a main industry area in the North of GS, the lowest number of managers who participated in MTP came from this area (15 courses from 220). It is also interesting to mention that the area with the second highest number of managers, who participated in training courses, after Gaza City, is Khanyones (16, 15 per cent), and the number of courses attended was 28.

Table 4.11   SME establishment year and participants in TPs

Year	UNRWA	DRC	GTZ	MAAN	Women	NFID	Agri.	Total
Before 1980s	8	2	1	2	1	3	0	17
1981-1990	14	12	12	8	6	5	8	65
1991-2000	46	13	14	17	15	10	14	129
Total	68	27	27	27	22	18	22	211

Source: Data analysis

The reason for the above analysis is to identify the relation between the business establishment year, and the percentage of participants in MTP courses during 1995-2000. First of all, it should be mentioned that three different establishment year groups are used in this study (before the 1980s, 1981-1990, and 1991-2000). The majority of the participants' firms (61, 62.9 per cent) were established in the period 1991-2000, while 25 (25.8 per cent) were established in 1981-1990, and the lowest percentage is for the businesses established before the 1980s (11, 11.3 per cent).

The data on the cross-tabulations of SME establishment and MTP courses are presented in Table 4.11 which shows that the total was 211 courses, 129 courses for businesses established in 1991-2000, 65 courses for those established during 1980s, and only 17 courses for the businesses established before.

Analysis of this result indicates that the main percentage (62.9 per cent) of SMEs were established after 1990. The high percentage (75.3 per cent) of SME managers was from the young age group (20-40 years), while 48.4 per cent of the SME managers from businesses established in 1991-2000 were from the same age group. It is important to note that this age category formed the majority (77.4 per cent) of respondents who participated in MTP courses. Furthermore, 47.1 per cent from this category (20-40 years) have a university degree, leading to a conclusion that the managers who have a degree attend the MTP courses more (Table 4.12). It is interesting to note the lesser participation with only 17 courses for businesses established before the 1980s, which seems to be for opposite reasons to the above.

Table 4.12   Age and establishment year

		Establishment Year			Total
		Before 80s	81-90	91-00	
20-30	No.	3	7	34	44
	%	3.2%	7.5%	36.6%	47.3%
31-40	No.	5	12	11	28
	%	5.4%	12.9%	11.8%	30.1%
41-50	No.	2	6	12	20
	%	2.2%	6.5%	12.9%	21.5%
Over 50	No.			1	1
	%			1.1%	1.1%
Total	No.	10	25	58	93
	%	10.8%	26.9%	62.4%	100%

Source: Data analysis

Firm sector and MT course attended

Is there any relation between the type of firms and the number of MT courses attended during 1995-2000? First of all, it should be mentioned that the research uses data from four different sectors of firms (services, industry, agriculture, construction).

The majority of the businesses (55, 53.9 per cent) were from the service sector, 40 (39.2 per cent) were from the industry sector, 4 (3.9 per cent) were from the agriculture sector, while the lowest percentage belongs to the construction sector 3 (2.9 per cent).

As shown in Table 4.13a the data from the firm sector cross-tabulation with MTP courses indicate that the total courses attended was 224: 122 for services firms, 78 for industry firms, 22 for agriculture firms, and only 2 courses for construction firms.

Table 4.13a Firm sector and MT courses

Sector	UNRWA	DRC	GTZ	MAAN	Women	NFID	Agri.	Total
Service	37	20	15	11	16	11	12	122
Industry	26	9	12	10	5	7	9	78
Agriculture	5	0	1	13	1	1	1	22
Reconstruction	2	0	0	0	0	0	0	2
Total	70	29	28	34	22	19	22	224

Source: Data analysis

Table 4.13b Firm sector and site of business (cross-tabulation)

Firm Sector		Site Of Business					Total
		Gaza	Khanyones	Rafah	North GS	Middle GS	
Service	No.	36	10	3		5	54
	%	35.6%	9.9%	3.0%		5.0%	53.5%
Industry	No.	25	4	3	2	6	40
	%	24.8%	4.0%	3.0%	2.0%	5.9%	39.6%
Agriculture	No.	2	1		1		4
	%	2.0%	1.0%		1.0%		4.0%
Construction	No.	2	1				3
	%	2.0%	1.0%				3.0%
Total	No.	65	16	6	3	11	101
	%	64.4%	15.8%	5.9%	3.0%	10.9%	100%

Source: Data analysis

Analysis of this result indicates that, as mentioned above (see table 4.13b), the main percentage (53.9 per cent) of SMEs were from service firms. Also, the high percentage (35.6 per cent) of these firms was in Gaza City; as mentioned earlier, it is the main area for the MT courses in GS.

Type of owner and MT courses

The relationship between the type of owner and the percentage of participants in MTP courses during 1995-2000 revealed that there are three different categories: partners, single owner and family (see Table 4.14).

There were 37 (37.4 per cent) participants from partners-owned firms. Nearly the same percentage, 36 (36.4 per cent), was from single-owner firms, and the lowest percentage was from family-owned firms (26, 26.4 per cent).

Table 4.14   Type of owners and participants in TPs

Owner	UNRWA	DRC	GTZ	MAAN	Women	NFID	Agri.	Total
Single	22	8	5	9	11	7	8	**70**
Family	15	5	9	8	5	4	4	**50**
Partners	31	16	14	10	7	8	9	**95**
Total	**68**	**29**	**28**	**27**	**23**	**19**	**21**	**215**

Source: Data analysis

The total number of courses attended was 215. From partners-owner type firms, managers attended 95 courses; from single-owner type, managers attended 70 courses; and from family-owner type, managers attended 50 courses.

Business success and MT courses

Was there any link between business successes and attending MTP courses? To answer this question, managers were asked to choose from the five point scale: from very successful to very unsuccessful.

The majority of the managers (60, 57.7 per cent) responded favourably that their business was successful, 21 (20.2 per cent) answered that it was very successful, 20 (19.2 per cent) commented that it was just satisfactory. Only three respondents felt that their businesses were not successful. It is interesting to see that managers who describe their businesses as 'very successful' and 'successful' (77.9 per cent) also find there is a clear relation between the MT and success.

The cross-tabulation of the data on 'business success' and participation in 'MTP courses' shows that managers who participated in 136 (out of 221) MTD courses responded that their businesses are successful; those who participated in 42 courses also answered that their businesses are more than successful.

Arguably, the main percentage (77.9 per cent) of SME managers who participated in MT courses answered that their businesses have been more than successful. This category of managers attended in 178 courses from a total of 221 courses (more than 80 per cent). This is a particularly interesting finding, because for the first time, a study has been able to confirm that SMEs do benefit from the participation of their managers in management training courses.

Profit and MT courses

Equally, when managers were asked to make comments on the profit made in relation to their participation in MTP courses (using a choice of three different answers namely: profit increasing, constant and decreasing) during 1995-2000, their response was generally favourable. The majority of the participant managers (49, 50.5 per cent) answered that their profits were increasing, 36 (37.1 per cent) answered that they were constant, while the lowest percentage (12, 12.4 per cent) belonged to group that found their profits were decreasing. Therefore, again we see the evidence that the majority of managers see a link between increasing profit and participation in MTP courses (87.6 per cent). Some 50.5 per cent think that, yes, there is a relation between MT and the increase in profit; the other 37.1 per cent could not decide if there is any relation. But 12.4 per cent saw no relation between the MT and the increase in profit.

The data shows (see Figure 4.3) that SME managers who participated in 110 MT courses from a total of 200 answered that their profit was increasing, participants in 70 MT courses answered that it was constant, and managers participating in 20 MT courses reported that it was decreasing.

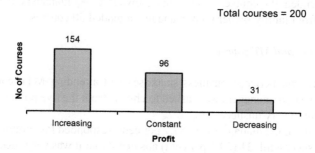

Figure 4.3   Participation in MTP and SMEs' profit

Source: Data analysis

Investment and MT courses

To identify the relation between the investment made and the participation in MTP courses during 1995-2000 two criteria were used (increasing and decreasing investment). The majority of the managers (80, 76.9 per cent) answered that the MT encourages them to increase investment; also, they felt that they have the ability and hope to do so. SME managers from this category participated in 177 (from 221) MT courses. The lowest proportion (24, 23.1 per cent) answered that the managerial training did not encourage them enough to increase investment; also, they do not have the ability to do so. On the whole, SME managers from this category participated in just 44 MT courses from the total of 221.

As shown (see Table 4.15) managers who participated in 19 courses (from a total of 44) in the MT programmes claimed that training courses did not encourage them enough to increase investment in their business. This also seems to be high a percentage compared with the total number of courses organised by the SMET programme (71 courses in all). It may be that the subjects of the mentioned training courses did not relate to new investment. Managers who participated in 3 courses (from a total of 44) in the NFID programme answered that the managerial training did not encourage them enough to increase investment. This seems to be not a high percentage. But it is very high compared with the total number of courses organised by the NFID programme (19 courses). On the whole, it can be argued that it would be difficult to find a direct relationship between factors such as increasing business profit or investment made and the attendance in training courses. What is certain however is that managers probably feel more confident and thus feel able to make such decisions once they have received relevant management training.

Table 4.15   Investment and number of participants in TPs

Investment	UNRWA	DRC	GTZ	MAAN	W-men	NFID	Agri.	Total
Increasing	52	24	25	22	20	16	18	177
Decreasing	19	6	4	5	3	3	4	44
Total	71	30	29	27	23	19	22	221

Source: Data analysis

Businesses' work

The total number of respondents was 103 from 106. The majority of the managers when asked about the nature of their business (85, 82.5 per cent) described their business as 'independent', 7 (6.8 per cent) described their business work as 'mixed', while 10 (9.7 per cent) reported that their business worked on the basis of 'subcontracting' with Israeli companies. Only one manager (1 per cent) described their business as being subcontracted with Arab country companies.

Table 4.16   Businesses' work and participants in TPs (cross-tabulation)

Kind Of Work	UNRWA	DRC	GTZ	MA'AN	Women	NFID	Agri.	Total
Sub-contract	6	8	4	2	2	4	1	27
Independent	58	18	21	21	16	12	15	161
Mixed	8	3	4	3	5	3	2	28
Total	72	29	29	26	23	19	18	216

Source: Data analysis

The analysis shows (see Table 4.16) that from a total of 216 MT courses, managers participating in 161 courses explained that their business is independent; those participating in 28 courses described their businesses as mixed (independent and subcontract), and managers participating in 27 courses said that their businesses work on a subcontract basis.

Businesses' finance and MT courses

Also, the majority of the managers (33, 32.4 per cent) answered that they have their own finance; 28 managers (27.5 per cent) described their business as family owned; 22 managers (21.6 per cent) and 19 managers (18.6 per cent) described their businesses as being financed by partner and loan respectively.

Those who financed their businesses by loan used financial institutions, banks, and Islamic banks. The total respondents' number was 19 from 106. As shown in Table 4.17, the majority (8, 42.1 per cent) secured loans from financial institutions. Some managers (7, 36.8 per cent) arranged loans from an Islamic bank. It is worth noting that, despite popular belief, the interest rate of Islamic banks is high when compared with other financial institutions and banks. However, there are many business owners who prefer to obtain a loan from an Islamic bank because of religious loyalty.

Table 4.17   Source of loan and participants in TPs (cross-tabulation)

Loan source	SMET	DRC	GTZ	MAAN	Women	NFID	Agri.	Total
Financial Institutions	3		1	1	6	0	0	11
Banks	1	1	1	1	1	0	1	6
Islamic Banks	4	1	1	2	2	1	1	12
Total	8	2	3	4	9	1	2	29

Source: Data analysis

An additional reason is that the Islamic bank pays for the equipment used in the business and uses this equipment as collateral. The lowest percentage of this group (4, 21.1 per cent) obtained a loan from banks.

Factors keeping the business running

What factors keep the business running? Three different factors were reported (money, managerial skills and technical skills). The application of the alpha model resulted in the extraction of all accounting factors (alpha = 0.69).

As shown in Table 4.18, the majority of the managers (51, 49 per cent) answered that money seemed to be the main factor in keeping their business running, 28 managers (26.9 per cent) placed money as the second and 24 managers (23.3 per cent) in the third position respectively in so far as running their business was concerned.

When they were asked about the role and importance of managerial skills in running their business the majority (48, 46.2 per cent) placed the acquisition of skills as the second most influential factor. Only a third of the managers (30, 28.8 per cent) felt that management skills should be regarded as first and the remaining managers (26, 25.2 per cent) referred to them as the third factor. Interestingly, the managers involved in the survey distinguished between 'managerial skills' and 'technical skills' with the former providing the competencies and know how for dealing with people, as opposed to the latter, which provides the competency to deal with the hard end of the business like finance and marketing. Almost half of the managers (53, 51.5 per cent) regarded technical skills as being the lowest influencing factor in running the business and only 23 and 28 managers treated this category of skills as the first and second most important factors (see Table 4.18).

Table 4.18   Factors keeping business running

Factors Keeping Business Running	First		Second		Third	
	No.	%	No.	%	No.	%
Money	51	49	28	26.9	24	23.3
Managerial skills	30	28.8	48	46.2	26	25.2
Technical skills	23	22.1	28	26.9	53	51.5

Source: Data analysis

Allocating an aggregate value to the above reveals a composite measure of factor importance. This composite measure reflects an aggregate view of each factor based on the level of elements to keep the business running. Three answers were designed to measure frequency loadings on each factor.

The majority of the participant managers answered that money is the first factor to keep the business running, and accounts for 77.6 per cent of total variance. Managerial skill occupies the second factor accounting for 70.6 per cent of total variance. Technical skills became the third overall factor and accounted for 59.3 per cent of total variance.

Training results

The reader should be reminded that training is crucial for development (Armstrong, 2001). However, it should be a continuous process to help managers and employees to become more effective in their present and future work. Such training is more important for the managers (Analoui, 1997), and the function of training programmes is to let managers practise an effective role. There should be deliberate provision for managers to understand and practise the training on-the-job or in the classroom (Armstrong, 2001). MTPs in Palestine tend to conduct their training in the classroom.

Percentage of participants in different programmes (1995-2000)

After the peace agreement, there were many efforts to provide training by several MTPs, typically financed by donors. In all there have been seven training programmes for managerial skills' development for SME managers in PT.

During 1995-2000 in all seven MTPs provided 133 training courses, responses show that 33 per cent, or the largest group of respondents, had attended 72 training courses with the SMET programme, 13 per cent had attended 30 training courses with the DRC programme, nearly the same percentage had attended 29 courses with the GTZ programme, and 12 per cent 27 training courses with the MA'AN programme. Participants (10 per cent) had also attended 23 courses with the Women's Affairs programme, the same number had attended courses with the Agriculture programme, and the lowest number of participants (9 per cent) had attended 19 training courses with the NFID programme (see Figure 4.4).

As expected, there was a high percentage of participants in the SME training courses. This result reflects that the SMET programme, as mentioned earlier, is the biggest and the oldest running TP in GS working with SME managers. This programme started in 1995, while some other programmes commenced in 1996 or 1997. It is interesting to mention that there were some training programmes, such as DRC and MA'AN, established even before the SMET programme; however, the target groups for these programmes were not just SME managers. Furthermore, the SMET programme is organising a large number of courses for SME managers every month.

And in the last two years studied (1999-2000), the programme opened two branches in Khanyones and in the middle of GS. On the other hand, there are no conditions for the participants to attend the courses, like some other MTPs, such as Women's Affairs, which organises courses just for women, and the Agriculture programme, which organises courses for just the agriculture sector. Furthermore, the SMET programme is part of the United Nations' development and planning department in GS, and from the researcher's observation, the Palestinian people are more confident in the work organised by the UN rather than by any other organisation. Since the development and planning department offers loans to the SMEs, maybe it is a significant reason for more people attending SMET courses.

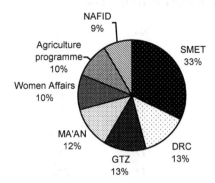

Figure 4.4   MTPs and percentage of participants (1995-2000)

Source: Data analysis

TP courses topics and attendance

There are seven training programmes dedicated to the development of managerial skills for SME managers in PT. There are also others organised for the public sector that provide for many different skills.

The seven MTPs conducted 133 training courses during the five years 1995-2000, and covered eight managerial topics, providing a total of 314 subject courses. Participation in each these courses were between 15 and 30. Some managers also participated in training courses organised by the TPs for the public sector.

Table 4.19 shows the distribution of the attendance of these courses, with 'Managerial skills' having the largest attendance (27 per cent) and 'How to start a business' the lowest (2 per cent).

The seven TPs arranged courses of different lengths and for many different skills. The objective of this item is to identify participation in courses of different lengths during 1995-2000, and the preferences of the participants.

The seven MTPs conducted two kinds of training courses, short and long; they specify a short course if it is between 9 and 30 hours, while if it is between 30 and 45 hours, the MTPs regard it as a long course. When managers were asked to identify and show their preference for the courses available, the majority of the participants attended 207 short courses from the total of 298 (69.5 per cent), and 91 long courses from the total 298 (30.5 per cent). 45.8 per cent of participants answered that they preferred the short course, while 13 per cent showed a preference for the longer duration courses (see Table 4.18).

Table 4.19   Training courses (1995-2000): Subjects, number of courses attended, percentage of total courses

Training Courses	No.	%
Managerial Skills	84	27%
Marketing	72	23%
Financial	53	17%
Production	37	12%
Human Resources	31	10%
Stock & Inventory	17	5%
Purchasing	15	5%
How to Start a Business	5	2%
Total No. of Courses	314	100%

Source: Data analysis

Training methods

What types of training methods were used, and which were more preferred by managers? During the training, the trainers used seven training methods: lecture, case study, video, seminars and conferences, role-playing, business games, and brainstorming. As shown in Table 4.20, the majority of the trainers (71.2 per cent) used the lecture as a first training method. This is not unusual. In most developing countries, management trainers and developers still use lectures (chalk and talk) as the main method for the transfer of learning. As shown only half of the respondents showed a preference for this method. The use of case study in training seems to offer a balanced activity. The respondents' preference for other methods clearly shows that SME managers prefer methods which help them learn the 'business' of managing enterprise in practical ways.

Table 4.20   Preference showed for training methods

Training Methods	Used	Preferred
Lecture	71.2%	39%
Case study	51.6%	56.7%
Video	37.1%	22.7%
Seminars and conferences	33.3%	23%
Role playing	30%	19.2%
Business games	20.5%	9.2%
Brainstorming	3.3%	6.2%

Source: Data analysis

MTPs' efforts and business success

In measuring the role and importance of MTPs in terms of effort, energy and their contributions in PT, five factors were identified. First, it was commented that the provision of MT is central to improved business performance; second, the MTPs are usually followed by the results of the training showing in the business; third that MTPs are designed to acquaint the managers with how to manage rather than what management is; fourth, the training programme trains in-house; and finally, they improve managerial skills quicker than experience.

On the whole, it was discovered that the majority of the participants (49.5 per cent) felt that their businesses were successful and this is as a direct result of attending the training courses, followed by 41.9 per cent of the SME managers who regarded the degree of success as 'satisfactory'. Such an outcome clearly shows the value of providing training for SMEs.

Results of the training programmes

Systematically, different MTPs conducted 15 training courses in 1995, attended by 368 participants; 25 training courses were conducted in 1996, attended by 565 participants; 4 per cent of participants were SME owners who had already established a business. In 1997, the number of training courses conducted was 29, attended by 496 participants; 48 per cent of the participants were SME owners (see Table 4.21). Also in 1997, TP introduced a series of one-day workshops with other institutions involved in training. In 1998, 445 managers attended 32 training courses; 42 per cent of the participants were SME owners (UNRWA, 1998, p.7). In the first six months of 1999, 323 participants attended 15 training courses; 33 per cent of participants were SME owners (Shaban, 1999).

Table 4.21 Number of courses, participants and owners

Year	Courses	Participants	Owners	% Owners
1995	15	368	154	42%
1996	25	565	231	41%
1997	29	496	240	48%
1998	32	445	240	54%
1999	32	518	255	49%
Total	133	2392	1120	47%

Source: Safi (1997); UNRWA (1998); Shaban (1999); Al-Efranjy (2000)

As discussed, during the first four years since the TP was established in 1995, the number of training courses has steadily increased. The best (highest) number of courses was 32 in 1998 and 1999. At the same time, the number of participants has been decreasing, with the best (highest) number of participants (565) in 1996. Nevertheless, the numbers of participants did not grow in the same way as the number of courses when comparison is made between the number of participants in 1996 and 1998 (565, 445), and the number of courses in the same years (25, 32). This means the courses had grown by 7, but at the same time, the number of participants had declined by 120. On the other hand, the increase in the number of participants in 1999 is because one course was given as a lecture (4 hours by international consultant); 130 participants attended this course. The percentage of owners and managers among the participants during the first 5 years did not increase from the best percentage for owners among the participants in 1998 (54 per cent). Yet the owners and the managers of SME are the main target group for the TP. The number of participants in the training courses is small (1120) when it is compared with the number of SMEs in the GS (20,470). During 5 years, these courses developed only 5 per cent of the owners and managers of SMEs.

Summary

The West Bank and Gaza (WBG) are parts of Palestine that were under Israeli occupation after 1967. The occupation continued until the peace treaty in 1993. The economy of the WBG is small, poorly developed and highly dependent on Israel. The Palestinians suffer from poverty, the number of families living below the poverty line being 33 per cent in GS.

With donors' assets, but with equally burdensome liabilities, the Palestinian economy is on a knife-edge between take-off and collapse.

After the peace agreement there were many efforts for training made by several TPs financed by donors. Some of these are dedicated to SME development. However, these TPs lack co-ordination and effective management.

UNRWA has contributed more effort and money to development in the GS since the peace agreement. The main part of these efforts goes to SME development. Since the size of the SME sector in the GS is large, it will play a critical role in the GS's future. However, the main problem is managerial weakness.

From the research results, it is clear that there is a good percentage of women who have their own businesses, and they are participating in MTP. The majority of the managers (76.5 per cent) are in the age group of below 40, and most of them are below 30 years of age. Furthermore, many managers are fresh graduates, and managers who have a university degree and who attend more MTP courses. Consequently, the majority of the respondents have a degree before they establish a business. As expected, the majority of the managers (62 per cent) have specialised their studies in commercial fields. It may be that study in these fields encourages starting a new business. While the majority of the managers have managerial experience only from their own business, 43.6 per cent of the managers had no managerial experience before establishing their business. On the other hand, the managers of small businesses participated in more MT courses than the managers of micro business. The span of supervision is very large and this may be taken as evidence that there is probably a lack of general knowledge of basic management.

Training programmes operate in different ways. Examples of methods employed during the last four years are long-term courses, workshops, trainers' programmes, printing new manuals for the training courses, and the small library for SME education.

Chapter Five

Categories of Skills for the Development of SME Managers

Introduction

Many authors have considered the success of the business to be directly related to the support managers are provided with in terms of managerial skills and knowledge or, to put it simply, in order to ensure the success of a business, support the manager with relevant managerial skills. Since managers play such a crucial role in determining the success or failure of a business or an enterprise, their development should be regarded as an investment rather than a cost (Drucker, 1954; Katz, 1974; Laird, 1978; Peels, 1984; Mol and Vermeulen, 1988; Kuber and Prokopenko, 1989; Davis, 1990; Analoui, 1993, 1997; Liedholm and Mead, 1999; MacMahon and Murphy, 1999; Analoui and Husseini, 2001; Al Madhoun and Analoui, 2002). SME managers, too, are no exception; to ensure the success of their business they need to attend MTPs. Furthermore, it has been shown in various studies that major managerial problems are the most frequently voiced reasons for SME failure (Schmitz, 1995; McCortnick and Pedersen, 1996; Van Dijk and Rabellotti, 1997; Burke and Collins, 2001).

In the previous chapter, the discussion focused on the efforts and the obstacles faced by MTPs in PT. However, the result confirmed the significant contribution of the MTPs in dealing with these difficulties. The main objective of this chapter is to focus on the contribution of MTPs to the development of managers and their businesses. Factor analysis will be attempted to use the results to explore managers' development of skills in three main categories: self-related, people-related and task-related skills. Also, using logistic regression analysis, the relationship between the developments of the categories of managerial skills for SME managers will be tested. Also, a comparative analysis of the development of the three categories of skills will be presented before reaching salient conclusions.

Cluster of managerial skills

What managerial skills were developed during the five years of effort by the MTPs in PT? Using factor analysis, an exploration was made into the nature of managerial skills acquired by dividing them into self-related, people-related and task-related categories of skills. Then the relation between these and the MTPs and successful businesses have been explored.

Factor analysis

The factor analysis technique is used to test the 26 variables chosen. The aim is to find the possible relationships between the different variables (managerial skills) and to summarise the information into a smaller set of new composite dimensions (factors), with a minimum loss of information, and use the result to construct a model.

With regard to the level of measurements and sample size, the study meets both requirements. Application of both the Bartlett Test of Sphericity (BTS) and Kaiser-Meyer-Olkin (KMO) tests of appropriateness for factor analysis revealed that the data is appropriate for factor analysis. Statistically, this means that the variables do have relationships between them and therefore they can appropriately be included in the analysis (Bryman, 1989).

Data analysis

All 26 items (variables) from the reliability analysis were entered for factor analysis, resulting in a six-factor solution (using PCA, principal component analysis) for the different variables of the manager's skills (see Table 5.1). It has been found that there are six variables extracted which have a significant relationship. These represent how to:

1. manage change effectively in the business;
2. use computers efficiently in daily management of affairs in the job;
3. be more confident;
4. manage conflicts to settle disputes effectively;
5. have clear ideas and arrive at the correct conclusions;
6. how to have an overall control of business operations.

Common patterns and interrelationships

This study also sought to determine analytically the presence of patterns of relationships and interrelationships amongst the managerial knowledge and skills that are required for development of SME managers. It was further hypothesised that some managerial skills for SMEs managers were improved by the MTPs efforts. Therefore, those skills that had been improved for the managers were subjected to the test. To further test the possible grouping of the skills identified in the literature, and to investigate the existing patterns of the interrelationships in the data, factor analysis was considered to provide the appropriate model for the required analysis. It was hoped that this analysis would also shed some light on the relative importance of the identified sets of skills.

Table 5.1   Factor analysis (total variance*)

No.	Initial Eigenvalues			Extraction Sums of Squared Loadings			Rotation Sums of Squared Loadings		
	Total	% of Variance	Cumul** %	Total	% of Variance	Cumul %	Total	% of Variance	Cumul %
1	9.203	35.395	35.395	9.203	35.395	35.395	4.762	18.315	18.315
2	2.256	8.679	44.074	2.256	8.679	44.074	2.824	10.863	29.178
3	1.984	7.630	51.704	1.984	7.630	51.704	2.744	10.553	39.732
4	1.595	6.136	57.840	1.595	6.136	57.840	2.652	10.201	49.933
5	1.186	4.563	62.403	1.186	4.563	62.403	2.263	8.705	58.638
6	1.110	4.268	66.671	1.110	4.268	66.671	2.089	8.033	66.671
7	.990	3.808	70.479						
8	.869	3.341	73.820						
9	.820	3.154	76.974						
10	.794	3.055	80.028						
11	.641	2.464	82.492						
12	.607	2.333	84.826						
13	.548	2.109	86.935						
14	.457	1.760	88.694						
15	.410	1.577	90.271						
16	.392	1.507	91.778						
17	.352	1.354	93.132						
18	.317	1.220	94.353						
19	.310	1.192	95.545						
20	.258	.991	96.535						
21	.251	.966	97.501						
22	.168	.647	98.149						
23	.149	.575	98.724						
24	.129	.496	99.220						
25	.121	.465	99.685						
26	.081	.315	100.00						

*   Extraction Method: Principal Component Analysis
**   Cumulative

Source: Data analysis

Briefly, as a multi-dimensional vector space, as defined by the cases, the presentation of the selected managerial skills (variables) is highly meaningful. It simply means, the smaller the angle between any two variables (vectors), the closer their association. The common patterns, distinct from each other, emerge by passing orthogonal axes through the centre of gravity of possible clusters of variables. Such patterns are defined by the loading of variables on these imaginary axes (factors). In other words, the common factors are defined by a set of closely associated variables. Naturally, such interrelationships and patterns may differ from sector to sector (Figure 5.1).

The principal component model of factor analysis (PCA) was therefore employed for this purpose as it was intended to search mainly for the basic dimensions of data that would define the total variance. In choosing the number of factors, we were guided by a combination of:

1. the magnitude of the eigenvalues;
2. the percentage of variance accounted for by successive factors;
3. a relatively significant drop in the percentage of variance accounted for by the last factor left out.

These criteria resulted in extracting six factors with eigen values greater than 1.00 accounting for 70 per cent of the total variance. The criterion used for rotation was to look for 'simple structure' in data, as this would search for highly interrelated clusters of variables as specific to the cluster as possible. This was expected to make the interpretation for factors more meaningful. Thus, the Varimax rotation procedure was employed for this purpose.

Reliability analysis

Scale (alpha) model resulted in the extraction of six common factors accounting for 92 per cent of total variance. This indicates that the measurement has a standard level of reliability. Furthermore, a reliability analysis was conducted, and Cronbach's alpha was calculated for each of the six factors to be sure about their reliability. The last row of Table 5.2 reveals the reliability coefficient (alpha) accounted for by the derived factors.

The last column in Table 5.2 shows the communalities range from 0.542 to 0.818. Extraction provides communality for each variable; the square root of each communality is equal to the length of the variable-vector in the vector space which remains unchanged through rotation. On the whole, most variables have high commonalities, indicating a relatively high degree of explanation offered for them by the extracted factors. The last two rows of Table 5.2 reveal the percentage of total variance (Vt), and cumulative total variance (Cum Vt).

Factor I: Analytical and self-related skills (cluster 1)

Factor I accounts for 55.9 per cent of total variance, and the alpha = 0.879. It is clearly dominated by self-related skills variables. Factor I consists of 9 variables that were developed through the training efforts for the SME managers. The nature of these skills comprises the following variables: transfer the training to practice, how to be more flexible, how to be more confident, how to cope effectively with stress in the job, how to manage own time effectively, negotiation, how to manage change effectively, effective communication, and how have clear ideas and arrive at correct conclusions. The values are all closely grouped, with the highest being 'transfer the training to practice' (0.77), and the lowest 'how to have clear ideas and draw correct conclusions' (0.47).

In this cluster 'Transferring the training to practice' has the highest loading (0.77) on this factor. The next highest loading belongs to dealing with 'How to be more flexible' (0.768), again it is an analytical and self-related skills factor. 'How to be more confident', once again it is an analytical and self-related skill, has a high loading of 0.699 on this factor, and the next high loading belongs to 'how to cope effectively with stress in the job' (0.696). 'How to manage own time effectively' (0.688) is the next high loading, it also is an analytical and self-related factor.

The 'Negotiating' skill (0.554) is once again an analytical and self-related skills factor. It is also interesting to note the moderate loading of this variable on Factor II (0.512), which is basically an analytical and self-related skills factor as well. 'Manage change effectively' (0.531) was initially thought to belong to the people-related variable, having a moderate-high loading with the analytical and self-related category. 'Effective communication' (0.524) was initially considered to be a people-related factor; however, it may be argued to have an analytical dimension. It is interesting to note the moderate loading of this variable on Factor V, task-related skills (1), (0.498). The low-moderate loading of 'How to have ideas and draw correct conclusions' (0.471), an analytical and self-related category, on this factor is also notable. The moderate loading of 'Effective communication' on this factor (0.524) seems very meaningful.

Factor II: Analytical and self-related skills (cluster 2)

Factor II accounts for 14.2 per cent of the total variance, and the alpha = 0.791. It is clearly dominated by self-related skills variables. Factor II consists of 4 variables that were developed through the training efforts for the SME managers. The nature of these skills is that they are comprised of the following variables: writing reports, using computer in management, managing meetings and presenting own ideas. The values are all closely grouped, with the highest being 'writing reports' (0.784) and the lowest 'presenting own ideas' (0.598).

It is also interesting to note the moderate loading of this variable on Factor I (0.548), which is basically an analytical and self-related skills factor as well. The

Table 5.2   Factor analysis (varimax rotated factor matrix for managerial skills) Alpha 92

Factors*	I	II	III	IV	V	VI	Extr
Factor I – Analytical and self-related skills (1):							
Transfer the training to practice	**.770**	.107	.112	-.035	.036	-.042	.621
Being more flexible	**.768**	.078	-.017	.035	.198	.224	.687
Being more confident	**.699**	.164	.115	.245	.338	.109	.715
Coping effectively with stress in the job	**.696**	.055	.098	.166	.163	.299	.641
Managing own time effectively	**.688**	.092	.133	.232	.111	.354	.692
Negotiating	**.554**	**.512**	.122	.144	.107	-.258	.682
Managing change effectively	**.531**	-.011	.358	.132	-.226	.249	.542
Communicating effectively	**.524**	-.0004	.0004	.356	**.498**	.097	.658
Drawing correct conclusions	**.471**	.063	.357	.223	.099	-.042	.415
Factor II – Analytical and self-related skills (2):							
Writing reports	-.019	**.784**	.139	.198	.098	.187	.718
Using computers in management	.172	**.758**	-.048	.242	-.123	.188	.716
Managing meetings	.091	**.740**	.198	.008	.150	**.448**	.818
Presenting own ideas	**.548**	**.598**	.122	-.007	.262	-.133	.759
Factor III – People-related skills (1):							
Creating business loyalty	.073	.040	**.855**	.165	.117	.167	.806
Managing team work/participation	.037	.242	**.759**	.017	.270	-.022	.709
Dealing with conflict and disputes	.336	.022	**.700**	.114	.224	.102	.677
Factor IV – People-related skills (2):							
Using other languages	.197	.189	.165	**.814**	-.067	.151	.792
Using new communication methods	.067	.163	-.055	**.750**	.179	.146	.650
Help people to develop their skills	.106	.035	.311	**.614**	**.445**	.056	.687
Managing people	**.438**	.152	.256	**.501**	.042	.187	.568
Factor V – Task-related skills (1):							
Controlling	.177	.174	.213	.253	**.694**	.106	.664
Solving problems	.149	-.026	.332	.008	**.671**	.029	.584
Making decisions effectively	.334	.135	**.402**	-.071	**.409**	.371	.602
Factor VI – Task-related skills (2):							
Job description	.183	.199	.157	.299	.070	**.707**	.693
Designing business structures	.148	.370	.021	.377	.018	**.609**	.673
Planning effectively	.349	.184	.118	.026	.395	**.489**	.565
Vt	55.9	14.2	9.4	7.8	7.1	5.6	
Cum Vt	55.9	70.1	79.5	87.3	94.4	100	
Alpha	.879	.791	.803	.767	.645	.738	

*   All loadings of .40 and above highlighted as moderate to high.
Source: Data analysis

conclusion for Factor II is that it is clearly the analytical and self-related factor which, in terms of the variations it accounts for, is the most important pattern emerging.

Factor III: People-related skills (cluster 1)

Factor III accounts for 9.4 per cent of the total variance and the alpha = 0.803. It is clearly dominated by people-related skills variables. Factor III consists of 3 variables that were developed through the training efforts for the SME managers. The nature of these skills is comprised of the following variables: 'creating organisational loyalty', 'managing team work/participation' and 'dealing with conflict and disputes'. The values are all closely grouped, with the highest being 'creating organisational loyalty' (0.855), and the lowest 'dealing with conflict and disputes' (0.70). 'Dealing with conflict and disputes' (0.70) was initially thought to belong to the self-related variables, having a moderate-high loading with the people-related category. The conclusion is that Factor III is clearly a people-related factor, which, in terms of the variations it accounts for, is the most important pattern emerging.

Factor IV: People-related skills (cluster 2)

Factor IV accounts for 7.8 per cent of the total variance and the alpha = 0.767. It is clearly dominated by people-related skills variables. Factor IV consists of 4 variables that were developed through the training efforts for the SME managers. The nature of these skills is comprised of the following variables: using other languages, using new communication methods, helping people to develop their skills and managing people. The values are all closely grouped with the highest being 'using other languages' (0.814), and the lowest 'managing people' (0.501).

'Managing people' (.501) is once again a people-related skills factor. However, it is interesting to note the moderate loading of this variable on Factor I, a self-related skill (.438). The conclusion is that Factor IV was regarded as being of a people-related nature. It is clearly a people-related factor, which, in terms of the variations it accounts for, is the most important pattern emerging.

Factor V: Task-related skills (cluster 1)

Factor V accounts for 7.1 per cent of the total variance and the alpha = 0.645. It is clearly dominated by task-related skills variables. Factor V consists of 3 variables that were developed through the training efforts for the SME managers. The nature of these skills is comprised of the following variables: 'controlling skills', 'solving problems' and 'effective decision-making'. The values are all closely grouped, with the highest being 'controlling skills' (0.694), and the lowest 'effective decision-making' (0.409).

'Effective decision-making' (0.409) is once again a task-related skills factor. However, it is interesting to note the moderate loading of this variable on Factor III, a people-related skill (0.402). The conclusion is that Factor V is clearly a task-related factor, which, in terms of the variation it accounts for, is the most important pattern emerging.

Factor VI: Task-related skills (cluster 2)

Factor VI accounts for 5.6 per cent of the total variance and the alpha = 0.738. It is clearly dominated by task-related skills variables. Factor VI consists of 3 variables that were developed through the training efforts for the SME managers. The nature of these skills is comprised of the following variables: 'job description', 'designing the business structures' and 'effective planning of the work'. The values are all closely grouped, with the highest being 'job description' (0.707), and the lowest 'effective planning of the work' (0.489). 'Effective planning of the work' (0.489) is once again a task-related skills factor. However, it is interesting to note the moderate loading of this variable on Factor V, a task-related skill, nearly 0.40. Overall, this factor is regarded to be of a task-related nature.

The results of the above factor analysis support the proposition that though managerial skills are interrelated, they form various clusters that may be more distinct than the broad categories referred to in the literature. While the analytical and self-related skills are by far more strongly interrelated, and should be regarded as an integrated set of skills, the same does not apply, at least not to the same extent, to the other two categories of skills. With respect to SMEs in the Palestinian Territories, data on task-related skills form, though rather weakly linked, two distinct patterns. Similarly, the people-related skills do not form an integrated single group of skills, rather they seem to form distinct clusters of subsets of such skills. The reader should be reminded that while these results are suggestive in various ways, they are nevertheless relevant to the SME managers in PT.

The relation between the managerial skills and development of SMEs

In the previous analysis, the factor analysis (PCA) was used to uncover the main factors from the different variables that were developed by attending the MT courses during the years 1995 to 2000 in Palestine.

The main objective in this part is to discuss a number of independent variables that affect some important dependent variables related to the characteristics of TD. To achieve this aim, we used the logistic regression model. The reason for using logistic regression is because all dependent variables concerned are dichotomous or dummy variables.

In the logistic analysis, the model chi-square is analogous to multivariate F test for the linear regression. If the model chi-square is statistically significant (P less or equal to 0.05), then we reject the null hypothesis that the dependent variable equals to 0, and accept the existence of the event. Statistical packages usually produce the log-likelihood multiplied by 2 as a proxy for the chi-square distribution; this has a positive value because log-likelihood for any number between 1 and 0 is negative (Menard, 1995).

Furthermore, the output from performing the logistic regression analysis gave us some important information, of which the point that led us to test the overall model was the information about the likelihood ratio x^2 (called in the output -2 log-likelihood). It provides information about the goodness of fit of the logistic regression model. In this respect Hair et al. suggest that 'the overall measure of how well the model fits has been given by the likelihood value. A well-fitting model will have a small value for 2 log-likelihood' (1998).

The six main factors were:

1. Analytical and self-related skills (1);
2. Analytical and self-related skills (2);
3. People-related skills (1);
4. People-related skills (2);
5. Task-related skills (1);
6. Task-related skills (2).

There are 26 variables that were accepted as skills developed according to the SME managers.

The dependent variables that need to be explained are related to the characteristics of TD which are: increasing investment (I), increasing number of markets (NM), success of the business (S), increasing profit (P), number of courses (NC), and the kind of course (KC) whether short or long. The independent variables that we need to know can be divided into two groups:

First Group: (1) (I) Analytical and self-related skills (1), (II) Analytical and self-related skills (2), (III) People-related skills (1), (IV) People-related skills (2), (V) Task-related skills (1), and (VI) Task-related skills (2).

Second Group: Skills developed by attending MT courses and which have a significant relation with the dependent variables. These variables are: Manage change effectively (Ch), Using computers in management (CM), Confidence (Con), Loyalty (L), Business structure (B), Manage meetings (M), Time management (T), Languages skills (Lg), Negotiation (N), and Controlling (Ct). In this chapter the following abbreviations will be used:

Table 5.3   Abbreviations used

SD1	Analytical and self-related skills (Cluster 1)
SD2	Analytical and self-related skills (Cluster 2)
PD1	People-related skills (Cluster 1)
PD2	People-related skills (Cluster 2)
TD1	Task-related skills (Cluster 1)
TD2	Task-related skills (Cluster 2)
Ch	Manage change effectively
CM	Using computers in management
Con	Confidence
L	Create a business loyalty
B	Business structure
M	Managing meetings
T	Time management
Lg	Languages skills
N	Negotiation
Ct	Controlling
NC	Number of courses
P	Increase of profits
I	Increase of investment
NM	Increase number of markets
S	Success of business
KC	Kind of course (short or long)

Logistic regression analysis

For analysing the dummy dependent variables we use the logistic model. The logistic regression analysis shows not only the independent variables affecting the dependent dummy variables, but also the probability of the dependent variable occurring. This analysis has been used to analyse successful and less-successful businesses; here, by asking SME managers if they had more or less success after attending training courses. Also, the logistic model is used for analysing the increase in investment during the five years following the managers' attending the training courses. In the same way, it can be used for testing the increase in the number of markets and the relation between the profit of the business and the kind of skills most improved, to find the relation between the number of courses that managers attended and the kind of skills most improved and, also, to test if there is any relation between the length of the courses (short or long) that managers attended and the kind of skills most improved.

Regression analysis is suitable for continuous dependent variables, but it is not suitable for dichotomous ones. There are some dichotomous dependent variables that need to be analysed. The main ones are dummy variables signifying if the investment of the business is growing or not, if the business gains sufficient profit or not, if the SME managers attended less than one course or more than one, if the course was short or long, if the business is successful or not, and if the number of the business markets increased or not. The suitable model for this analysis is the logistic regression model as illustrated at the beginning of this chapter.

Factors affecting increase of investment

Here the logistic technique is used to explain the increasing and decreasing of investment in the businesses during the years of the training courses. The independent variable in this case is dichotomous. It is a dummy variable for investment; it is a dummy variable that equals zero if I is decreased after the training, and equals 1 if I is increased after the training. The logistic equation for the relationship with the two main positive independent variables affecting I is:

$$\text{Logit (I)} = -3.36 + 1.61(\text{SD2}) + 1.29\ (\text{PD1})$$
$$\qquad\quad (.002) \quad (.005) \qquad (.016)$$

Where SD2 is self-development (cluster 2), and PD1 is people-development (cluster 1), and they are continuous variables. The logistic model shows that –2 log likelihood = 81.94, the Chi-square for the model = 18.725 (df = 6), with significance at the 0.00 level, which means that the model significantly fits the data, and the goodness of fit equals 79. The number of missing cases is 15 out of 106 cases in the sample. The characteristics that relate positively with the event are significant at less than the 0.05 level for all independent variables. The probability of the business increasing investment, if it is a SD2 and PD1, equals 39 per cent. If other independent variables that have a negative effect on the probability of the event occurring are taken into consideration, the equation will be:

$$\text{Logit (I)} = -3.315 + .74\ (\text{L}) - .82\ (\text{B}) + .98\ (\text{M})$$
$$\qquad\quad (.000) \quad (.01) \quad (.02) \qquad (.002)$$

Where L creates business loyalty, B design business structure, M managing meetings, are continuous variables. I investment is a dummy variable which equals (1) if I increased after the training, and equals zero if I decreased after the training.

The logistic model shows that –2 log likelihood = 85.506, the Chi-square for the model = 22.349 (df = 3) with significance at the 0.000 level, which means that the model significantly fits the data, and the goodness of fit equals 83.268. The number of missing cases is 6 out of 106 cases in the sample. The characteristics that relate positively with the event are significant at less than the 0.05 level for all independent variables. The probability of the business increasing investment, if it is a L, M, and B, equals 92 per cent.

Factors affecting increased number of markets

The logistic technique is used here to explain the increase and decrease of the number of markets for the businesses during the years of the training courses. The independent variable in this case is dichotomous. It is a dummy for the number of markets, and equals (1) if NM increased after the training, and equals zero if NM decreased. The independent variables = SD1, SD2, PD1, PD2, TD1 and TD2, and they are continuous variables. After running the logistic regression analysis for increase in the number of markets as a dependent variable, it was found that there is no relation between them.

However, if other independent variables that have a negative effect on the probability of the event occurring are taken into consideration, the equation will be:

$$\text{Logit (NM)} = -.195 - 1.03 \ (T) + .54 \ (M) + .52 \ (Lg)$$
$$(.826) \quad (.01) \qquad (.05) \qquad (.05)$$

Where T is time management, M is managing meetings, and Lg is languages skills; these are continuous variables. NM is the increased number of markets; it is a dummy variable that equals 1 if NM is increased after the training, and equals zero if NM decreased.

The logistic model shows that -2 log likelihood = 95.781, the Chi-square for the model = 12.199 (df = 6), with the significance at the 0.05 level, which means that the model significantly fits the data, and the goodness of fit equals 84.081. The number of missing cases is 27 out of 106 cases in the sample. The characteristics that relate positively with the event are significant at less than the 0.05 level for all the independent variables. This will affect the probability of the positive result of the managerial skills that attending the training courses developed. Under these results, the probability of the number of markets increasing positively is 46 per cent.

Factors affecting increased success of business

For a successful analysis, in this section any businesses achieving success are considered, using the logistic technique to explain the increase and decrease of success for the businesses during the years of the training courses. The independent variable in this case is dichotomous. It is a dummy for success, which equals (1) if S increased after the training, and equals zero if S decreased. Unfortunately, none of the six factors has a significant relation with success as a dummy variable. Furthermore, no single variable from the 26 skills has such a relation with success.

Factors affecting increase of profit

For profitability analysis, in this section businesses that have gained profit are considered, using the logistic technique to explain the increase and decrease of profit for the businesses during the years of the training courses. The independent variable in this case is dichotomous. It is a dummy variable for profit that equals 1 if P increased after the training, and equals zero if P decreased. The logistic equation is for the relationship with the one positive independent variable affecting P. Unfortunately, none of the six factors has a significant relation with profit as a dummy variable. Furthermore, no single variable from the 26 skills has such a relation with profit.

Factors affecting number of courses

In this section, logistic technique is used to explain the increase in the number of courses that the managers attended during the five years and the relation to the skills that were developed further. The independent variable in this case is dichotomous. It is a dummy variable for the number of courses, which equals 1 if a) NC is equal to two courses or more courses, and b) equals zero if NC equals two courses or fewer. The independent variables = SD1, SD2, PD1, PD2, TD1 and TD2, and they are continuous variables. After running the logistic regression analysis for increase in the number of courses as a dependent variable, it was found that there is no relation between them.

Furthermore, when the other independent variables that have a negative effect on the probability of the event occurring are taken into consideration, the equation will be:

$$\text{Logit (NC)} = -.333 - .617 \text{ (N)} + .63 \text{ (Ct)}$$
$$\quad\quad\quad (.687) \quad (.03) \quad\quad\quad (.04)$$

Where N is negotiation skills, and Ct is controlling skills; they are continuous variables. NC is the increased number of courses; this is a dummy variable that equals 1 if NC is equal to two courses or more, and equals zero if NC equals two courses or fewer. The logistic model shows that -2 log likelihood = 120.577, the Chi-square for the model = 11.214 (df = 6) with the significance at 0.05 level, which means that the model significantly fits the data, and the goodness of fit equals 99.871. The number of missing cases is 6 out of 106 cases in the sample. If the increase in the number of the courses is the main objective, this will affect the probability of the positive result of the managerial skills that attending the training courses developed. Under these results, the probability of the number of courses increasing positively is 42 per cent.

Factors affecting length of courses (short or long)

In this section, the logistic technique is used to explain the length of courses that the managers attended during the five years, and the relation with the skills which were developed more. The independent variable in this case is dichotomous. It is a dummy variable for the number of courses, which equals (1) if KC is a long course, and equals zero if KC is a short course. The independent variables = SD1, SD2, PD1, PD2, TD1 and TD2, and they are continuous variables. After running the logistic regression analysis for increase in the number of courses as a dependent variable, it was found that the relation between the variables affecting KC is:

$$\text{Logit (KC)} = + .0728 + 1.02 \text{ (PD2)} - 1.34 \text{ (SD1)}$$
$$\quad\quad (.956) \quad\quad (.05) \quad\quad\quad (.05)$$

Where SD1 is self-development (cluster 1) and PD2 is people-development (cluster 3), and they are continuous variables. KC is the kind of course, and is a dummy variable that equals 1 if KC is a long course, and equals zero if KC is a short course. The logistic model shows that -2 log likelihood $= 71.383$, the Chi-square for the model $= 9.593$ (df $= 6$) with significance at the 0.05 level, which means that the model significantly fits the data, and the goodness of fit equals 64.466. The number of missing cases is 34 out of 106 cases in the sample. The characteristics that relate with the event are significant at the less than 0.05 level for all independent variables.

The probability of a relation between the kind of course and the skills that were developed equals 60 per cent.

On the other hand, when the other independent variables that have a negative effect on the probability of the event occurring are taken into consideration, the equation will be:

$$\text{Logit (KC)} = .-1.77 - 1.61 \text{ (Con)} + .85 \text{ (L)} + .65 \text{ (Ch)}$$
$$\quad\quad\quad (.105) \quad (.002) \quad\quad (.02) \quad\quad (.05)$$

Where Con is confidence, L is loyalty, and Ch is managing change, and they are continuous variables. KC is the kind of the courses; it is a dummy variable which equals 1 if KC is a long course, and equals zero if KC is a short course. The logistic model shows that -2 log likelihood $= 73.418$, the Chi-square for the model $= 15.976$ (df $= 5$) with the significance at the 0.00 level, which means that the model significantly fits the data, and the goodness of fit equals 89.784. The number of missing cases is 27 out of 106 cases in the sample. The characteristics that relate positively with the event are significant at the less than 0.05 level for all the independent variables. If increasing the number of the courses is the main objective, this will affect the probability of the positive result of the managerial skills that attending the training courses developed.

Measurement for development of managerial skills

Respondents were asked to indicate agreement or disagreement with statements relating to a five-point Likert-type scale, ranging from 1 = strongly disagree to 5 = strongly agree; the totals of each of the five agreement scores were then multiplied by their respective importance ratings. The resulting five scale scores were averaged to construct a composite measure of firm performance. This composite measure reflects an aggregate view of performance based on the level of skill development satisfaction.

Following the discussion of the factor analysis, the pattern of factor loading suggests that the three factors may be interpreted as information related to three major aspects of self development (Factor 1), people development (Factor 2), and task development (Factor 3). Composite measures representing each factor were computed by summing the scores of the variables with loading on the factor.

Self-development skills

This factor accounts for 41.1 per cent of total variance. Three variables have high loadings on this factor. Analytical and self-related skills (Clusters 1 and 2) seem to have clustered together. Initially, this variable was considered to be a self-related variable; however, it may be argued to have an analytical dimension. This factor was therefore regarded as being of an analytical and self-related nature.

Analytical and self-related skills (cluster 1) The objective of the questions posed was to identify the factors which were developed more in the opinion of SME managers. The application of the alpha model resulted in the extraction of all accounting factors (alpha = 0.88).

Nine indices were designed to measure the frequency of self-development skills. Self-development skills that load on this factor are: confidence, effective communication, draw correct conclusions, time management, cope with stress in my job, flexibility, transfer of training, negotiation and managing change. As shown in Table 5.4, the majority of the participant managers (84.2 per cent) answered that displaying confidence is developed as a result of attending MT courses; the total number of respondents was 104 from 106. 84 per cent answered that effective communication is the second skill developed more as a result of attending MT courses. On the other hand, 83.5 per cent answered that finding out how to have clear ideas and arrive at the correct conclusions is the third skill to be developed. 83 per cent answered that time management is the fourth skill developed. The total number of respondents was 106 from 106. Coping with stress in the job (82 per cent) is the fifth skill developed as a result of attending MT courses. The total number of respondents was 103 from 106. 83.2 per cent answered that flexibility is the sixth skill developed. The total number of respondents was the same. 80 per cent answered that transfer of the training to practice is the seventh skill developed. The total number of respondents was 104 from 106. 78 per cent of the managers answered that negotiation is the eighth skill developed. The total number of respondents was 102 from 106.

Table 5.4   Managers' perception of their analytical and self-related skills development (cluster 1)

Skills	Per cent	Priority
Being more confident	84.2	First
Communicating effectively	84.0	Second
Making correct conclusions	83.5	Third
Managing own time effectively	83.0	Fourth
Coping effectively with stress in the job	82.0	Fifth
Flexibility	83.2	Sixth
Transfer of training to practice	80	Seventh
Negotiation	78	Eighth
Manage change effectively	75.8	Ninth

Source: Data analysis

The lowest answer (75.8 per cent) was that manage change effectively is the skill developed as a result of attending MT courses. The total number of respondents was 104 from 106.

Analytical and self-related skills (cluster 2) This factor is regarded as being of an analytical and self-related skills nature. The objective of these questions was to identify the factors that were developed in the opinion of the SME managers. The application of the alpha model resulted in the extraction of all accounting factors (alpha = 0.79).

Four a priori indices were designed to measure frequency of analytical and self-related skills. The four that load on this factor are presentation skills, managing meetings, writing reports and using computers in management.

As shown in Table 5.5, the majority of the participant managers (79.6 per cent) answered that presentation of own ideas is the first skill developed as a result of attending MT courses. The total number of respondents was 101 from 106. On the other hand, managing meetings (75.7 per cent) is the second skill developed. The total number of respondents was 103 from 106. Furthermore, the third skill to be developed was writing reports (71 per cent). The total number of respondents was 105 from 106. The lowest number of answers (66.4 per cent) was that using the computer in management is the skill developed as a result of attending MT courses. The total number of respondents was 103 from 106 (see Table 5.5).

Table 5.5   Managers' perception of analytical and self-related skills for their development (cluster 2)

Skills	Per cent	Priority
Presenting own ideas	79.6	First
Managing meetings	75.7	Second
Writing reports	71.0	Third
Using computers in management	66.4	Fourth

Source: Data analysis

People development skills

This factor accounts for 22.9 per cent of total variance. Two factors have high loadings on this factor; people-related skills (Clusters 1 and 2) seem to have clustered together.

People-related skills (cluster 1)   Initially, this variable was considered to be a self-related variable; however, it was decided that it has an analytical dimension, thus, this factor is regarded as being of a people-related nature. The objective was to identify whether or not SME managers viewed their skills in this cluster as having been developed. The application of the alpha model resulted in the extraction of all accounting factors (alpha = 0.80).

Three indices were designed to measure the frequency of people-related skills. The three a priori indices designed to measure frequency of people-related skills that load on this factor are managing teamwork, create organisational loyalty, and conflict resolution.

As shown in Table 5.6, the majority of the participant managers (83.5 per cent) answered that managing teamwork is the skill that was developed the most as a result of attending MT courses. The total number of respondents was 104 from 106. On the other hand, creating organisational loyalty (81 per cent) is the second skill to be developed. The total number of respondents was 103 from 106. The skill that was developed the least (76.9 per cent) was conflict resolution. The total number of respondents was 104 from 106.

Table 5.6   Managers' perception of people-related skills for their development (cluster 1)

Skills	Per cent	Priority
Managing team work	83.5	First
Creating organisational loyalty	81.0	Second
Dealing with conflict and disputes	76.9	Third

Source: Data analysis

Analytical and people-related skills (cluster 2) Initially, this variable was considered to be a people-related variable; however, it may be argued to have an analytical dimension. Therefore, this factor was regarded as being of an analytical and people-related nature. The application of the alpha model resulted in the extraction of all accounting factors (alpha = 0.77).

Five indices were designed to measure frequency of people-development skills. The four that load on this factor are managing people, using new communication skills, helping people develop skills and using other languages.

As shown in Table 5.7, the majority of the participant managers (80 per cent) answered that they were helped to develop their 'managing people' skills as a result of attending MT courses. The total number of respondents was 103 from 106. Using the new communication methods (78.1 per cent) is the second most developed skill. The third is 'help people to develop skills' (74.8 per cent), and the least developed skill (70.7 per cent) is the use of other languages. The total number of respondents was 103 from 106 for above categories of skills. Managers ought to be helped to develop use of other languages.

Table 5.7   Managers' perception of their analytical and people-related skills development (cluster 2)

Skills	Per cent	Priority
Managing people	80.0	First
Use new communication methods	78.1	Second
Help people to develop skills	74.8	Third
Use other languages	70.7	Forth

Source: Data analysis

Task development skills

This factor accounts for 36 per cent of total variance. Two factors have high loadings on this factor. Task-related skills (Clusters 1 and 2) seem to have clustered together. The objective was to learn about the opinion of the SME managers for the development of the skills in task-related clusters.

Task-development skills (cluster 1) This factor was regarded as being of an analytical and task-related nature. The application of the alpha model resulted in the extraction of all accounting factors (alpha = 0.65).

Three indices were designed to measure the frequency of task-development skills. The three that load on this factor are controlling, effective decision-making and solving problems.

As shown in Table 5.8, the majority of the participant managers (85 per cent) answered that controlling is the most developed skill as a result of attending MT courses. The total number of respondents was 103 from 106. On the other hand, effective decision-making (84.4 per cent) is the second skill developed more. The total number of respondents was 104 from 106 and the lowest answer (83.5 per cent) was solving problems. The total number of respondents was 103 from 106.

Table 5.8   Managers' perception of task-related skills for their development (cluster 1)

Skills	Per cent	Priority
Controlling	85.0	First
Managing effective decision	84.4	Second
Solving problems	83.5	Third

Source: Data analysis

Task-development skills (cluster 2) The application of the alpha model resulted in the extraction of all accounting factors (alpha = 0.74).

Three indices were designed to measure the frequency of task-development skills. The three that load on this factor are planning, designing the business structure and job description.

As shown in Table 5.9, the majority of the participant managers (80.2 per cent) answered that planning is the most developed skill as a result of attending MT courses and the lowest answer (63.4 per cent) was writing job description skills. The total number of respondents was 99 from 106.

Table 5.9   Managers' perception of their task-related skills development (cluster 2)

Skills	Per cent	Priority
Planning work effectively	80.2	First
Designing business strategies	71.0	Second
Writing job description	63.4	Third

Source: Data analysis

Comparison between skills developed and skills to be developed

To shed light on the importance of the acquired skills and those that need to be developed by managers in the future, a comparison was made between the two categories. First of all, it should be mentioned that the research has used three different answers (analytical and self-related, people-related, and task-related skills).

As shown in Table 5.10 below, respondents were asked to indicate development of the three factors on a three-point scale. The cumulative number of responses received was averaged to construct a composite measure of factor development. This composite measure reflects an aggregate view of each factor based on the level of development elements.

Three answers were designed to measure frequency loadings on each factor. The total number of respondents was 103 from 106. As shown in Table 5.10, the majority of the participant managers (85 per cent) answered that self-related skills are the ones that were developed the most. 68.6 per cent answered that task-related skills came second, and 43 per cent answered that the people-related skills were the least developed factor.

On the other hand, the respondents were asked to specify the skills they wished to develop. Three answers were designed to measure frequency loadings on each factor. The total number of respondents was 104 from 106. As shown (see Table 5.10), the majority of the participant managers (69 per cent) answered that self-related skills is the first factor they wish to develop, 63.6 per cent answered that people-related skills is the second, and 60 per cent answered that task-related skills is the third factor.

Table 5.10   Comparison between the acquired categories of skills, and the categories that are still to be developed

Category	Per cent	Level	Per cent	Level
	Acquired skills		To be developed	
Self-development	78.3	First	69.0	First
People-related	43.6	Second	63.6	Second
Task-related	68.6	Third	60.0	Third

Source: Data analysis

Summary

The prime purpose of this chapter was to discuss the contribution of MTPs to manager and business development. To assess the impact of MTPs on SME managers' development, different sets of variables were used. These variables assess the validity of the research hypotheses. In order to achieve this objective, this chapter has explored the skills' development for managers by dividing the managerial skills into three broad main categories: self-related, people-related and task-related skills.

Since the findings of this research appear to indicate that analytical and self-related skills have the highest influence on the effectiveness of SME managers, we feel that more attention needs to be paid to developing relevant competencies in the people-related skills category. These results also suggest that task-related skills must be given a high degree of priority in the formulation of the human resource development policies and strategies, while at the same time some efforts need to be directed towards eliminating those obstacles that are hindering managers' development. It should be pointed out that the relative degrees of importance attached to such skills are likely to change with respect to circumstances. The results clearly show that the degree of importance attached to each set of skills tended to vary according to the position of the managers in the hierarchy of the organisation. Nonetheless, generalisation about managerial activities is likely to be at least partially incorrect for any particular manager or group of managers.

Also, in order to find out and analyse the main independent variables that affect some dependent variables, a logistic regression model was used. The results indicated that there is a relation between the development of some managerial skills and the increase of investment in the enterprise. There is also a relation between the number and the length of courses that the SME managers attended and the managerial skills that they developed.

Managers in different sectors, various cultural backgrounds, and different places are likely to have different perceptions of the importance of such skills and their interaction for their increased effectiveness and development as a whole. For the development of managers, the implications of these findings are many.

On the whole, the emerging pattern of variations and the forming of categories of skills show that managers perceive effectiveness to be a function of self-related (41.1 per cent) and task-related (36 per cent) categories of managerial skills, rather than people-related skills (22.9 per cent).

Chapter Six

Obstacles and Weaknesses Facing Training and Development

Introduction

Having paid attention to the SME managers and their business background, here the focus will be on the main obstacles and weaknesses facing training and development in Palestine. Using factor analysis, the results from data analysis are used to explore the training obstacles and weaknesses faced by MTPs.

Following a brief discussion of factor and logistic regression analysis, the second section describes the weaknesses inherent within a conflict zone situation. Then, the management training programmes and their weaknesses will be the focus of attention before attempting to explore the weaknesses associated with the trainers involved in MPT programs. Since SME managers are an integral part and parcel of the process of training, we will look at their specific obstacles and weaknesses, as they see them. Finally, a summary of the discussion will be presented and relevant conclusions will be reached.

Factor analysis

The factor analysis technique is used for testing twenty-two variables to discover the relationships between the different variables, to summarise the information into a smaller set of new composite dimensions, with a minimum loss of information, and also to build a model for analysis. All requirements for the use of factor analysis have been met. These include, level of measurements, sample size, the Bartlett Test of Sphericity (BTS) and Kaiser-Meyer-Olkin (KMO) tests of appropriateness.

As shown (see Table 6.1) the result of the BTS test is large, which is at 498.065, and the level of significance is $P = 0.000$. These results indicate the data are appropriate for the use of factor analysis. Statistically, this means that the variables do have relationships between them, and therefore they can appropriately be included in the analysis (Bryman, 1989).

Table 6.1   Factor analysis: KMO and BTS

Kaiser-Meyer-Olkin Measure of Sampling Adequacy (KMO)		.537
Bartlett's Test of Sphericity (BTS)	Approx. Chi-Square	498.065
	df	231
	Sig.	.000

Source: Data analysis

The KMO result of sampling adequacy is 0.537; accordingly, it can be classified as mediocre. However, the KMO measure result supports the appropriateness of factor analysis technique.

All 22 items (variables) from the reliability analysis were entered for factor analysis, resulting in a nine-factor solution (using PCA principal component analysis) for the different variables of the obstacles and weaknesses (see Table 6.2), and it was found that there are nine variables, which have a significant relationship. These represent:

1. Conflict zone lack professional MTP;
2. SME managers don't need managerial skills;
3. SME managers don't know about the training courses;
4. Trainers don't follow the modern training methods;
5. MTPs don't specify the training needs;
6. SME managers' of lack of time;
7. MTPs lack professional trainers;
8. SME managers don't believe that management training is important;
9. MTPs are designed to acquaint the manager with what management is.

Common patterns and interrelationships

Since the aim is to analytically determine the presence of patterns of relationships and interrelationships, if any, amongst the obstacles and weaknesses facing the training process, some hypotheses had to be introduced. Thus, it was decided to test some obstacles and weaknesses which have been stopping the development of the training process, and to further test the possible grouping of the obstacles and weaknesses identified in the literature in order to investigate the existing patterns of the interrelationships in the data.

Briefly, in a multi-dimensional vector space, as defined by the cases, the presentation of the selected obstacles and weaknesses (variables) is highly meaningful. The smaller the angle between any two variables (vectors), the closer would be their association. The common patterns, distinct from each other, emerge by passing orthogonal axes through the centre of gravity of possible clusters of variables. Such patterns are defined by the loading of variables of these imaginary axes (factors). In other words, the common factors are defined by a set of closely associated variables. Naturally, such interrelationships and patterns may differ from sector to sector.

Table 6.2   Factor analysis (total variation) total variance explained

Component	Initial Eigenvalues			Extraction Sums of Squared Loadings		
	Total	% of Variance	Cumulative %	Total	% of Variance	Cumulative %
1	3.117	14.168	14.168	3.117	14.168	14.168
2	2.701	12.279	26.448	2.701	12.279	26.448
3	2.086	9.483	35.931	2.086	9.483	35.931
4	1.892	8.601	44.532	1.892	8.601	44.532
5	1.460	6.636	51.168	1.460	6.636	51.168
6	1.258	5.720	56.888	1.258	5.720	56.888
7	1.137	5.169	62.058	1.137	5.169	62.058
8	1.112	5.056	67.114	1.112	5.056	67.114
9	1.053	4.787	71.900	1.053	4.787	71.900
10	.872	3.964	75.864			
11	.763	3.466	79.330			
12	.698	3.174	82.505			
13	.635	2.884	85.389			
14	.609	2.768	88.157			
15	.469	2.132	90.289			
16	.427	1.941	92.230			
17	.397	1.803	94.033			
18	.368	1.671	95.704			
19	.295	1.343	97.047			
20	.273	1.241	98.288			
21	.224	1.019	99.307			
22	.153	.693	100.000			

Extraction Method: Principal Component Analysis

Source: Data analysis

The principal component model of factor analysis (PCA) was therefore employed for this purpose, as it was intended to mainly search for the basic dimensions of data, which would define the total variance. In choosing the number of factors we were guided by a combination of:

1. the magnitude of the eigenvalues;
2. the percentage of variance accounted for by successive factors;
3. a relatively significant drop in the percentage of variance accounted for by the last factor left out.

These criteria resulted in extracting four factors with eigenvalues greater than 1.00 accounting for 71.9 per cent of total variance. The criterion used for rotation was to look for simple structure in data as this would search for highly interrelated clusters of variables as specific to the cluster as possible. Simple structure is based on the principle of parsimony, where the variance of the variable is accounted for by one or two factors rather than by several factors. The purpose is to find factors delineating separate groups of highly intercorrelated skills. This was expected to make the interpretation of factors more meaningful. Varimax rotation procedure was employed for this purpose.

Reliability analysis Using the scale (alpha) model resulted in the extraction of four common factors accounting for 63 per cent of total variance. This indicates that the measurement has a standard level of reliability. Furthermore, a reliability analysis was conducted, and Cronbach's alpha was calculated for each of the four factors to be sure about their reliability. The last row of Table 6.3 reveals the reliability coefficient (alpha) accounted for by the derived factors.

The last column of Table 6.3 shows the communalities range from 0.570 to 0.796. Extraction provides communality for each variable; the square root of each communality is equal to the length of the variable-vector in the vector space, which remains unchanged through rotation. On the whole, most variables have high communalities, indicating a relatively high degree of explanation offered for them by the extracted factors. The last two rows of Table 6.3 reveal the percentage of total variance (Vt) and cumulative total variance (Cum Vt).

Following the discussion of the factor analysis, the pattern of factor loading suggests that the four factors may be interpreted as information related to three major aspects of conflict zone situation weaknesses, MTPs' weaknesses, trainers' weaknesses and SME managers' weaknesses. Composite measures representing each factor were computed by summing the scores of the variables with loading on the factor.

Respondents were asked to indicate agreement or disagreement with statements on a five-point Likert-type scale, ranging from 1 = strongly disagree to 5 = strongly agree; the totals of each of the five agreement scores were then multiplied by their respective importance ratings. The resulting five scale scores were averaged to construct a composite measure of firm performance. This composite measure reflects an aggregate view of performance based on the level of obstacles and weaknesses.

Conflict zone situation weaknesses

This factor (alpha = 0.51) is clearly dominated by conflict zone situation obstacles and weaknesses variables. It consists of 5 variables, which are acting as obstacles to the development of SME managers in training efforts (see Table 6.3).

Table 6.3   Factor analysis (varimax rotated factor matrix for obstacles and weaknesses) Alpha = 0.63

Factors	I	II	III	IV	Extraction
Factor I: MTPs and Trainers' Weaknesses					
MTPs lack professional trainers	**.618**	.383	.260	-.079	.665
Trainers don't follow modern training methods	**.612**	.026	.07	.327	.718
Conflict zone lacks professional MTPs	**.566**	.350	-.142	.297	.737
Numbers of trainers not enough	**.552**	.231	-.095	-.328	.667
MTPs do not specify training needs	**.536**	**.442**	-.168	.237	.699
SME managers don't know about training courses	**.462**	.021	.295	.134	.666
Factor II: Training Process and Conflict Zone Situation					
SME managers don't need managerial skills	-.112	**.515**	.369	-.115	.717
SME managers prefer that MTPs train them in-house	.098	**.458**	-.347	-.406	.762
Closure of conflict zone stopped some training courses	-.019	**.424**	-.141	-.293	.707
MTPs have no clear policies and plans	-.475	**.423**	.039	.341	.735
MTPs designed to acquaint manager with what management is	-.002	**.408**	.308	-.498	.744
Factor III: Trainers' Weaknesses					
Trainers are not qualified enough	-.564	.253	**.471**	.257	.796
Trainers have no practical experience	-.496	.246	**.409**	.243	.769
Trainers did not speak Arabic	.102	.380	**.403**	-.221	.643
Factor IV: SME Managers' Weaknesses					
SME managers' lack of time	.280	.118	.084	**.622**	.642
SME managers did not believe that management training is important	.256	.300	.082	**.486**	.726
SME managers prefer short courses	-.114	.188	.194	**.486**	.570
MTPs did not follow up training results in business	-.084	.266	-.458	**.443**	.783
Vt	29.1	0.00	51.1	19.8	
Cum Vt	29.1	29.1	80.2	100	
Alpha	.69	.51	.60	.50	

Rotation Method: Varimax with Kaiser Normalisation. A Rotation converged in 8 iterations
Extraction Method: Principal Component Analysis

*   All loadings of .40 and above highlighted as moderate to high.
Source: Data analysis

The nature of these obstacles and weakness comprise the following variables:

1. SME managers don't need managerial skills;
2. Trainers don't follow modern training methods;
3. SME managers prefer in-house MTPs training;
4. Closure of the conflict zone stopped some training courses;
5. MTPs have no clear policies and plans;
6. MTPs are designed to acquaint the manager with what management is.

The values are all closely grouped, with the highest being 'SME managers don't need managerial skills' (0.515), and the lowest being 'MTPs are designed to acquaint the manager with what management is' (0.408).

The variable 'SME managers don't need managerial skills' has the highest loading (0.515) on this factor, and seems to be an SME managers-related obstacle. The next highest loading belongs to 'SME managers prefer that MTPs train them in-house' (0.458), and it is a MTPs-related obstacle. 'Closure of the conflict zone stopped some training courses', a conflict zone situation-related obstacle, has a loading of 0.424 on this factor, and the next loading belongs to 'MTPs have no clear policies and plans' (0.423), which is another factor related to MTPs obstacles and weaknesses. The low-moderate loading of 'MTPs designed to acquaint the manager with what management is' (0.408) on this factor, once again a MTPs-related obstacle, is also notable.

MTPs in the conflict zone suffer from some serious weaknesses related to the training process and conflict zone situation. A composite measure was obtained as described earlier. The application of the alpha model resulted in the extraction of all accounting factors (alpha = 0.51).

Five factors may be interpreted as information related to obstacles and weaknesses associated with the training process and the conflict zone situation. MTPs did not train SME managers in-house (Factor 1). MTPs are lacking clear policies and plans (Factor 2), MTPs are designed to acquaint the manager with what management is (Factor 3), Closure of the conflict zone stopped some training courses (Factor 4), and SME managers do not need managerial skills (Factor 5). Composite measures representing each factor were computed by summing the scores of the variables with loading on the factor.

For Factor 1, the total number of respondents was 104 from 106. Almost 80 per cent of the managers answered that MTPs did not train SME managers in-house. For Factor 2, the total number of respondents was 102 from 106. Here 77 per cent of the managers answered that the MTPs are lacking clear policies and plans. For Factor 3, the total number of respondents was 103 from 106. 72 per cent of the managers answered that MTPs are designed to acquaint the manager with what management is. For Factor 4, the total number of respondents was 101 from 106. More than half, 62 per cent of the managers answered that the closure of the conflict zone stopped some training courses. For the last factor (5), the total number of respondents was

101 from 106. Only 47 per cent of the managers answered that managers do not need managerial skills.

Weaknesses of the management training programmes

This factor accounts for 29.1 per cent of the total variance, and the alpha = 0.69. It is clearly dominated by MTPs' and trainers' weaknesses obstacle variables. This factor consists of 6 variables, which are acting as obstacles for development of the SME managers in the MTD training efforts. These variables are:

1. MTPs lack professional trainers;
2. Trainers don't follow modern training methods;
3. Conflict zone lacks professional MTPs;
4. Numbers of trainers not enough;
5. MTPs do not specify training needs;
6. SME managers don't know about the training courses.

The values are all closely grouped, with the highest being 'MTPs lack professional trainers' (0.62), and the lowest 'SME managers don't know about the training courses' (0.46). 'MTPs lack professional trainers' has the highest loading (0.62) on this factor, a MTPs and trainers-related obstacle. The next highest loading belongs to 'trainers don't follow the modern training methods' (0.610), a trainers-related obstacle. 'conflict zone lacks professional MTPs', once again an MTPs-related obstacle, has a high loading of 0.566, and the next high loading belongs to 'Numbers of trainers are not enough' (0.552), which is another trainers-related factor. 'MTPs do not specify the training needs' (0.536), once again a MTPs-related obstacle. The low-moderate loading on this factor of 'SME managers don't know about the training courses' (0.462), an MTPs-related obstacle, is also notable (see Table 6.4). The objective here is to identify the factors that are perceived as obstacles and weaknesses to the training process for developing SME managers in the conflict zone. The application of the alpha model resulted in the extraction of all accounting factors (alpha = 0.69).

Trainers' weaknesses

This factor accounts for 51.1 per cent of the total variance (the alpha = 0.60). It is clearly dominated by trainers' weakness obstacles and weaknesses. This factor consists of 3 variables, which are stopping the development of SME managers in their training efforts. The nature of these obstacles and weaknesses comprises the following variables:

1. 'Trainers are not qualified enough';
2. 'Trainers have no practical experience';
3. 'Trainers do not speak Arabic'.

The values are all closely grouped, with the highest being 'Trainers are not qualified enough' (0.471), and the lowest 'Trainers do not speak Arabic' (0.403).

'Trainers are not qualified enough' has the highest loading (0.471) on this factor, and it is a trainers-related obstacle. The next highest loading belongs to 'Trainers have no practical experience' (0.409), once again a trainer's weakness-related obstacle. The low-moderate loading of 'Trainers do not speak Arabic' was .403, and this variable was regarded as being of a trainers-related obstacle nature. On the other hand, it seems that the SME managers prefer Palestinian trainers.

Table 6.4   Obstacles and weaknesses related to MTPs in conflict zone

Obstacles and Weaknesses	Per cent	Order of Importance
Number of trainers not enough	79.4	First
Lack of good MTP trainers	75.8	Second
Areas of training needs not specified	74.4	Third
Trainers do not follow modern training methods	64.8	Fourth
Do not know about training courses	64.6	Fifth
Shortage of professional trainers	59.8	Sixth

Source: Data analysis

MTPs in the conflict zone suffer from some serious weaknesses related to the trainers issue. A composite measure was obtained in the same way as for other obstacles and weaknesses in the MT process in the conflict zone. The application of the alpha model resulted in the extraction of all accounting factors (alpha = 0.60).

Three factors may be interpreted as information related to trainers' weaknesses. Trainers did not speak Arabic (Factor 1). Trainers are not qualified enough (Factor 2), and Trainers have no practical experience (Factor 3). Composite measures representing each factor were computed by summing the scores of the variables with loading on the factor (see Table 6.4).

Table 6.5   Obstacles and weaknesses related to trainers

Obstacles and Weaknesses	Per cent	Order of Importance
Trainers do not speak Arabic	69.4	First
Trainers are not qualified	68.0	Second
Trainers have no practical experience	67.6	Third

Source: Data analysis

With regard to the first obstacle, the majority of the SME managers do not speak any language other than Arabic, and the SME managers did not want to attend training courses presented in other languages and have a translation into Arabic (see Table 6.5). For the second trainers' weakness, the trainers not being qualified enough, the majority of MTP managers accepted this argument, with a small reservation that they especially mentioned, that such weaknesses may now have disappeared with the programmes now being organised especially for the development of Palestinian trainers, and by inviting some trainers from Arab countries. Also, during the five years, the number of Palestinian trainers with more relevant knowledge has increased. However, it is an interesting point mentioned by the MTP managers that the problem is not their qualifications but actually it is the practical experience on the part of the trainers, and that the majority of the trainers in the training market used to be lecturers or teachers, and most of their experience is theoretical rather than practical in its nature. This matched with the third trainers' weaknesses recognised by the SME managers, that trainers have no practical experience. In this case, the MTP managers completely accepted this argument.

SME managers' and their weaknesses

This factor accounts for 19.8 per cent of total variance, and the alpha = 0.50. It is clearly dominated by SME managers' obstacles and weaknesses. This factor consists of 4 variables, which are stopping the development of SME managers in the training efforts (see Table 6.6). The nature of these obstacles and weaknesses comprises the following variables:

1. SME managers' lack of time;
2. SME managers do not believe that the management training is important;
3. SME managers prefer short courses;
4. MTPs do not follow up the training results in the business.

The values are all closely grouped, with the highest being 'SME managers' lack of time' (0.622), and the lowest 'MTPs did not follow up the training results in the business' (0.443).

Table 6.6   Obstacles and weaknesses related to managers

Obstacles and Weaknesses	Per cent	Order of Importance
MPTs do not follow up training results in the business	84.6	First
SME managers lack time	75.6	Second
SME managers prefer short courses	72.6	Third
SME managers do not believe in the importance of management training	46.6	Fourth

Source: Data analysis

SME managers' lack of time is an obstacle which has the highest loading (0.622) on this factor, and it is related to SME managers' obstacles and weaknesses. The next highest loading belongs to 'SME managers did not believe that the management training is important' (0.486), again an SME managers-related obstacle. 'SME managers prefer short courses', once again an SME managers-related obstacle, has a high loading of 0.486. The low-moderate loading is of 'MTPs did not follow up the training results in the business' (0.443). The application of the alpha model (alpha = 0.50) resulted in the extraction of all accounting factors.

SME managers' and their preferences for training

Five factors could be interpreted as information related to managers' preferences. SME managers prefer following up the training results in their own business (Factor 1), MTPs following up the training results in the business (Factor 2), SME managers training in-house (Factor 3), and MTPs training in the firm's location (Factor 4). Composite measures representing each factor were computed by summing the scores of the variables with loading on the factor.

For Factor 1, the total number of respondents was 103 from 106. 84 per cent of the SME managers answered that they prefer to follow up the training results in their own business. For Factor 2, the total number of respondents was 104 from 106. 63.8 per cent of the managers answered that MTPs are followed by the training results in the business. For Factor 3, the total number of respondents was 103 from 106. 78 per cent of the managers answered they prefer to train in-house. For Factor 4, the total number of respondents was 101 from 106. 53.4 per cent of the managers answered that MTPs are training in the firm's location.

Comparison between obstacles and weaknesses facing training and development

On the whole, the emerging pattern of variations and the forming of categories of obstacles and weaknesses show that the training process is facing different obstacles and weaknesses: SME managers' weaknesses (68.4 per cent), MTPs' weaknesses (65.8 per cent), trainers' weaknesses (64.6 per cent), and training process and conflict zone situation weaknesses (52.4 per cent). Among the obstacles and weaknesses the training process is facing in the conflict zone, it seems clear that SME managers' weaknesses form the highest percentage. MTPs and trainers constitute the most important category for the obstacles and weaknesses, irrespective of their position in the hierarchy. Subsequently, managers look forward to overcoming these obstacles and weaknesses as seen in Figure 6.1.

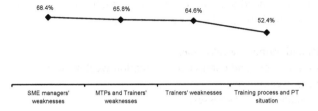

Figure 6.1   Comparison between perceived obstacles and weaknesses facing MTPs

Source: Data analysis

The relationship between the obstacles and weaknesses and development

The main objective in this part is to discuss a number of independent variables that affect some important dependent variables related to the characteristics of TD. To achieve this, the logistic regression model will be used. The reason for this is because all dependent variables concerned are dichotomous or dummy variables.

In the logistic analysis, the model chi-square is analogous to multivariate F test for the linear regression. If the model chi-square is statistically significant ($P \leq 0.05$), then we reject the null hypothesis that the dependent variable equals 0, and accept the existence of the event. Statistical packages usually produce the log-likelihood multiplied by -2 as a proxy for the chi-square distribution; this has a positive value because log-likelihood for any number between 1 and 0 is negative (Menard, 1995).

Furthermore, the output from performing the logistic regression analysis gave us some important information, of which the point that led us to test the overall model was the information about the likelihood ratio x^2 (called in the output -2 log-likelihood). It provides information about the goodness of fit of the logistic regression model. In this respect Hair et al suggest, 'the overall measure of how well the model fits has been given by the likelihood value. A well-fitting model will have a small value for 2 log-likelihood' (1998).

The main four factors were: (1) MTPs and trainers' obstacles and weaknesses, (2) Training process and conflict zone situation obstacles and weaknesses, (3) Trainers' obstacles and weaknesses, and (4) SME managers' obstacles and weaknesses. On the other hand, 18 variables were accepted as obstacles and weaknesses after asking the SME managers.

The dependent variables that need to be explained are success of MTPs (SP), success of the business (S), and development of MTPs (D). The independent variables, which we need to know, can be divided into two groups of obstacles and weaknesses (see Table 6.7). The first group includes:

1. MTPs and trainers' weaknesses;
2. Training process and conflict zone situation weaknesses;
3. Trainers' weaknesses;
4. SME managers' weaknesses.

The second group includes obstacles and weaknesses facing MTPs and which have a significant relation with the dependent variables. These variables are:

1. Closure stopped some training courses (C);
2. MTPs lacked clear policies and plans (P);
3. Trainers are not qualified enough (Q);
4. Number of trainers (N);
5. Trainers have no practical experience (TX);
6. Professional trainers (T).

Table 6.7   Abbreviations used

SP	Success of MTPs
S	Success of Business
D	Development of MTPs
TSW	Training process and conflict zone situation weaknesses
TW	Trainers' weaknesses
TPW	MTPs' and trainers' weaknesses
MW	SME managers' weaknesses
C	Closure stopped some training courses
P	MTPs missed clear policies and plans
Q	Trainers are not qualified enough
N	Number of trainers
TX	Trainers have no practical experience
T	Professional trainers

Logistic regression analysis

For analysing the dummy dependent variables we use the logistic model. The logistic regression analysis shows not only the independent variables affecting the dependent dummy variables, but also the probability of the dependent variable occurring. This analysis has been used to analyse successful and less-successful businesses. SME managers were asked if they had more or less success after attending training courses. Also, the logistic model is used for analysing the increase of investment during the five years following the managers' attending the training courses. In the same way, for testing the increase in the number of markets, and also, the relation between the profits of the business, the numbers of courses attended, the kinds of courses (short or long) and the kind of skills most improved.

Regression analysis is suitable for continuous dependent variables, but it is not suitable for dichotomous ones. There are some dichotomous dependent variables that need to be analysed. The main dependent variables that need to be analysed in this section are dummy variables signifying whether the investment in the business is growing or not; whether the business gains were sufficient profit or not; if the SME managers attended more than one course and whether those courses were short or long; whether the business is successful or not; and if the number of business markets had increased or not. The suitable model for this analysis is the logistic regression model as illustrated at the beginning of this section.

Factors affecting success of MTPs

Here, logistic technique is used to explain the success of the MTPs during the years of training courses. The independent variable in this case is dichotomous. It is a dummy for the success of the MTPs (SP), which equals zero if SP is negative, and equals (1) if SP is positive. The logistic equation is for the relationship with the main four positive independent variables affecting S. The independent variables equal TW, TPW, MW and TSW, and are continuous variables. After running the logistic regression analysis for success of MTPs as a dependent variable, it was found that there is no relation between them.

If other independent variables that have a negative effect on the probability of the event occurring are taken into consideration, the equation will be:

$$\text{Logit (SP)} = -5.66 + .99 \text{ (P)} + 1.04 \text{ (Q)} + .57 \text{ (C)}$$
$$(.002)(.01)(.02)(.04)$$

Where P is MTPs lacked clear policies and plans; Q, Trainers are not qualified enough; C, Closure stopped some TPs (continuous variables). SP, Success of the training programmes is a dummy variable which equals zero if SP decreased after the training, and equals (1) if SP increased after the training.

The logistic model shows that -2 log likelihood $= 95.361$, the Chi-square for the model $= 24.919$ (df $= 14$), with significance at the 0.03 level, which means that the model significantly fits the data, and the goodness of fit equals 88.573. The number of missing cases is 15 out of 106 cases in the sample. The characteristics that relate positively with the event are significant at less than the 0.05 level for all the independent variables. The probability of a business increasing an investment, if it is a P, Q and C, equals 4 per cent.

Factors affecting development of MTPs

What kind of courses did the managers attend during the five years? What relationship was there with the obstacles and weaknesses? The independent variable in this case is dichotomous. It is a dummy for TPs need more development (D) which equals zero if TPs do not need more development and equals 1 if TPs need more development.

The independent variables TW, TPW, MW and TSW are continuous variables. After running the logistic regression analysis for increasing the number of courses as a dependent variable, it was found that the relation between the variables affecting D is:

$$\text{Logit (D)} = -.5018 + 2.19 \text{ (TW)} - 3.33 \text{ (MW)}$$
$$\quad\quad\quad (.183) \quad\quad (.05) \quad\quad\quad\quad (.01)$$

Where TW is trainers' weakness and MW is SME managers' weaknesses, (continuous variables). The logistic model shows that -2 log likelihood = 27.03, the Chi-square for the model = 11.242 (df = 3) with significance at the 0.01 level, which means that the model significantly fits the data, and the goodness of fit equals 42.922. The number of missing cases is 19 out of 106 cases in the sample. The characteristics that relate with the event are significant at less than the 0.05 level for all independent variables. The probability of having a relation between the development of MTPs and the obstacles and weaknesses equals 16 per cent.

On the other hand, when the other independent variables that have a negative effect on the probability of the event occurring are taken into consideration, the equation will be:

$$\text{Logit (D)} = -.703 - .82 \text{ (C)} + .73 \text{ (N)}$$
$$\quad\quad\quad (.000) \quad (.04) \quad\quad\quad (.05)$$

Where C is Closure of the conflict zone, and N is number of trainers, which are continuous variables. D stands for TPs need more development; it is a dummy variable, which equals 1 if D represents TPs do not need more development, and equals zero if D is TPs need more development. The logistic model shows that -2 log likelihood = 42.217, the Chi-square for the model = 7.918 (df = 2) with significance at the 0.01 level, which means that the model significantly fits the data, and the goodness of fit equals 88.286. The number of missing cases is 10 out of 106 cases in the sample. The characteristics that relate positively with the event are significant at the less than 0.05 level for all the independent variables. If increasing the number of courses is the main objective, this will affect the probability of the positive result of the managerial skills. Under these results, the probability of the number of kinds of markets involved positively is 31.

Factors affecting business success

In this section, the logistic technique is used to explain business success during the relevant five years and their relationship with the obstacles and weaknesses. The independent variable in this case is dichotomous. It is a dummy for the success of the businesses (S), which equals zero if S is negative, and equals 1 if S is positive.

The independent variables TW, TPW, MW and TSW are continuous variables. After running the logistic regression analysis for increasing the number of courses as a dependent variable, it was found that the relation between the variables affecting S is:

Logit (S) = - .5704 + .931 (TP)
            (.00)   (.02)

Where TP is MTPs and trainers' weaknesses (continuous variables). S is the business success. The logistic model shows that -2 log likelihood = 83.799, the Chi-square for the model = 8.017 (df = 3), with significance at the 0.04 level, which means that the model significantly fits the data, and the goodness of fit equals 81.759. The number of missing cases is 18 out of 106 cases in the sample. The characteristics that relate with the event are significant at less than the .01 level for all the independent variables. The probability of there being a relationship between the kind of course and the obstacles and weaknesses that developed equals 59 per cent.

On the other hand, when taking into consideration the other independent variables that have a negative effect on the probability of the event occurring, the equation will be:

Logit (S) = -.985 +.70 (T) + 1.01 (N) + .84 (TX)
            (.00)   (.05)   (.05)   (.05)

Where T is professional trainers, N is the number of the trainers is not enough, and TX, trainers do not have practical experience (continuous variables). The logistic model shows that -2 log likelihood = 60.056, the Chi-square for the model = 28.723 (df = 22) with significance at the 0.05 level, which means that the model significantly fits the data, and the goodness of fit equals 89.374. The number of missing cases is 24 out of 106 cases in the sample. The characteristics that relate positively with the event are significant at less than the 0.01 level for all the independent variables. If increasing the number of the courses is the main objective, this will affect the probability of the positive result of the managerial obstacles and weaknesses that attending the training courses developed. Under these results, the probability of the number of the kinds of the markets involved positively is 83 per cent.

Summary

The issues related to the training process efforts, obstacles and weaknesses have been addressed in this chapter, given the exploratory training results' analysis.

To assess the impact of MTPs on SME managers' development, different sets of variables are used. These variables assess the validity of the research hypotheses. For this purpose, this chapter has discussed the obstacles and weaknesses faced by training and development, which are intended to meet the development of the managers and the businesses.

The results of the study highlighted the question of the interrelationship and interaction of the obstacles and weaknesses, and support the literature evidence in suggesting that obstacles and weaknesses should be analysed as a system of interrelated obstacles and weaknesses.

In this chapter, the researcher used the logistic regression model to find out and analyse the main independent variables that affect some dependent variables (SP, S and D).

It was found that the main independent variables that affect SP are P, Q and C, with a probability of 88 per cent. The variables TW and MW are the main independent variables that affect D, with a probability of 16 per cent. On the other hand, the main independent variables that affect D are N and C, with a probability of 31 per cent. It was found that the main independent variable that affects S is TP, with a probability of 59 per cent, while the main independent variables that affect the existence of S are T, N and TX, with a probability of 83 per cent. From these results, the conclusion reached is that there is a relationship between some obstacles and weaknesses and the development of MTPs.

From the results obtained, it is clear that there is a high percentage of different obstacles and weaknesses in the managers of SMEs (68.4 per cent). Having established this, it is notable that different items of MTPs and trainers' obstacles and weaknesses have a high percentage (65.8 per cent), while the different items of trainers' obstacles and weaknesses have 64.6 per cent. A lower percentage in comparison was the training process and conflict zone situation obstacles and weaknesses (52.4 per cent).

Chapter Seven

Summary and Conclusions

Introduction

Probably the best point of departure for assessing Palestinian management development needs is to turn to those attending the MT courses organised by MTPs financed by donors and who have gained managerial skills and run successful SMEs.

This volume, based on a first time empirical study, is primarily concerned with the effectiveness of Management Training and Development Programmes (MTPs), especially those which are expected to benefit the managers of Small and Micro Enterprises (SMEs) in Palestine.

The main purpose of this research was to test the effectiveness of training in MTPs using SME managers' perceptions, views and feedback. The results of the study indicate partially that training has, by and large, enhanced managerial effectiveness and has led to the development of managerial skills. This indication at the individual skill level is also the same at the overall business skill level. A possible explanation for this finding is that the emphasis of the research framework has been on the development of managerial skills. The participants on the training courses would be urged to first develop some managerial skills. On the assumption that the participants had different profiles initially, the participants were encouraged to share and develop differing skills with each other. Therefore, any of the skills of a single participant would be visible in the profile of the participants overall.

The findings, based on the analysis of the empirical data collected from the study, suggest that there is a link between TD and a manager's individual performance at work. This link becomes even more critical when we consider the nature and varying needs of the managers for different categories of managerial skills.

The main objective of the study was to explore the contribution of MTPs to the development of managerial skills for SME managers in Palestine. Here, in the final chapter, following a brief review of the literature and the introduction of the respondents, the main conclusions will be presented. The host of managerial skills offered in these programmes will be divided into three main categories, namely self-related, people-related and task-related skills. Attempts will be made to explore the contribution of each of the categories, their interdependence and interactions in the development of the SME managers. Finally, based on the results, policy implications will be reached. Also, a framework for successful MTD programmes will be proposed. Then, the limitations of the study will be discussed. The last section will focus on the future need for more research programmes and their related activities.

Literature and its relevance

What constitutes relevant MTD literature? An attempt has been made to review all the relevant literature available relating to the topics of SMEs and their management, especially within conflict zones. As a starting point, some historical perspectives of the main field of this research, that is MD, have been reviewed. Although there are some differences in the understanding and approaches adopted towards developing managerial skills, most scholars tend to agree that both are basically similar and are coming from the same root, although the approaches are more concerned with the strategic aspect of management and development of the resources within an organisation.

Many writers (Drucker, 1954; Katz, 1974; Laird, 1978; Peels, 1984; Mol and Vermeulen, 1988; Kubr and Prokopenko, 1989; Davis, 1990; Analoui, 1993 and 1997; Liedholm and Mead, 1999; MacMahon and Murphy, 1999; Analoui and Husseini, 2001; Al-Madhoun and Analoui, 2002; Yukl, 2002) consider that, for businesses to be successful, managers with adequate managerial knowledge and skills must support them. Various studies find that managerial problems are at the root of the most frequently voiced reasons for the failure of the SMEs in developing countries (Schmitz, 1995; McCormick and Pedersen, 1996; Van Dijk and Rabellotti, 1997; Burke and Collins, 2001). A significant component of the change programme was to educate the managers in role-related concepts as a means of self-appreciation of appropriate role behaviour. A significant complementary development in recent years has been the changing of management styles and administrative practices in the SMEs (Das, 2001).

Since managers play a critical role in the success of the business, one way to develop managerial competencies and effectiveness, as a result, is to provide the managers with opportunities to attend MTPs (Pickett, 1998; Willcocks, 1998; Analoui, 2002). A number of analysts have argued that geographical concentrations of such programmes, like those in Palestine, provide significant benefits to those who participate in the training courses (Schmitz, 1995; McCormick and Pedersen, 1996; Van Dijk and Rabellotti, 1997).

Over the last few decades, the subject of management training for managers has been highlighted and has become the focus of much attention for a number of writers. This subject will also pose an enormous challenge for the management trainers and developers of tomorrow. Many writers such as Katz (1955), Mintzberg (1973), Stewart (1982), Margerison (1984), Jones and Woodcock (1985), Bramley (1996), Labbaf (1996), Analoui (1997, 2002), Pickett (1998), and Willcocks (1998), have carried out independent studies in this field and have come up with many interesting findings and conclusions.

Katz (1955), who can be considered as the founding father of the concept of managerial skills, was the first to put forward the MD model which is based on three basic categories of managerial skills: technical, human and conceptual. This development was closely followed by Mintzberg (1973) and a host of other writers.

Five of the most recent studies in the field of 'managerial skills' were carried out by Labbaf (1996), Analoui (1995 and 1997), Analoui et al (2000), Analoui and Hosseini (2002), and Al-Madhoun and Analoui (2002). Labbaf's work mainly focused on managerial effectiveness and the required categories of skills in the Iranian Steel Industry. On the other hand, Analoui's last two studies were concerned with the MTD of officials/managers in the Indian Railways Organisation, and 22 private and public organisations in Romania.

Both of the above writers and researchers (Labbaf and Analoui) came to almost the same conclusion in their studies, whereby they suggest that there appears to be a hierarchy of skills that managers require in order to be effective in their job. They have managed to identify three categories of managerial skills, which they argue are essential for the successful performance of managers:

1. Analytical and self-related skills;
2. People-related skills;
3. Task-related skills.

Hence, Management Training and Development in a country like Palestine is gaining momentum. In this developing country, the PNA has listed giving human resource development as one of its top priorities, and has considered it to be one of the main strategies for the future development of Palestine (MOBIC, 1999).

In this context, the present study is concerned with the skills developed by the SME managers in the private sector in Palestine in order to perform their job more effectively, and it is also concerned with the development of SMEs as a result of managerial development interventions (programmes).

As a developing country, the economy of the PT is small, poorly developed and highly dependent on Israel; at the same time, the land is limited, Israel controls 80-85 per cent of the Palestinian water, and there is large-scale unemployment. Faced with this situation, SMEs have come to play a critical role in the economy.

Donors, the PNA and UNRWA have recognised that many of the managers suffer from managerial weaknesses, and training is one of the long-term solutions to promoting the development of SMEs and alleviating the problem of persistent unemployment in the PT.

To support the peace agreement, the international community promised to support the Palestinian economy. Part of this aid has been spent on SMEs' development, and on establishing MTPs. These programmes aim to encourage economic development of the PT, through supporting small business education and entrepreneurship training. With donors' assets, but with equally burdensome liabilities, it would not be an exaggeration to contend that the Palestinian economy is on a knife-edge between take-off and collapse.

These programmes suffer from various problems, such as a lack of professional trainers, only a minority of the managers attended the TP courses, and some of these programmes lacked funding. Therefore, some TPs were closed during the last two years studied and the managers of small businesses continue to suffer from various managerial problems.

The study also explored the effects of the MTPs, which are designed to meet the needs of the SME managers on SMEs' development in the PT. Also, the study has attempted to test the relevance and validity of the managerial skills training which has been developed for the SME managers in Palestine. The main purpose was to assess the skills and knowledge required by the managers in order to be effective in their job, and to explore the major factors that hinder the positive and effective development of managerial skills to occur at their workplace.

Subsequently, based on the results and findings of the study, a conceptual framework, in the form of a model, has been proposed in order to provide a holistic approach or view of developing managerial skills. It is hoped that this will shed light on the existing situation in most SMEs, and thus enable the provision of a more effective MTP for the SME managers.

Much of the recent literature on the subject states that the design of effective MTPs has a key role in developing SME managers in Palestine. And that should be driven by the stated needs of the managers themselves. This is true in relation to the obvious need for skills as asserted by the managers in this study, who readily acknowledged the need to acquire skills in relevant areas, and who gave very positive feedback to the initial training provided by the MTPs. However, if one of the major impediments to the growth of SMEs is to be removed, MTPs that deal with these issues must also be developed and accepted by SME managers.

An overview of one of the main functions of MTD was undertaken, and later expanded to its main focus in the developing countries, since the study was carried out in one of those countries – Palestine. It was deemed to be appropriate that the overall picture of the development of this subject in that part of the world was examined in more detail.

Throughout, many writers have come up with ideas of how vital the two activities of MTD, that is training and development, are, and how important their effective implementation is for any organisation. This is for the immediate benefit and future development of their managers and SMEs as a whole. When discussing this subject (training and development) today, the topic of management development is considered to be a must. Not surprisingly, a number of writers have paid attention to what it means and how to organise its activities and programmes in order to gain maximum return. Yet, in most cases, the problematic nature of MT has been ignored.

Subsequently, the distinction between management education and training was made. This was a deliberate attempt on our part to differentiate between the two concepts, since there is lately much confusion and misinterpretation regarding the two. Here, too, some writers have given their definitions and explanations on those concepts, which we hope may give a clearer understanding of them.

As shown in Chapters Two and Three, we are in agreement with most of what has been mentioned and proposed by many writers before on this subject, especially what was aptly stated and stressed by Bramley (1996) and Analoui (1997, 2002).

Nevertheless, as a conclusion to this part, it is felt that the subject of MTD in relation to managers' training should be taken into serious consideration in the context of developing managerial skills in today's ever challenging and competitive world of business, and also the many challenges of tomorrow. More studies should be done in order to formulate ways and means to ensure that whatever training is being conducted for the SMEs, managers should be able to transfer it to their workplace. If the failure to do so continues, the amount of money, time and effort spent on training can be considered to be a great waste.

Methodological approach

We focused on research design and methodology as the most important aspects related to the collection of relevant and adequate data. Firstly, the appropriateness of employing qualitative and quantitative data collection was considered. The discussion included the differences between methods, assessing their strengths and weaknesses, and also gaining insights into the detail of some of the instruments used in this study. Explaining some of the considerations when using those methodologies in this research then followed this task. Further elaborations were then given on some of the constraints and choices present in undertaking the study. From here, the design of the questionnaire was explained and discussed in more detail. Some statements followed this on the interviews that have been conducted with heads of MTPs. After this, a brief note on the secondary data used and the pilot study was given.

Based on the survey instruments chosen (questionnaires, interviews, observation and secondary data), the process of the data collection was completed in about a three-month period. The questionnaire was designed on the basis of the literature review and the training process in PT. It was designed first in English and then discussed with experts who had experience in using questionnaires in developing countries. As a consequence of this consultation, it was modified and then translated into Arabic, the formal language of Palestine. After the pilot study, the full-scale fieldwork was carried out with selected SME managers, 106 in all. After accumulating all the relevant data and information, and then analysing them, the importance of the findings of this study should be judged in the light of the strengths and limitations of the methods by which the data were collected and analysed. The findings summarised below were the result.

Major findings

From the analysis and findings of this study, it is very clear now that most MTPs for the managers of SMEs are aimed more at the self and task-related category than people-related. This means that the programmes are not tailor-made to the needs of the managers. Besides that, there are many other factors or obstacles that hinder or inhibit the managers from developing managerial skills. If managers are not given the chance to demand and decide on their own training needs for their self-development, and also for their SMEs' benefit and future progress, the situation will remain as it is.

Background of managers and SMEs in Palestine

To assess the impact of MTPs on SME managers' development, different sets of variables are used. These variables assess the validity of the research hypotheses. For this reason, this part has explored the SME managers' background. It has also explored the relation between the business characteristics and the MT courses, which are intended to meet the development needs of the SME managers and their businesses.

After the peace agreement, there were many training efforts made by several MTPs, financed by donors, and especially by UNRWA, who made the most effort and provided funding for development of the above in the PT. The main part of these efforts was dedicated to SME development. However the TPs lacked co-ordination with each other. Furthermore, co-ordination with the PNA is needed. In addition, MTPs need to make greater efforts towards playing more effective roles in the TD activities. These efforts include linking the training system to promotion, incentives and career development according to established criteria, a rigid system of participant selection, and a systematic process of assessment of training needs and evaluations. MTPs usually do their evaluation at the end of the day. However, they may also need to do an evaluation at the end of the course in order to evaluate the change of behaviour in the SME managers. The groups targeted by the MTPs varied widely. Therefore, the MTPs should focus only on the main target group, which is development of the SME managers.

The size of the SME sector in the PT is large and it plays a critical role for the future. But the number of participants is relatively small when compared with the SME sector size. MTPs for SME managers only developed 5 per cent of the managers of SMEs in the years 1995-1999. Therefore, the SME managers need more efforts directed at them, and a more active media role in raising the awareness of SME managers about the critical role of management in SMEs' success. However, the percentage of the managers from the total participants who attended courses during the last five years has been described as steady. Furthermore, the number of training courses has grown during the last four years, but the number of participants has grown at a slower rate. The reason could be the general overall problems faced by the Palestinian economy.

MTPs operate in different ways. Examples of methods employed during the last four years are long-term courses, workshops, trainers' programmes, preparing new manuals for the training courses and establishing a small library for SME education. However, the main problem facing SME managers is the managerial weakness.

From the research results, it is clear that there is a good percentage of women who have their own businesses, and they are participating in MTPs. The majority of the managers (76.5 per cent) are in the age group of below 40, and most of them are below 30 years of age. The fact that SME managers attending MT courses are on average younger is mainly due to the younger start-up age. As seen already, and also because of the nature of some of the management programmes for new start up businessmen, the MTPs for SME management development often gather young entrepreneurs. Young people were most frequently motivated to start a business on their own. Also, a set of differences in start-up motivations for the group of SME managers was disclosed: the challenge of an opportunity, a new product and the everlasting wish to be independent.

Furthermore, many managers who are attending MTP courses are fresh graduates. Consequently, the majority of the respondents have a degree before they establish a business. As expected, the majority of the participant managers (62 per cent) have specialised in commercial fields. It may be that study in these fields encourages starting a new business. While the majority of the managers have only managerial experience gained from running their own business, 43.6per cent of the managers had no managerial experience before establishing their business. The managers of small businesses participated more in the MT courses than the managers of micro businesses. Furthermore, the span of supervision is very large, and this may be taken as evidence that there is probably a lack of general knowledge of basic management.

The majority of the businesses (64.7 per cent) are located in Gaza City. Also, a large number of courses attended were conducted in Gaza City itself (146 courses from a total of 220). The main percentage (62.9 per cent) of all SMEs was established after 1990. The largest group of SMEs (53.9 per cent) belongs to the service sector firms, a high percentage (35.6 per cent) of which are located in Gaza City, which is also the main area for MT courses in GS. The biggest percentage (77.9 per cent) of SME managers who participated in MT courses answered that their businesses were successful or very successful, and 55 per cent of them answered that their profits were increasing, 35 per cent answered that their profits were constant, and just 10 per cent answered that their profits were decreasing. In comparison, 76.9 per cent answered that the training encouraged them to increase their investment. The main percentage of SME managers who were participants in MT courses answered that their businesses work as independent firms. The majority of the participants on MT courses for managers have a loan from the Islamic banks. 77.6 per cent of the participant managers answered that money is the major factor in the ability to keep the business running, while 70.6 per cent thought that managerial skills are the second most important factor.

The results show the significant efforts made by MTPs: the seven MTPs conducted 133 training courses during the five years 1995-1999. There are eight different courses offered for different managerial skills. The responses show the majority of the participants had attended 84 training courses (27 per cent) under the title of managerial skills. The majority of the participants (33 per cent) had training courses with the SMET programme, the biggest and the oldest training programme in PT working with SME managers. The SME managers prefer to attend the short courses. MTPs are central to improving business performance, and 88.6 per cent of the SME managers answered that the MT courses developed their businesses.

The MTPs need to make greater efforts towards more effective roles in TD activities. These efforts include linking the training system to promotion, incentives and career development according to established criteria, a rigid system of participant selection and a systematic process of assessment of training needs and evaluation.

So far, the conclusion to this part of the descriptive analysis might be that SME managers join MTPs to learn the techniques and ways of dealing with their shortcomings and how to trouble-shoot, while working out their own business concept or idea. In most cases, the SME managers learn while being confronted with the daily 'family' businesses. In any case, partly due to the SME managers' motivations, partly due to the pre-start-up experience and expertise (age, education and entrepreneurial household), SME managers indeed show a different pre-start-up entrepreneurial profile. In the following part, elements will be emphasised that also underscore the issue that participating in one or more MTPs influences survival and growth rate of SMEs.

Contribution of MTPs to the development of managers and SMEs

The main objective of this analysis was to explore the contribution of MTPs to SME managers' development. The principal component model of factor analysis (PCA) was employed for this purpose. In all, 26 variables were tested, and the aim here was to find relationships between the different variables and to establish the factors from different variables, which were improved by attending MT courses. These variables assess the validity of the research hypotheses. For this reason, the analysis was focused on exploring the manager skills' development by dividing the skills into six main categories. These were:

1. Analytical and self-related skills (two sub-groups);
2. People-related skills (two sub-groups);
3. Task-related skills (two sub-groups).

From the results, the different items of self and task-development skills have a high percentage, while those of people-development skills have a lower percentage. On the whole, the emerging pattern of variations and the forming of categories of skills show that managers perceive effectiveness to be a function of self-related (41.1 per cent) and task-related (36 per cent) categories of managerial skills, rather than people-related skills (22.9 per cent).

One interesting issue which has emerged from all this is that in reality the identified managerial skills are so overlapping that it is difficult to make a clear-cut distinction between the three categories. The line of demarcation can therefore only be drawn theoretically and only for the ease of analysis. As Katz (1974) aptly states, 'In practice these skills are so closely interrelated that it is difficult to determine where one ends and another begins' (p.102). Furthermore, there is clear indication that managers, irrespective of their SMEs, require a comprehensive range of managerial skills for their increased effectiveness. Mintzberg (1975) also claims that the required managerial skills form an integrated whole, thus implying that no single managerial skill can be ignored if the manager is to do his job effectively. In a study of managerial skills (Boyatzis, 1982), the American Management Association and McBer Consultants suggested a MD model based on three clusters of skills. These clusters were identified empirically on the basis of the magnitude of correlation between skills. In their view, a set of managerial skills is a system in which each part is in relation to other parts, and managers' skills should be examined in the context of the entire set. The results of the study highlighted the question of interrelationship and interaction of managerial skills, and support the above literature evidence in suggesting that managerial skills should be analysed as a system of interrelated skills.

It is deemed imperative to pay more attention to the development of people skills. These results also suggest that task skills must be given a high degree of priority in the formulation of the human resource development policies and strategies, while at the same time some efforts need to be directed towards eliminating those obstacles, which are hindering managers' own development. It must be noted that the relative degree of importance attached to such skills is likely to change with respect to changes in circumstances.

These results clearly support the view that analytical and self-related skills have the highest level of managerial skills development in PT, therefore more attention needs to be paid to developing competence in people skills. These results also suggest that task skills must be given a high degree of priority in the formulation of the MD policies and strategies, while at the same time; some efforts need to be directed towards eliminating those obstacles, which are hindering managers' development. It should be pointed out that the relative degrees of importance attached to such skills are likely to change with respect to circumstances.

It also became clear that the degree of importance attached to each set of skills tended to vary according to the position, education level, field of study and managerial experience of the managers in the hierarchy of the business.

In this part of the study, the relation between the managerial skills which were developed and the SMEs' development has been tested by using the logistic regression model to find out and analyse the main independent variables that affect some dependent variables (Increase of investment, Increased number of markets, Success of business, Increase of profit, Number of courses, and Kind of course).

It was found that the main independent variables that affect increase of investment are Analytical and self-related skills development (cluster 2), and People-related skills development (cluster 1), with a probability of 39 percent, while the main independent variables that affect increase in investment are 'Create a business loyalty', 'Organisation structure' and 'Managing meetings', with a probability of 92 per cent. The variables 'Time management', 'Managing meetings' and 'Languages skills' are the main independent variables that affect increase number of markets, with a probability of 46 per cent. On the other hand, the main independent variables that affect the number of courses are 'Negotiation' and 'Controlling', with a probability of 42 per cent. It was found that the main independent variables that affect the length of course are Analytical and self-related skills development (cluster 1), and People-related skills development (cluster 2), with a probability of 60 per cent, while the main independent variables that affect the length of course are 'Confidence', 'Create a business loyalty' and 'Manage change effectively', with a probability of 13 per cent.

From these results, it can be concluded that there is a relation between the development of some managerial skills and the increase of investment. On the other hand, there is a relation between the number and the kind of courses that the SME managers attended and the managerial skills which were developed.

Managers from different private sectors, various cultural backgrounds and different places are likely to have different perceptions of the importance of such skills and their interaction for their increased effectiveness and development as a whole. For the development of managers, the implications of these findings are many. These are to be presented and dealt with in the concluding part. In the next part of this chapter, therefore, attempts will be made to draw relevant conclusions based on the findings of the research, and hence explore the likely implications for future research and its application within developing countries.

Through logistic regression analysis, evidence has been found for the direct and predictive or causal relation between managerial skills and sound planning behaviour leading to business growth. There is, however, no manifest indication that one by one these differentiating entrepreneurial and managerial variables priori determine a profitable business-planning attitude.

In order to learn about (causal) relationships between MT and managerial characteristics, planning attitudes and the economic profit for the enterprise, the reader should keep the above schema in mind. In this part, arguments in favour of, or against the fact that SMEs show a growth rate because of their specific planning mix and elementary entrepreneurial and managerial attitudinal profile will be searched for. Therefore, firstly, the relationship between the managerial skills and enterprise growth will be examined. Secondly, resulting positive relationships will be looked at from the perspective of the relationship, with possible underlying causes, that is entrepreneurial and managerial characteristics.

These might help to uncover the tight relationship between MT and SMEs' growth. Logistic regression shows that the relation between the growth of SMEs and managerial skills for the managers is significantly positive. Previous findings and research results suggest that any significant entrepreneurial or managerial parameter can be used to enhance the strategic planning and hence the performance of SMEs (Ballantine et al, 1992; Schamp and Deschoolmeester, 1998). Certain entrepreneurial and managerial attitude combinations, however, have a relative high predictive value towards planning behaviour and the resulting firm growth pattern (Schamp and Deschoolmeester, 1998).

Obstacles and weaknesses facing the training process

To discover what the obstacles were between the MTPs and the SME managers' development, the principal component model of factor analysis (PCA) was therefore employed, as it was intended to search mainly for the basic dimensions of data, which would define the total variance. In all, 23 variables were chosen to be tested. By using factor analysis we divided the obstacles into four categories: MTPs' and trainers' weaknesses, training process and the PT situation, trainers' weaknesses, and SME managers' weaknesses.

From the results obtained, it is clear that there is a high percentage of different obstacles and weaknesses on the part of the managers of SMEs (68.4 per cent). Whilst on the other hand, the different items of MTPs' and trainers also have a high percentage of weaknesses (65.8 per cent). While the trainers' weaknesses have a different set of shortcomings (64.6 per cent). The SME managers' and trainers' main weaknesses were training process and awareness of the PT situation (52.4 per cent).

In this part also, the logistic regression model was used to find out and analyse the main independent variables that affect some dependent variables (Success of MTPs, Success of business, and Development of MTPs). It was found that the main independent variables that affect the success of MTPs are that the MTPs do not have clear policies and plans, Trainers are not qualified enough, and Closure stopped some training courses, with a probability of 88 per cent. The variables Trainers' weaknesses and SME managers' weaknesses are the main independent variables that affect the development of MTPs, with a probability of 16 per cent. On the other hand, the main independent variables that affect the development of MTPs are Number of trainers and Closure, with a probability of 31 per cent. It was found that the main independent variable that affects the success of a business is MTPs' and trainers' weaknesses, with a probability of 59 per cent, while the main independent variables that affect the success of business are Lack of professional trainers, Number of trainers, and Trainers with no practical experience, with a probability of 83 per cent. From these results, it can be concluded that there is a relation between some obstacles and the development of MTPs.

Policy implications

As the twenty-first century begins, it is important for Arab TP specialists to chart the future of MTD in the Arab world, and to consider the themes that will dominate at the beginning of this new millennium. Admittedly, MTD in the Arab countries in general and in Palestine in particular has been a subject of increasing interest and debate in recent years, especially after the peace agreement. The bulk of literature is still faddish in nature, and yet very little attention has been directed at how to help corporate MTD programmes to create successful implementation. Therefore, this section is designed to clarify the main prerequisites for success. Finally, Arab researchers have criticised the training providers. In contrast, this section stresses the point that unless the MTPs themselves co-operate with each other and with PNA, it is difficult to assess the MTD efforts, and it is hard to judge the MTP success without understanding the MTP functions. It is intended in this section, based on the findings of this study in the field of MTD, in addition to the researchers' own experience in the field of management and training in Palestine, to clarify the major prerequisites for successful programmes. Also, to address all weaknesses and obstacles facing MTPs in Palestine (weaknesses related to the MTPs, SME managers, the PT situation, trainers and donors), the following lists the major dimensions of the policy implications for MTD in Palestine:

1. Need to adopt an MTD systems approach

According to these policy implications, the assessment of SME managers' needs is an important stage at the beginning of any MTD programme design. Assessment is necessary to expose the gap between what is happening and what ought to be happening in terms of managerial performance. Errors in training need assessment (TNA) can be disastrous in terms of costs, loss of credibility and interest, and failure to contribute effectively to the achievement of SME goals. Therefore, MTPs should begin their functions by seeking clarification on the true status of MTD. They should then arrive at a common understanding of the definition of the TD function, its goal and strategies, and enlist the co-operation of all parties concerned. Also, the advice here is to diagnose needs before proposing solutions, and not to limit concerns to matters that have a direct link with profitability; the career needs of managers must also be taken into account in TNA.

Since MTPs are able to influence significantly TD plans and policies, this study urges them to take the necessary steps to formulate a comprehensive training plan that is clearly defined and forms part of the overall SME plan. As for the MTD strategy, it should cover three horizons: long, medium and short term, all coherently coordinated and aiming to achieve common objectives. An accurate assessment enables the limited training budget to be directed more specifically to achieving MTP strategy. Furthermore, the distinction between operational needs and managerial needs should be taken into account in order to design acceptable MTD programmes.

Kubr and Prokopenko (1989) have outlined different techniques that can be used to gather TNA information. These include interviews, surveys, planning, self-assessment, performance appraisals, tests and examinations, report analysis and the use of assessment centres. Briefly, all the steps of MTD systematic approaches are mainly based on the manager TNA. It is worth noting that without manager TNA, it is impossible to continue in the application of an MTD systems approach which includes objectives' setting, programme design, programme implementation, evaluation and follow-up (Taylor, 1989). Therefore, MTPs should insist on operating within a long-term TD strategy that is clearly related to the SME managers' needs. Also, it should be brought to MTPs' attention that the latest thinking in HRD supports the view that MD ought to be conceived as a continuous and long-term process available to all managers at various stages in their careers, rather than a process that merely reacts to immediate needs.

To complete this job of the system approach to TD, evaluation must be made an integral part of the process of training. Only through evaluation can success or failure be measured and lessons learnt. However, difficult it may be, it must not be skipped. Evaluations are difficult and require special skills. MTPs in Palestine are advised to use the help of specialist consultants to acquire those skills and apply them in their MTPs. MTPs need to remember that evidence of success that can be derived from the evaluation phase may be the best weapon they have to defend MTD programmes and make the case for future investments in TD activities.

2. *MTPs' commitment to MTD efforts*

MTPs must realise that if TD is to be taken seriously, it must be based on a rational process rather than on personal subjective judgments in its design and implementation. There is no doubt that it is necessary for MTD specialists to secure MTP support and commitment before any training courses, if good results are to be achieved. Securing support is easier if management in general, and top managers in particular, feel that there are certain pressures that demand initiatives. In support of this argument, Mol and Vermeulen (1988) have stated management of businesses and in particular top managers, are the key to the success of MD programmes. Scherer (1978) further argues that the TP should accept responsibility for the development of managerial skills.

MTPs should also endeavour to develop other measuring techniques and accumulate experience of, and information on, TD and its association with business success and profitability. Quoting previous success or the success of others could impress SME managers and trigger their support for TD activities.

From the HRD perspective, the economically developed centre is serviced by typical free-market mechanisms of TD, that is, training MTP, which offers the entire gamut of MTD activities. It should be noted, however, none has the plethora of options that are available in the central region, mainly in Gaza. It should be noted, also, that MTPs should reflect the particular needs of each sector according to its development stage, as well as the particular needs of the Palestinian environment. Moreover, the future MTPs should design special instructional modes that deal with both the acute weaknesses and the ideal characteristics identified by the surveyed Palestinian SME managers and dealt with here.

Suitable MTPs offered to SME managers ought to reflect the need for a balanced mixture of managerial skills. They should also cater for MD needs, with people-development as a built-in component for their future MD.

MTPs should be specifically designed, depending on the level of SME managers and the position held by the trainees, to meet the people-related aspects of their job effectively. Awareness by the trainers of the organisational and cultural context and background from which the trainees originate is of the utmost importance, and a major consideration when designing the content of such courses.

MTPs cannot be regarded solely as empirical-rational change strategies and they must be treated as cultural-symbolic interventions (Mathiassen et al, 1999) in order to identify their likely implications for the participants. The authors recommend using a symbolic perspective to foresee possible significant outcomes of TPs instead of simply relying on SME managers' responsiveness to side effects.

We recommend initiating other parallel activities, which are loosely coupled to the TP, to exploit information about the business, the programme and the participants, that is created as the process unfolds, to reduce the risk of unwanted or dysfunctional effects, to address defensive routines and actions evoked by the programme, and finally to exploit the unintended positive side-effects and opportunities created.

One of the methods for conducting TD is through technological 'incubation centres', where MTPs are readily available and set-up costs are subsidised. Another support system functions through special programmes through which expert consultants are assigned to the small business. These consultants guide an inexperienced manager of a new venture for nominal fees and, in essence, supply on-the-job training in real time. While success rates are not yet available, interviews with seven members of MTPs revealed a high level of satisfaction with MT for entrepreneurs. Clearly, the market will have to be the final judge of the success of this method.

There are a few females working as owner/managers of SMEs in Palestine. MTPs for women in Palestine have a good success rate when compared with other developing countries, but still MTPs need special commitment to develop the managerial skills of female managers. For the effectiveness of this training, the authors suggest organising training courses only for females, and this would be in keeping with the Palestinian culture.

There is a significant relation between the location of SMEs and the rate of attendance at MT courses. Therefore, MTPs should organise MT courses everywhere to cover all Palestinian cities. This does not mean the TPs should have branches everywhere; only that they need to find a suitable place or places that will service all areas. Possibly, co-operation between the institutions in PT will offer these places. Also, MTPs should establish a body that will ensure co-operation and co-ordination between themselves and the SMEs and PNA.

As shown, 61 per cent of the courses were attended by the managers of SMEs that were established between 1991 and 1999. There is a need for more effort on the part of the MTPs to promote and explain the importance of the training and managerial skills, especially for the managers who had established the SMEs before the 90s. The majority of SMEs (55, 53.9 per cent) were from the service sector, therefore, MTPs may need to encourage the managers of other sectors, especially the industrial sector, to join the MT courses. Also, MTPs can organise some special courses in the industrial areas, such as Beet Hanoon and Carni, which lie between Israel and GS. That is because the majority of industrial SMEs are only working in the industrial areas. Also, MTPs ought to try to support the industrial SME managers with some special courses, even if they have an Israeli partner. That will be a helpful step for the future to establish an independent Palestinian economy.

Most respondents (69.5 per cent) attended short courses. Obviously, the SME managers prefer the short courses. Therefore, MTPs consider short courses as a first alternative when they are designing the MT courses. Also, due to the busy schedule of SME managers, MTPs are advised to provide MT courses during the weekend or at the end of the day. Moreover, it is better to follow up the MT results on the site with SME managers. MTPs may have to consider the possibility of training some SMEs on an in-house basis. Furthermore, MT courses should focus on how to manage, rather than what is management. To train managers, they must be provided with not only cognitive learning, but practice combined with performance feedback (Mintzberg, 1975).

Supporting the weaknesses of trainers should be one of the main targets of MTPs. This can be done through organising some special training of trainers' courses. Also, MTPs can try to open the market for the new Palestinian trainers.

In conclusion, experience and findings suggest that action learning is a useful approach to developing managerial skills in SMEs, but management's attention and willingness to improvise are important prerequisites to successful exploitation of the potential of the above approaches as a change strategy.

3. Need to adopt new strategy for development of trainers

It is now being gradually realised that management trainers need not have benefited solely from specialisation in only one or two areas of management-related subjects, they should also have sufficient skills related to learning design, training methods, communication and interpersonal skills, and the transfer of training.

MTPs ought to be involved seriously in management research. It has been argued that those MTPs which ignore the importance of research and development reduce the impact of the institution on the socio-economic environment and impair its reputation, which results in its becoming a second-rate institution (Stewart, 1967).

MTPs ought to become more sensitive to the clients' needs and strive consciously towards the creation of a 'task' as well as a 'service' culture (Analoui and Kakabadse, 2000). This means that trainers should be supported through the provision of adequate resources and training, so that they can assume the responsibilities of the modern management educator. Only in this way can it be assured that trainers themselves continuously develop and evolve to meet the ever-increasing needs of their trainees and their businesses. From the view of the Palestinian trainers to achieve more effective management training, the MTPs ought to ensure that:

1. Trainers are advised to attend courses, workshops and conferences, designed for 'training the trainers' at home and abroad to update and improve their skills (68 per cent of SME managers answered that the trainers are not qualified enough).

2. Trainers are assisted to become familiar with various 'operating cultures' within the private sector in which the trainees work, and be aware of cultural differences and their effect on learning among their participants. Therefore, trainers are made aware of the importance of understanding the Palestinian culture for effective learning, training and transfer. SME managers prefer a Palestinian trainer or at least a trainer who can speak Arabic (69.4 per cent of SME managers answered that trainers not speaking Arabic is the first obstacle facing the training process in Palestine).

3. Trainers need to use different training methods, especially the case study method, as the majority of the respondents (56.7 per cent) prefer the case study method as a first technique.

4. Trainers are assisted to identify their personal need and understanding of people-related knowledge, information and 'know how' skills in subject areas such as perception, communication, motivation, leadership, and the like.

5. Trainers are enabled to design course content in such a way that ample opportunity to learn is provided for SME managers.

6. Trainers are encouraged to adopt participatory styles of training to facilitate learning and to be more practical (SME managers need to know how to manage, not what management is). Also, 67.6 per cent of SME managers answered that the trainers need some more practical experience of training. Such knowledge will enable them to be regarded as competent professionals who are able to apply training solutions to business problems.

7. Trainers are made aware of the need for ensuring that trainees have become aware of developing their managerial skills for when they re-enter their actual workplace.

8. Trainers should become aware of the importance of evaluating and assessing the TP, based on acquired knowledge and skills.

To sum up, MT plays a crucial role in achieving development, whether in the case of an individual manager or an individual business. However, realisation of this objective requires conscious attempts on the part of MTPs and of management trainers to meet the developing needs of managerial skills of the trainees and their businesses. For the clients, effective development requires suitable planned change, and MT and trainers can play a decisive role in realising this goal (Analoui, 1994).

4. SME managers' motive for change

Nowadays, managers operate in an environment of constant change due to both new developments and intense national and international competition. To be successful in this environment, they need to develop managerial skills, knowledge, and competencies which will keep them up-to-date with these changes. SME managers who are aware of this, and who are concerned with the success of their business, are likely to have strong motives for implementing MTD policies and programmes to solve any current managerial problems resulting from change.

The results showed that there appears to be a direct relationship between the SME managers and the managerial skills and knowledge that they require for their effectiveness. These findings supported the hypothesis that, for SME managers, in the hierarchy of MTD needs, people-related skills take a lower position than task-related and self-development, in that order. The implications of this discovery are that:

1. SME managers require MTD for their increased effectiveness. Also, SME managers were all aware of their need for a combination of management skills, namely managing people and task, self- and career development. However, it is of the utmost importance that SME managers' TD needs are explored and not assumed.
2. SME managers must be prepared to transfer their managerial skills and competencies in to their businesses. Therefore, they should not neglect the transfer of the managerial skills that they acquired to the workplace. Also, they must remember that total commitment from them is imperative if SMEs are to meet with success.
3. SME managers are also reminded that they should regard their managerial skills as a valuable strategic resource that can help their businesses to obtain competitive advantage and superior performance.
4. SME managers are advised to discover their own managerial weaknesses and specify their needs for overcoming such weaknesses.
5. SME managers should be encouraged to bring into the business external managerial personnel on a consultative basis for a short period to deal with specific problems and to demonstrate good management practice. This intervention could help develop a management system which is appropriate to the firm and which, subsequently, may be developed and maintained. Such practice would be particularly relevant where businesses, being small, are not in a position to recruit individual management personnel in the various areas of management on a permanent or full-time basis.

As result of the above steps, SME managers may well be advised to conduct an assessment of their current MTD provision, and measure it against prescriptive advice in the field to discover its strengths and weaknesses, and act on them constructively.

5. MTPs and donors need to understand the Palestinian culture and situation

With regard to the findings of the study, since the environment in which Palestinian SMEs are working is different from that of Western countries, business management theories and practices developed in those countries might have only limited applicability.

The present study is the first of its kind in the field of business management directed at developing managerial skills in Palestine. It is hoped that in the light of these findings business management programmes could be designed better and closer to the skills and knowledge required by SMEs managers.

MTPs' funding agencies are becoming increasingly aware of the importance of the transferability of material learned in a Western institute situation into the workplace environment in a developing country. It is being accepted increasingly that TD institutions and donors require a more dynamic and 'task-oriented' culture, which is capable of responding to change quickly and easily.

Furthermore, due to the special situation in PT and the presence of Israeli checkpoints, MTPs should organise the MT courses in different places to give more opportunities for the managers to attend these courses without any difficulties.

6. Congruence between corporate formal systems and the nature of MTD programmes

In this context, it would be prudent to pose the question whether practices and policies generate the business culture or if it is the culture which generates management practices and policies. Since the early 1980s, the emphasis on culture in businesses has been accelerated, and getting the right culture has become an essential requirement for the continuity of a business's life cycle and MD programmes. But in either case, it is the management's responsibility to lead the necessary changes in their corporate culture, so that change is acceptable by the rest of the business's members.

The managers are the key determinant in the success or failure of MTD programmes (McDonald, 1989). Supporting this idea, McDonald (1989, p.9) postulated, 'an in-depth understanding of the business is extremely important to those who are trying to make management happen'.

The question is whether Western MT can be effectively transferred to Arab countries where there is a different business culture. This view is consistent with that of other researchers (Roy, 1977; Atiyyah, 1993; Abu-Doleh, 1996; Al-Bahussain, 2000; Al-Athari and Zairi, 2002; Al-Madhoun, 2002).

MD must be linked to a business's strategy. In ensuring that MT plans are constructed in the same context and the same process, the business plan should do this. More recently, the current approach to defining management needs is based on a thorough analysis of a business's formal system, which includes promotion, vacancies and decentralisation opportunities. Indeed, unless formal business procedures are supportive of MT by giving the managers the opportunity to apply what they have learned in TPs, MTD programmes will not be effective. As mentioned, Hussey (1988) has argued for those training objectives, especially for MD, and for a shift in thinking regarding the training. For him, training should be for the benefit of the business; therefore, there are some key words here that warrant attention. First, MD should be considered as a continuous part as well as an integral part of management work and, to be successful, it must provide and maintain a balance between the changing needs and nature of jobs and businesses. In short, for MTD to produce results, it should not be in conflict with existing corporate policies, culture and management practices. In this context, it is important to understand the role of business systems in the following areas:

1. They should create or reinforce the desire within managers to be developed;
2. They should ensure that the content of MTPs is acceptable within the SMEs;
3. Effective evaluation procedure should be implemented to monitor the results of MTPs, on the one hand, and to give direct feedback reward to the new managerial behaviour that has been acquired through programmes, on the other.

7. *Trust and understanding between SME managers and MTPs*

Trust plays a critical role in making MTs work effectively. SME managers ought to provide the necessary support for the training specialists so that their duties are carried out in an effective manner. SME managers should regard trainers as their partners throughout the whole process of MD. Clear understanding on the part of SME managers regarding SMEs that require training intervention and those that have no training relevance. Unfortunately, it is often assumed by SME managers that training should be the panacea for all managerial and business problems; therefore the only way for the training specialist to change the attitudes of managers is by gaining more direct support from the SME managers who are responsible for SME management policies. In short, the success of all MD initiatives, in the final analysis, depends on a willingness to be developed and on the ability of the training specialists.

In developing countries, however, MD needs to be taken a step further. Although it should be concerned with the development of both required managerial knowledge and skills, it is also a measure that is usually taken to ensure the smooth operation of economic growth and development programmes. The importance of MD has reached its highest position in developing countries. MD is not a choice, it is a 'must', a requirement of the economic systems for transitional economies, a process imposed on enterprises in both developed and developing countries as a result of globalisation, business growth, changing technology, changing conditions (politically, socially) and changing environment in its broadest sense (Bettignies, 1975).

Many businesses in Southeast Asia and in Arab countries are now conscious of the need to change their work-related cultures. The recent dramatic changes in technology and products, fluctuations in economic activity, and business restructuring, demand a new breed of trained managers who will be more proactive, more accountable, and more persistent in changing corporate culture, structure, strategy and operations, to stay competitive. There are numerous indications that the impact of a TP is reduced considerably if the business culture is not receptive to a new approach (Abu-Doleh, 1996).

8. Strategy of planners and policy makers for successful MTPs

In relation to the delivery of policy, the importance of the development of human capital should be fully recognised and should become a central part of the policies of the PNA, donors and NGOs.

These consist of self, people, and task-related skills categories. These categories of skills were contributing to managers' increased effectiveness at work. On the other hand, in reality, the identified managerial skills are so overlapping that it is difficult to make a clear-cut distinction between the three categories.

Mintzberg (1975) and Analoui (1993) take this issue further and claim that the required managerial skills form an integrated whole, thus implying that no single managerial skill can be ignored if the managers are expected to do their job effectively.

However, there is still a gap between managers' required skills based on the needs of their businesses, and the range of skills and knowledge offered by the MTPs. MTPs that are canned or packaged quite often fail because they do not meet the needs of the audience (Murrell, 1984). To avoid this failure, more loosely structured programmes can provide better flexibility for creating tailor-made training activity. Therefore, in view of recent findings in developing countries, the traditional approaches employed for training and developing managers, in particular in the business management programmes, are not suitable for increasing managers' effectiveness, since they tend to place inappropriate emphasis on theoretical and cognitive learning as opposed to the required skills and practical applications.

The findings of the present study strongly recommend that in order to ensure the increased effectiveness and efficiency of managers at work, there is a need to acquire relevant managerial skills and knowledge in all three identified skills categories of analytical and self-development, people-related, and task-related, with emphasis on the latter two categories rather than the former, through a tailor-made programme.

To address the weaknesses and obstacles facing MTPs in Palestine, the PNA, the MTPs, the SME managers, trainers and donors need to adopt a new strategy for self-finance as a long-term future plan. Finance is a serious problem that MTPs are facing in WBG. Donors finance the majority of the TPs. Some of TPs closed during the last two years studied due to stoppage of funds. It is evident that should there not be a new strategy for finance, the main part of the TPs will close down. This problem needs to be looked at from different angles by the PNA, donors, TPs and SMEs, in order to find a solution. One of the options open to MTPs would be to consider extending grants, introducing a TD voucher scheme, or funding sector-based training in areas of acute shortage. It is logical to mention here that the policy of MT should be specified through TNA rather than through the policy of the donors. It is hoped that this study will contribute to that understanding.

The findings of this study indicate that the planners and policy makers have a predominantly soft approach on the issues of TD. So far, the attitude has been to appeal to MTPs' sense of responsibility, with little or no intervention in these matters. In our considered view, the time has now come for the higher authorities to adopt a new approach combining inducements and pressure in equal measures. However, it is advisable to keep MT sustainable, using a combination of effectiveness and flexibility.

Positive action by planners and policy makers could be initiated through the commissioning of a research team to look into the real factors that influence MTPs' attitudes towards TD. Solutions can subsequently be devised to combat complacency or address the difficulties appropriately through support or sanctions and through establishing clear policies and strategy plans for the MD future in Palestine, especially with the unsettled situation. This is vital for the future development of Palestine.

Planners and policy makers should from now on place greater emphasis on providing practical guidance on how to design and implement good TD rather than on persuasive measures to increase the volume of its provision within MTPs. Planners and policy makers could assist MTPs through a programme of funding for consultancies, and by making expert advice widely available, for example through the local or regional Chambers of Commerce and/or higher education institutions.

Again, planners and policy makers should find ways to improve the operation of the training market to make it easier for SMEs to obtain the training they require. For example, they ought to consider publishing a list of training providers in Palestine so that SMEs can be made aware of the opportunities that are already available. It could also encourage and assist them in forging links so that effective co-operation exists between training needs and provision. Another supportive measure would consist of promoting and backing collaborative training ventures between firms, for example by establishing or sharing existing MTPs to organise collective TD provision.

There is also an urgent need in Palestine for a National Qualification System, to provide a coherent structure for individuals to obtain appropriate training and a recognised qualification. Such a system could help managers articulate their training needs, as well as enable managers to structure their careers.

Positive incentives could also take the form of a planners' and policy makers' initiative to develop and regulate 'training managers', which would confer such titles to high-training levels and incite others to emulate them. Also, planners and policy makers should encourage and generously reward any attempts to produce relevant, up-to-date, and culturally sensitive training materials designed for wide use.

Finally, planners and policy makers must continue to reinforce the message of the importance and urgency of the task of equipping the nation with the necessary skills to enable it to face the future with confidence. It must make sure that TD remains planners and policy makers' priority and is promoted as a high profile issue.

Proposed framework for successful MTD programmes

Therefore, we propose a system with which the different sides involved in the training in PT to could work together with more co-operation and co-ordination, and to find an independent body to finance the TD in Palestine based on a long-term strategy (see Figure 7.1).

Also, to address some other weaknesses facing MTPs in Palestine (MTPs did not assess the needs of the SME managers before designing the training courses, MTPs do not use performance appraisal or have any clear guidelines or policies in terms of the training needs and development of the SME managers), this research has led to the development of a MTP framework, which can be used to enable MTPs to measure the development of the managerial skills of SME managers.

The proposed framework was created by bringing together aspects from the works of Warr et al, (1970), Kirkpatrick (1994), Wilson (1999), and Tennant and Roberts (2002) and incorporating the authors' own personal perspectives. For measuring the effectiveness of MT, it should consider important aspects such as context, inputs and reactions, which should be measured before the training is delivered. However, positive attributes for the four models have been combined with new elements, which consider measuring the change during the actual training.

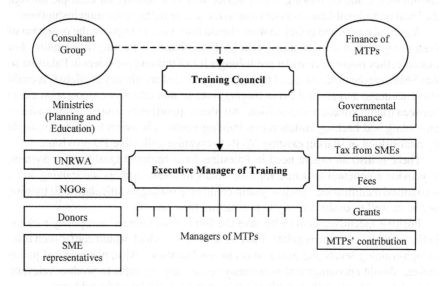

Figure 7.1   Proposed framework of unified system for MTPs in Palestine

Source: Data analysis

This aspect was considered to be as important as measuring before and after training, because it gives the training provider an opportunity to improve the quality of the training in the real-time situation.

The framework (see Figure 7.2) shows that the SME's effectiveness has to be measured concurrently with the MTP's. Before delivering the MT courses, the MTPs as providers have to measure the initial factors, which will influence the ability of the MTP to provide the managers with the required new skills. Measurement should also be carried out during the actual training in order to allow the training provider to respond to the individual needs of particular managers in real-time.

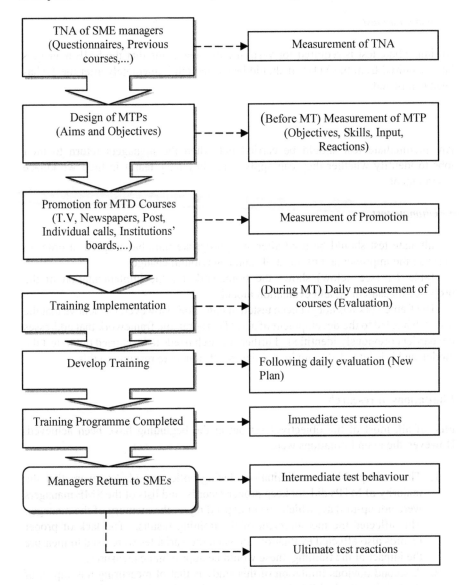

Figure 7.2   Proposed framework for successful MTD programmes

Source: Data analysis

After completion of MTP, three additional measurement steps are recommended. These are as follows:

1. Immediate test

An immediate test is required for verifying the new skills that the SME managers have acquired from the MTP. It should be carried out immediately after the TP has been completed.

2. Intermediate test

An intermediate test should be carried out when the managers return to their jobs to identify whether they can apply what they have learnt in their workplace environment.

3. Ultimate test

An ultimate test should be used after an appropriate time has elapsed in order to measure the improvement of the skills and behavioural changes.

Table 7.1 (see below) shows the framework for the implementation of the proposed measurement and evaluation model.

The framework has not yet been tested in Palestine. However, we believe that the research has led to the development of a MTD programme framework that addresses the barriers previously identified. Further research needs to be carried out to test the model, and it is intended to invite training practitioners to respond to this.

Limitations of research

First of all, most of the objectives set out at the beginning have been achieved. However, the main limitations were:

1. The main problems or limitations facing collection of data were that the majority of MTPs did not keep proper records, and lists of the SME managers were not up-to-date, which meant depending on the memory of the manager. This affected the measurement of the training results. The lack of proper records also affected evaluation, so when the variables were used to measure the impact of the training, these would be approximate measures.
2. A second obvious limitation of this study is that of measuring the impact of the training, the inability to measure actual results of changes in performance in the SME managers. Kirkpatrick (1976) identifies this as the highest of four levels of rigour in assessing the effectiveness of training. Some evidence exists to support the expectation that if performance had been measured, improvements would have been found. However, this is speculative, and future

research should include such measurement. Some would argue that the act of withholding the results of the survey is unethical because it violates the needs of the participants and could contaminate attitudes within the organisation against future surveys. In addition, failure to provide feedback could create turmoil within the SMEs that the managers were not willing to risk.

3. A third limitation of this study was that many SME managers found it difficult to provide data that can measure profit or revenue, so it took time to pursue the owners to give financial data. This problem faced us due to the fear of tax imposed by the Israeli Authority.

4. A fourth limitation of the study is that dividing the SMEs into sector groups meant that when one group provided only a small number, which may have affected the results. The sample realistically could not be increased due to limited time and resources, and the unstable situation in the GS and the PT as a whole.

5. A fifth limitation is that it is difficult to generalise the results over all sectors in the PT. However, most of the results of this study are compatible with what has been written before about the GS and the WB or elsewhere, and others are consistent with MD theory. This encouraged making some generalisations and drawing policy implications for the MTPs in PT. Church (1997), however, indicated that more research is needed with diverse and larger samples to both understand the multilateral process and justify the use of it. This study at least provides some support for both additional research and for the need for training to obtain optimal results.

6. A final and obvious limitation to this study is that it investigates only seven TPs that could be developed for SME managers. Other training programmes could be developed for some other SME managers.

Areas of future research

The subject of developing managerial skills, especially in management training, is a new field of study in Palestine. Not much writing has been produced nor much reliable empirical research has been carried out in this field. As indicated earlier, there are a few works which seem to have lightly touched this subject. These include Shaban (1998), Safi (1999), and Al-Madhoun (2002). For these reasons, the work by Analoui (1997) and his model of developing managerial skills for managers was chosen as a starting point in this study.

Certainly, there is a need for more studies to be carried out in the future. These could include:

Table 7.1   Training measurements and evaluation framework

What?	Who?	When?	Where?	Why?	How?
Objectives	MTP	Before training	At MTP	To ensure that requirements of SME managers will be met	Define SME objectives and new managerial skill levels required
Inputs	MTP	Before training	At MTP	To ensure that inputs will satisfy training needs	Test training inputs against objectives
Reactions	MTP & SME managers	Before training	At MTP	To identify attitude prior to training	Issue questionnaire to SME managers
Skills	Trainer and SME managers	Before training	At MTP	To identify initial skills prior to training	Monitor and record managers' current job performance
Measurement during training	Trainer and SME managers	During training	At training venue	To identify progress and develop training material	Practical tests and examinations
Immediate test	Trainer and SME managers	After training	At training venue	To identify new skills and attitudes after training	Practical tests, questionnaires and module reviews.
Intermediate test	MTP & SME managers	Upon return to SMEs	At SMEs	To identify any changes in SME managers' performance	Monitor new work performance and environment
Ultimate test	MTP & SME managers	Ongoing process	At SMEs	To identify skills retention and impact on SME's performance	Monitor new work performance and environment

Source: Data analysis

1. Conducting a series of case studies to explore in more depth the nature and extent of MTD provision within a selected number of private sector organisations in Palestine. Such studies would leave no stones unturned, and would uncover details and insights that are often overlooked by survey research.

2. Studying the problem of developing managerial skills in the public sector (in one or more organisations) in Palestine. This study could be limited to the SME officers only or to different levels of staff.

3. Investigating the ways of evaluating the planned and implemented programmes in the private and public sectors. A comparative study of these programmes would lead to identification of strengths and weaknesses in the TPs in both sectors, which in turn would furnish appropriate policy information. On the other hand, a comparison and correlation study could tackle the difficult issue of the link between business success and managerial skills.

4. Finding out how many TPs really have specific guidelines and procedures for training in developing managerial skills, and if they really care whether what has been taught is being transferred to the participants' workplaces. If not, what is/are the problem/s.

5. Discover the actual and perceived needs of managers/officers and other staff in the private or public sectors, and ascertain whether or not the training that they have received could be regarded as compatible to their work-related needs.

6. Looking into whether or not, in the long run, MTD is the best approach to build and retain the skilled workforces of organisations, and whether or not recruiting already trained workers is an acceptable and cheaper alternative for businesses and the nation as whole.

7. Testing further the suggestion that the Western body of knowledge and experience in developing managerial skills is not wholly applicable for SME managers in Palestine. By employing more empirical studies focusing on the extent to which the Western theories are applicable in increasing managerial skills of SME managers, and indeed how such developments can be incorporated into the policy and MTPs designed for managers in Palestine.

Closing remarks

Finally, it must be noted that sustainability of the TD policies, procedures and practices, in terms of programmes and activities, are by and large determined by the attention paid to facilitating factors that result in positive management training. This may be done by removing as many obstacles and inhibiting factors in the path of the SME managers as possible to help them advance towards greater effectiveness at work.

Bibliography

Abd Alkareem, N. (1996), 'Strategy for the Good Future of the Palestinian Economy', *Alquds* newspaper, 18 November, Ramallah, Palestine.

Abdalla, A. and Al-Homoud, M. (1995), 'A Survey of Management Training and Development in the State of Kuwait', *Journal of Management Development*, Vol. 14, No. 3, pp. 14-25.

Abdol Shafi, K. (1998), 'The Laws of the Palestinian Authority Did Not Encourage the Investment in Palestine', *The Voice of the Islamic University*, No. 18, Gaza, Palestine.

Abdullah, S. (1994), 'The Cairo Accord and Economic Agreement: Did They Solve the Problem of Development?', *Journal of Al-Siyasa Al-Filastiniyya*, Vol. 1, No. 3-4, Palestine.

Abu-Doleh, J. (1996), *Human Resource Management: Management Training Development in the Jordanian Private Sector – Attitudes, Policies and Practices in the 1990s*, Ph.D. Thesis, Management Centre, University of Bradford, UK.

Abu Eljedian, Y. (1996), 'Small-Scale Enterprises in the Gaza Strip: A Case Study of the Plastics Rubber Industry', *Third World Planning Review*, Vol. 18, No. 4, pp. 455-475.

Abu Shukur, A. (1990), 'The Industry in the Occupied Territories', *Alkateb Journal*, No. 117.

Abu-Zarifa, S. (1997), *A Suitable Strategy for Industrial Sector Development*, Paper presented at a Workshop on the Industrial Sector in Palestine, Ministry of Industry, Gaza, Palestine.

Ackroyd, S. and Hughes, J. (1992), *Data Collection in Context*, 2nd Ed., Longman, London.

Aker, A., Kumar, V. and Day, G. (1995), *Marketing Research*, 5th Ed., John Wiley, USA.

Al-Ali, A. (1999), *Human Resource Development: Training and Development Practices and Related Organisational Factors in Kuwaiti Organisations*, Ph.D. Thesis, Management Centre, University of Bradford, UK.

Al-Ali, A. and Taylor, D. (1997), *Factors Affecting Management Training and Development in Kuwaiti Organisations*, Paper presented at Arab Management Conference, 29-31 July, Bradford, UK.

Al-Athari, A. and Zairi, M. (2002), 'Training Evaluation: An Empirical Study in Kuwait', *Journal of European Industrial Training*, Vol. 26. No. 5, pp. 241-251.

Al-Ayyam newspaper (1996-2000), Rammalah, Palestine.

Al-Bahussain, S. (2000), *Human Resource Management: An Investigation into the Nature and Extent of Training and Development in the Saudi Private Manufacturing Sector*, Ph.D. Thesis, Management Centre, University of Bradford, UK.

Albanese, R. (1989), 'Competency-based Management Education', *Journal of Management Development*, Special Issue, Vol. 8, No. 2, pp. 66-76.

Albert, J. S. (1963), 'Toward an Understanding of Inequity', *Journal of Abnormal and Social Psychology*, Vol. 67, pp. 422-436.

Al-Efranjy, E. (2000), 'Year's Report from SMET Programme', *Alquds* newspaper, 14th January, Rammalah, Palestine.

Al-Falah, K. (2002), *An Empirical Study of World-class Manufacturing Implementation*, Ph.D. Thesis, Management Centre, University of Bradford, UK.

Al-Faleh, M. (1987), 'Cultural Influences on Arab Management Development: A Case Study of Jordan', *Journal of Management Development*, Vol. 6. No. 3, pp. 19-33.

Al-Hayat Aljadeda newspaper (1997-1999), Rammalah, Palestine.

Ali, A. and Al-Shakis, M. (1985), 'Managerial Value Systems for Working in Saudi Arabia: An Empirical Investigation', *Group and Organisation Studies*, Vol. 10, pp. 135-51.

Al-Madhoun, M. (1997), *The Role of Needs Analyses for the Training Programmes' Success in the Gaza Strip*, Second Workshop for Training in the Gaza Strip, UNRWA, SMET Programme Office, Gaza Strip, Palestine.

Al-Madhoun, M. (2002), 'Training Programmes for the SMEs in the Gaza Strip', in Analoui, F. (ed.), *The Changing Patterns of Human Resource Management*, Ashgate, UK and USA, pp. 169-180.

Al-Madhoun, M. and Analoui, F. (2002), 'Developing Managerial Skills in Palestine', *Journal of Education and Training*, Vol. 44, No. 8/9, pp. 431-442.

Al-Madhoun, M. and Analoui, F. (2003), *Weaknesses and Obstacles Facing Small Businesses' Development*, A paper presented to the 8th Annual Conference of the European Council for Business Education, Birmingham, UK.

Al-Muraifea, K. M. (1993), *Employees' Training Programmes of Public Authority for Applied Education and Training*, Ph.D. Thesis, University of Hull, UK.

Al-Nearab, F. (1997), *Case Study from the Palestinian Association for Vocational Training, (PAVT)*, Second Workshop for Training in the Gaza Strip, UNRWA, SMET Programme Office, Gaza Strip, Palestine.

Al-Qady, J. (1997), *The Local Lending Institutions*, Palestinian Authority, Office of President, Planning Centre, Economic Department, Gaza Strip, Palestine.

Alquds Al-Araby newspaper (1999-2000), London, UK.

Alquds newspaper (1996-1999), Rammalah, Palestine.

Al-Rasheed, M. A. (1994), *Bank Managers in Jordan: A Case Study of Motivation, Job Satisfaction and Comparative Organisational Practices*, Ph.D. Thesis, University of Kent at Canterbury, UK.

Al-Rashidi, T. (2000), *Human Resource Management, Human Resource Development and Performance*, Ph.D. Thesis, Management Centre, University of Bradford, UK.

Al-Risala al Uropia (European Message) newspaper (1997-1999), Gaza, Palestine.

Al-Risala weekly newspaper (1999), Gaza, Palestine.

Al-Tayeb, H. A. (1984), *Arab Management Development Institutes*, Arab Organisation for Administrative Sciences, Amman-Jordan (in Arabic).

American Society for Training and Development (2000), *Human Resource Development Quarterly*, Jossey-Bass, San Francisco, CA.

Analoui, F. (1990), 'Managerial Skills for Senior Managers', *International Journal of Public Sector Management*, Vol. 3, No. 2, pp. 121-154.

Analoui, F. (1993), *Training and Transfer of Learning*, Avebury, UK and USA.

Analoui, F. (1994), 'Training and Development: The Role of Trainers', *Journal of Training and Development*, Vol. 13, No. 9, pp. 61-72.

Analoui, F. (1995), 'Workplace Sabotage: Its Styles, Motives and Management', *Journal of Management Development*, Vol. 14, No. 7, pp. 48-65.

Analoui, F. (1996), *Training and Transfer of Learning*, Avebury, UK and USA.

Analoui, F. (1997), *Senior Managers and Their Effectiveness*, Avebury, UK and USA.

Analoui, F. (1998), 'Managerial Perspectives, Assumptions and Development of the Human Resource Management', in Analoui, F. (ed.), *Human Resource Management Issues in Developing Countries*, Ashgate, UK and USA.

Analoui, F. (1999), 'Eight Parameters of Managerial Effectiveness: A Study of Senior Managers in Ghana', *Journal of Management Development*, Vol. 18, No. 4, pp. 362-390.

Analoui, F. (2002), 'Politics of Strategic Human Resource Management: A 'Choice' Model', in Analoui, F. (ed.), *The Changing Patterns of Human Resource Management*, Ashgate Publishing, UK and USA.

Analoui, F. and Hosseini, M. (2001), 'Management Education and Increased Managerial Effectiveness: The Case of Business Managers in Iran', *Journal of Management Development*, Vol. 20, No. 9, pp. 785-794.

Analoui, F. and Karami, A. (2003), *Strategic Management in Small and Medium Enterprises*, Thomson, UK.

Analoui, F., Labbaf, H. and Noorbakhash, F. (2000), 'Identification of Clusters of Managerial Skills for Increased Effectiveness: The Case of the Steel Industry in Iran', *International Journal of Training and Development*, Vol. 4, No. 3, pp. 217- 234.

Anderson, D. C. (1970), *Factors Contributing to the Success of Small-Services Type Businesses*, Ph.D. Thesis, Georgia State University, USA.

Anon. (1999), 'Training Budgets', *Training Journal*, Vol. 63, No. 10, pp. 43-46.

Appley, L. A. (1956), *Management in Action*, Prentice Hall, Englewood Cliffs.

Appley, L. A. (1969), *A Management Concept*, American Management Association, New York, USA.

Argyris, C., Putnum, R. and Mclain Smith, D. (1987), *Action Science*, Jossey-Bass, San Francisco.

Armstrong, M. (1994), *How to be a Better Manager*, Kogan Page, London.

Armstrong, M. (2001), *Human Resource Management Practice*, 8th Ed., Kogan Page, UK and USA.

Arnberg, P. (1984), *International Training for Trainers Program*, Interview With Co-author, University of Southern California, Los Angeles, USA.

Ary, D., Jacobs, L. C. and Razavieh, A. (1972), *Introduction to Research in Education*, Holt, Rinehart and Winston.

Ashi, M. (1987), *Small Business in the Gaza Strip*, M.Sc. Dissertation, University of Wales, SHEIM, Cardiff, UK.

Ashi, M. (1989), *An Analysis of Small Business Management Training Needs in Jordan*, Ph.D. Thesis, University of Wales, SHEIM, Cardiff, UK.

Ashor, Y. (1995), *The Prospect of the Palestinian Banking System*, Gaza, Palestine.

Ashton, D. and Easterby-Smith, M. (1979), *Management Development in the Organisation*, Macmillan, London.

ASIR (Arab Scientific Institution for Research and Transfer of Technology) (1986), *Industry in the Occupied Territories and Scope of its Development*, ASIR, Palestine.

ASIR (Arab Scientific Institution for Research and Transfer of Technology) (1996), *The Scope and Problems in Marketing of Industrial Products in the Occupied Territories*, ASIR, Palestine.

Atherton, A. and Hannon, P. (1996), *Building Strategic Awareness Capability: The Cognitive Tools and Methods of Thinking of Small Business Owner-Managers*, Paper presented at 41st ICSB World Conference, Stockholm.

Atiyyah, H. (1992), 'Designing Management Training Programmes in a Developing Country: A Case Study', *Management Education and Development*, Vol. 23, No. 2, pp. 3-12.

Atiyyah, H. (1993), 'Management Development in Arab Countries: The Challenges of the 1990s' *Journal of Management Development*, Vol. 12, No. 1, pp. 3-13.

Awartani, H. M. (1979), *A Survey of Industries in the West Bank and Gaza Strip*, Birzeit University, West Bank, Palestine.

Badaway, M. K. (1980), 'Style of Mid-eastern Managers', *California Management Review*, Vol. 22, No. 3, pp. 51-58.

Badwan, A. (1996), 'The Palestinian Economic Future', *Al-Hayat Aljadeda* newspaper, November, Palestine.

Bahiri, S. (1987), *Industrialisation in the West Bank and Gaza*, The West Bank Data-base Project (WBDP), Jerusalem, Palestine.

Ballantine, J. W., Frederick, W. C. and Koeller, C. T. (1992), 'Characterizing Profitable and Unprofitable Strategies in Small and Large Businesses', *Journal of Small Business Management*, Vol. 30, No. 2, April, pp. 13-24.

Bancroft, G. and O'Sullivan, G. (1993), *Quantitative Methods for Accounting and Business Studies*, 3rd Ed., McGraw-Hill, London.

Barrington, H. and Reid, M. (1997), *Training Interventions*, IPD, London.

Bass, B. M. and Vaughan, J. A. (1966), *Training in Industry: The Management of Learning*, Tavistock, London.

Bedeian, A. N. (1989), *Management*, 2nd Ed., The Dryden Press, New York.

Behrman, A. N. and Levin, R. H. (1984), 'Are Business Schools Doing Their Job?', *Harvard Business Review*, January, pp. 140-147.

Bell, J. (1993), *Doing Your Research Project: A Guide for First-Time Researchers in Education and Social Science*, Open University Press, UK.

Bennett, R. and Brodie, M. (1979), 'A Perspective on Managerial Effectiveness', in Brodie, M. and Bennett, R. (eds), *Managerial Effectiveness*, Thames Valley Regional Management Centre, pp. 12-31.

Bettignies, H. (1975), 'Management Development: The International Perspective', in Taylor and Lippit (eds), *Management Development and Training Handbook*, McGraw Hill, UK.

Bharadwaj, S. B. L. (1975), 'Management Development in the Developing Countries', in Taylor, B. and Lippit, G. L. (eds), *Management Development and Training Handbook*, McGraw Hill, UK.

Bigelow, J. D. (1991), *Managerial Skills Development*, Sage, UK and USA.

Bird, M. (1991), *How to Make Your Training Pay*, Business Books, London.

Bir-Zeit University (1997), *Palestine Human Development Profile (1996-1997)*, Sustainable Human Development Project, Ramallah, Palestine.

Bloom, B. S. (1956), *Taxonomy of Educational Objectives Handbook I: Cognitive Domain*, David McKay, New York.

Bolton, R. (1979), *People Skills*, Prentice-Hall, USA.

Boomgard, J. S., Davies, S. and Haggblade, D. C. (1992), 'A Sub-sector Approach to Small Enterprise Promotion and Research', *World Development*, Vol. 20, No. 2, pp. 199-212.

Boyatzis, R. E. (1982), *The Competent Manager*, John Wiley, New York.

Bramley, P. (1996), *Evaluating Training*, IPD, London.

Bramley, P. (1991), *Evaluating Training Effectiveness: Translating Theory into Practice*, McGraw-Hill, UK.

Branine, M. (1996), 'Observations on Training Management Development in the People's Republic of China', *Personal Review*, Vol. 25, No. 1, pp. 25-39.

Broom, H. D. and Longnecker, J. G. (1979), *Small Business Management*, South-western Publishing, UK.

Brown, G. F. and Read, A. R. (1984), 'Personnel and Training Policies: Some Lessons for Western Companies', *Long Range Planning*, Vol. 17, No. 2, pp. 48-57.

Bryman, A. (2001), *Social Research Methods*, Oxford University Press, UK.

Bryman, A. and Cramer, D. (1992), *Quantitative Data Analysis for Social Scientists*, Routledge, London and New York.

Bryman, A. and Cramer, D. (1998), *Quantitative Data Analysis with SPSS for Windows: A Guide for Social Scientists*, Routledge, London.

Brynen, R. (1996), 'Buying Peace? A Critical Assessment of the International Aid to the West Bank and Gaza', *Journal of Palestine Studies*, No.3, pp. 79-92.

Burgoyne, J. and Stuart, R. (1991), 'Teaching and Learning Methods in Management Development', *Personnel Review*, Vol. 20, No. 3, pp. 27-33.

Burgoyne, J. G. (1976), *The Nature, Use and Acquisition of Managerial Skills and Other Attributes*, Ph.D. Thesis, Lancaster University, UK.

Burke, M. J. and Day, R. R. (1986), 'A Cumulative Study of the Effectiveness of Managerial Training', *Journal of Applied Psychology*, Vol. 71, pp. 232-245.

Burke, S. and Collins, K. (2001), 'Gender Differences in Leadership Styles and Management Skills', *Journal of Women in Management Review*, Vol. 16, No. 5, pp. 244-256.

Burr, P. L. and Heckman, R. J (1979), 'Why So Many Small Businesses Flop and Some Succeed', *Across the Board*, February.

Burrell, G. and Morgan, G. (1993), *Sociological Paradigms and Organisational Analysis*, Athenaeum, Newcastle and USA.

Bussom, R., Elsaid, H., Schermerhon, J. and Wilson, H. (1984), 'Integrated Management and Organisation Development in a Developing Country: A Case Study', *Journal of Management Development*, Vol. 3, No. 1, pp. 3-15.

Bygrave, W. D. (1994), *The Portable MBA in Entrepreneurship*, John Wiley, New York.

Campbell, J. P., Dunnette, M. D., Lawler, E. E. and Weick, K. E. J. (1970), *Managerial Behavior, Performance, and Effectiveness*, McGraw-Hill, New York.

Carnall, C. and Maxwell, S. (1988), *Management Principles and Policy*, ICS Publishing, Cambridge, UK.

Carnevale, A. and Schultz, P. (1990), 'Return on Investment: Accounting for Training', *Training & Development Journal*, Vol. 44, No. 7, pp. 41-72.

Carroll, S. J., Pain, F. T. and Ivancevich, J. (1972), 'The Relative Effectiveness of Training Methods: Expert Opinion and Research', *Personnel Psychology*, Vol. 25, pp. 495-510.

Carson, D. J. and Cromie, S. (1989), 'Marketing Planning in Small Enterprises: A Model and Some Empirical Evidence', *Journal of Marketing Management*, Vol. 5, No. 1, pp. 33-50.

Casey, T. (1976), *Perceptions of Managerial Work in South East Asia*, American Academy of Management Proceedings, USA.

Cassell, C. and Symon, G. (1994), *Quantitative Methods in Organizational Research*, Sage, London.

Castrogiovanni, G. J. (1996), 'Pre-Startup Planning and the Survival of New Small Businesses: Theoretical Linkages', *Journal of Management*, Vol. 22, No. 6, pp. 801-23.

Centre of Palestine Research and Studies, Economic Department (1997), *Prevailing Perceptions on Aid Management*, Research Reports Series, No. 9, Nablous, Palestine.

Changiz, P. (1978), 'Challenges to Management in the Arab World', *Business Horizons*, Vol. 21, pp. 47-55.

Christiananta, B. (1987), *Human Resource Development in Indonesia: Policies and Practices in East Javan Manufacturing Industry*, Ph.D. Thesis, Edinburgh University, UK.

Church, A. H. (1997), 'Managerial Self-Awareness in High-Performing Individuals in Organizations', *Journal of Applied Psychology*, Vol. 82, No. 2, pp. 281-92.

Churchill, S. (1995), 'Projecting a Career: Industry and Education Working Together in Bexley', *Journal of Education and Training*, Vol. 37, No. 5, pp. 28-31.

Cohen, L. and Manion, L. (1980), *Research Methods in Education*, Croom Helm, London.

Cole, G. A. (1988), *Personnel Management Theory and Practice*, D.P. Publications, London.

Collins, D. (1990), 'Getting Ready for the 1990s', *Journal of European Industrial Training*, Vol. 14, No. 4, pp. 21-24.

Conant, J. C. (1991), 'Management Development Revisited', *Journal of European Industrial Training*, Vol. 10, No. 2, pp. 15-19.

Cox, C. J. and Cooper, C. L. (1988), *High Flyers: An Anatomy of Managerial Success*, Blackwell, New York.

Crant, J. M. (1996), 'The Proactive Personality Scale as a Predictor of Entrepreneurial Intentions', *Journal of Small Business Management*, Vol. 34, No. 3, pp. 42-49.

Cunnington, B. (1985), 'The Process of Educating and Developing Managers for the Year 2000', *Journal of Management Development*, Vol. 4, No. 5, pp. 66-79.

Curran, J. (1986), *Bolton Fifteen Years On: A Review and Analysis of Small Business Research in Britain 1971-1986*, Small Business Research Trust, London.

Daft, R. and Marcic, D. (2001), *Understanding Management*, 3rd Ed., Harcourt College Publishers, New York and London.

Daibes, I. and Barghouthi, M. (1996), *Infrastructure and Health Services in the Gaza Strip*, Al-Amal Press, Jerusalem.

Dajany, M (1999), 'Preparing for the Training National Conference', *Journal Al-ayyam*, April, Economic Page, Ramallah, Palestine.

Das, T. K. (2001), 'Training for Changing Managerial Role Behaviour: Experience in a Developing Country', *Journal of Management and Development*, Vol. 20, No. 7, pp. 579-603.

Davis, T. R. (1990), 'Whose Job Is Management Development? Comparing the Choices', *Journal of Management Development*, Vol. 9, No. 1, pp. 58-70.

De Vaus, D. A. (1996), *Surveys in Social Research*, 4th Ed., Allen & Unwin, London.

Deal, T. E. and Kennedy, M. A. (1982), *Corporate Culture: The Rites and Rituals of Corporate Life*, Addison-Wesley, Reading, Massachusetts.

Delatte, A. P. and Baytos, L. (1993), 'Guidelines for Successful Diversity Training', *Journal of Education and Training*, January, pp. 55-60.

Dey, I. and Harrison, J. (1988), *'Training Needs and Attitudes of Small Firms: The UK experience'*, 11th Conference of Small Business, Cardiff, UK.

Dickinson, M. (2000), 'Giving Undergraduates Managerial Experience', *Journal of Education and Training*, Vol. 42, No. 3, pp. 159-169.

Dickson, D. L (1983), *Quantitative Training Needs Assessment of the Small Business Community of Grand Unction*, University of Northern Colorado, Colorado, USA.

Digman, L. A. (1980), 'Determining Management Development Needs', *Human Resource Management*, Vol. 19, No. 4, pp. 12-16.

Diwan, I. and Shaban, R. (1998), *Development Under Adversity: The Palestinian Economy in Transition*, Palestine Economic Policy Research Institute (MAS) and World Bank, Palestine.

Dooley, A. R. and Skinner, W. (1977), 'Casing Case Method', *Academy of Management Review*, April, pp. 277-289.

DRC (Development Resources Centre) (1997), 'Information Centre, Five Years for the Development', *DRC Journal*, Vol. 6, June, Gaza Strip, Palestine.

DRC (Development Resources Centre) (1998), *Development Resource Centre, Institutional Profile*, DRC, Gaza Strip, Palestine.

Drucker, P. F. (1954), *The Practice of Management*, Harper & Row, New York.

Drucker, P. F. (1964), *Managing for Results*, Harper & Row, New York.

Drucker, P. F. (1967), *The Effective Executive*, Harper & Row, New York.

Drucker, P. F. (1974), *Management: Task, Responsibilities and Practice*, Heinemann, London.

Drucker, P. F. (1979), *Management*, Pan Books, London.

Drucker, P. F. (1988), *The Effective Executive*, Heinemann, London.

Dun, I. and Bradstreet, G. (1987), *Key Business Ratios*, Dun and Bradstreet, London.

Dunham, R. B. and Smith, F. J. (1979), *Organizational Surveys: An Internal Assessment of Organizational Health*, Scott, Foresman, Glenview.

Dunn, S. and Thomas, K. (1985), 'Evaluating Training Via Multiple Baseline Designs', *Journal of Training and Development*, Vol. 22, October, pp. 28-40.

Dunnette, M. D. (1971), *Assessing Managerial Performance*, Proceedings of one-day seminar, Independent Assessment and Research Centre, August, pp. 38-53, London.

Durham (1984), *Education and Training in the Small Business Sector for Owner-Managers and Their Key Staff*, Small Business Club Limited New College, Durham, UK.

Durra, A. and El-Sabbagh, Z. (1990), 'Training of Top and Middle Managers in Commercial Banks in Jordan: An Empirical Study', *Abhath Al-Yarmok*, Vol. 6, No. 3, pp. 7-24, Jordan.

ECWA (Economic Commission for Western Asia) (1981), *The Industrial and Economic Trend in the West Bank and Gaza Strip*, UN, Economic Commission for Western Asia.

Edmunds, S. W. (1979), 'Differing Perceptions of Small Business Problems', *American Journal of Small Business*, Vol. III, No. 4, pp. 68-96.

Egan, G. (1994), 'Cultivate Your Culture', *Management Today*, April, pp. 39-42.

El-Fathaly, O. and Chackerian, R. (1983), 'Administration: The Forgotten Issue in Arab Development', in Ibrahi, M. I. (ed.), *Arab Resources: The Transformation of a Society*, Croom Helm, London.

El-Hifnawi, H. (1997), *Motivation of Multinational Work Force in Arab Culture*, Paper presented at Arab Management Unit Conference, University of Bradford, UK.

Ellis, S. (1989), *How to Survive a Training Assignment: A Practical Guide for the New Part-Time or Temporary Trainer*, Addison-Wesley, Canada.

El-Musa, S. and El-Jaafari, M. (1995), 'Power and Trade: The Israeli-Palestinian Economic Protocol', *Journal of Palestine Studies*, Vol. 22, pp. 19-24.

European Union (1996), *The Aid from European Union to the Palestinians*, European Union Report, Abroad Centre, Jerusalem, Palestine.

Falah, G. (1993), 'Demography and Division: A View from the Middle East', in Taylor, P.T. (ed.), *Political Geography of the Twentieth Century*, Belhaven Press, London.

Fayol, H. (1959), *General and Industrial Management*, in C. Storrs (trans), Pitman, London.

Filley, A. C., Foster, L. W. and Herbert, T. T. (1979), 'Teaching Organisational Behaviour: Current Patterns and Implications', *The Organisational Behaviour Teaching Journal*, Vol. 4, No. 2, pp. 13-18.

Fitz-enz, J. (1988), 'Proving the Value of Training', *Personnel Review*, March, pp. 17-23.

Follet, M. P. (1941), *Dynamic Administration: The Collected Papers of Mary Parker Follet*, Metcalf, H. C. and Urwick, L. F. (eds), Harper, New York.

Forcese, D. P. and Richer, S. (1973), *Social Research Methods*, Prentice-Hall, New Jersey.

Foster, G. and Swenson, D. W. (1997), 'Measuring the Success of Activity-Based Cost Management and Its Determinant', *Journal of Management Accounting Research*, Vol. 9, pp. 104-141.

Fowler, A. (1991), 'How to Identify Training Needs', *Personnel Management Plus*, Vol. 2, No. 11, pp. 22-23.

Fraser, R. F., Gore, J. E. and Cotton, C. C. (1978), 'A System for Determining Training Needs', *Personnel Journal*, December, pp. 682-697.

Frey, J. H. and Oishi, S. M. (1995), *How to Conduct Interviews by Telephone and in Person*, Sage, London.

Fuller, E. (1993), *Small Business Trends, Some Implications for Skills and Training into the Next Century*, Skills and Enterprises Network, UK.

Gharaibeh, F. (1985), *The Economies of the West Bank and Gaza Strip*, West View Special Studies on the Middle East, Boulder, USA.

Gibb, A.A. (1995), *The Role of Education and Training in Small and Medium Enterprise in Europe: Creating an Agenda for Action*, Inter-Ministerial Conference of Education and Employment Ministries of the European Union and Partner States on Small and Medium Enterprise Education, Italian Foreign Ministry & European Training Foundation, Italy, pp. 1-35.

Gilbert, N. (1993), *Researching Social Life*, Sage, London.

Gill, J. and Johanson, (1991), *Research Methods Management*, Paul Chapman, London.

Goldstein, I. L. (1980), 'Training in Work Organisations', *Annual Review of Psychology*, Vol. 31, pp. 229-272.

Goldstein, I. L. (1986), *Training in Organisations: Needs Assessment, Development, and Evaluation*, Brooks/Cole, Monterey, California, USA.

Gorsuch, R. L. (1983), *Factor Analysis*, Erlbaum, Hillsdale, N.J.

Gorton, K. and Dool, I. (1993), *Low-Cost Marketing Research*, John Wiley, Chichester.

Graham, J. L. (1983), 'Brazilian, Japanese, and American Business Negotiations', *Journal of International Business Studies*, Vol. 16, January, pp. 81-96.

Gray, C. (1989), *Distance Learning for Small and Medium Sized Enterprises*, Conference on the Planning and Management of Multi-Media Training Systems for Open Learning: The European Experience, 8-11 November.

Greenbank, P. (2000), 'Training Micro-business Owner-Managers: A Challenge to Current Approaches', *Journal of European Industrial Training*, Vol. 24, No. 7, pp. 403-411.

Grierson, J., Donald, C. M. and Sam, M. (1997), 'Business Linkages in Zimbabwe: Helping to Shape "Win-Win" Economic Structures', *Development in Practice*, Vol.7, No. 3, pp. 304-307.

Griffiths, P. and Allen, B. (1986), 'Assessment Centre: Breaking with Tradition', *Journal of Management Development*, Vol. 6, No. 1, pp. 18-29.

Gulick, L. and Urwick, L. (1954), *Papers of the Science of Administration*, Institute of Personnel Management, New York.

Hair, J. F., Rolph, E., Anderson, R. L. and Black, T. W. (1998), *Multivariate Data Analysis*, 5th Ed., Prentice-Hall, London.

Hair, M., Ghiseli, E. and Porter, L. W. (1966), *Management Thinking. An International Study*, Wiley, New York.

Hales, C. P. (1986), 'What do Managers Do? A Critical Review of the Evidence', *Journal of Management Studies*, Vol. 23, No.1, pp. 88-115.

Hall, D. and Hall, I. (1996), *Practical Social Research in the Community*, Macmillan, London.

Hamblin, A. C. (1974), *The Evaluation and Control of Training*, McGraw-Hill, Maidenhead and London.

Hambrick, D. C. (1988), *The Executive Effect: Concepts and Methods for Studying Top Managers*, JAI Press, London.

Hamed, O. (1998), *Informal Finance and Lending NGOs in the West Bank and Gaza Strip*, New Jersey, USA.

Hameed, R. (1999), *Human Resource Management and Development: Case Study of Management Training in Malaysia*, International Conference on Human Resource Development Practices and Practitioners Beyond the Year 2000, University of Bradford, Bradford, UK, 27-28 May.

Hankinson, A. (1991), *Small Business Management and Performance: Survival for Engineering Firms*, Avebury, London.

Hannon, P. D. and Atherton, A. (1998), 'Small Firm Success and the Art of Orienteering: The Value of Plans, Planning, and Strategic Awareness in the Competitive Small Firm', *Journal of Small Business and Enterprise Development*, Vol. 5, No. 2, pp. 102-119.

Harris, L. (1989), 'Money and Finance in the OT in the Under-developed Banking System', in El-Abed, G. (ed.), *Palestinian Economy Under the Occupation*, PNA, Palestine.

Harrison, R. (1995), *Training and Development*, Institute of Personnel and Development, London.

Has, A. (2000), Analysis of the World Bank Report About the Poverty in Palestine, *Harts* newspaper (in Hebrew), 28 May, Israel.

Hayes, J. L. (1983), *CEO's in Action*, American Graduate School of International Management, Glendale, USA.

Hemerson, M. F., Morris, L. L. and Gibbon, G. T. F. (1978), *How to Measure Attitudes*, Beverly Hills, Sage, London.

Hertzberg, F. (1968), 'One More Time: How do you Motivate Employees?' *Harvard Business Review*, Vol. 46, January/February, pp. 53-62.

Hicks, H. G. and Gullott, C. R. (1976), *The Management of Organisations*, 3rd Ed., McGraw-Hill, UK.

Hill, J. and Wright, L. (2001), 'A Qualitative Research Agenda for Small to Medium-Sized Enterprises', *Marketing Intelligence & Planning*, Vol. 19, No. 6, pp. 432-443.

Hinrichs, J. R. (1976), 'Personnel Training', in Dunnette, M. D. (ed.), *Handbook of Organisational and Industrial Psychology*, Rand McNally, Chicago.

Hirst, D. (1997), 'Shameless in Gaza', *The Guardian*, 12 April, UK.

Ho Sam, P. (1980), *Small-scale Enterprises in Korea and Taiwan, Development Economics Department*, Development Policy Staff, World Bank, D.C.

Hodgetts, R. and Kuratko, D. (2001), *Effective Small Business Management*, 7th Ed., Harcourt College Publishers, New York and London.

Hopelain, D. G. (1985), 'Teaching Organisation Behaving', *Organisation Behaviour Teaching Review*, Vol. 10, No. 3, pp. 33-76.

House, R. (1967), *Management Development: Design Evaluation and Implementation*, Bureau of Industrial Relations, University of Michigan, Ann Arbor, USA.

Huczynski, A. (1983), *Encyclopaedia of Management Development Methods*, Gower, Aldershot.

Human Development Project (1997), *Palestine Human Development Profile (1996-1997)*, Sustainable Human Development Project, Bir-Zeit University, Ramallah, Palestine.

Hussey, D. (1988), *Management Training and Corporate Strategy: How to Improve Competitive Performance*, Pergam on Richard Clay, UK.

Iftaimeh, S. M. (1993), *The Industrial Sector of the World Bank and the Gaza Strip*, Dar El-Carmel, Amman, Jordan.

ILO (International Labour Organisation) (2000), 'Year's Report', *Alquds* newspaper, 24th March, Rammalah, Palestine.

Institute of Management (1999), *Personnel Policies: Training and Development*, Hodder & Stoughton, London.

Iredale, N. and Cotton, J. (1995), 'Small Business Links With Education', 18th ISBA Small Firms Research and Policy Conference', in Deakins, D. (ed,), *Entrepreneurship in the 90s*, University of Paisley, UK, pp. 789-800.

Irmgard, N. (1997), 'Management Training for Women Entrepreneurs: An Evaluation Methodology and Case Studies from Africa', *International Labour Review*, Vol. 136, No. 4.

Iweada, B. (2000), 'Private Sector Role for the Palestinian Development', *Alquds* newspaper, 31 May, Rammalah, Palestine.

Jaber, H. (1992), 'Methods, Institutes and Possibilities of Industrial Finance', *Shu'un Tanmawiyyeh: A Quarterly Journal on Development in the West Bank and Gaza Strip*, Vol. 2, No. 4, pp. 20-27.

Jacobs, T. O. and Jaques, E. (1987), 'Leadership Complex System', in Zeidner, J. (ed.), *Human Productivity Enhancement: Organisations, Personal, and Decision Making*, Vol. 2, pp. 7-65.

Jones, J. E. and Woodcock, M. (1985), *Manual of Management Development*, Gower, Aldershot.

Jorkedal, A. (1967), *Top Management Education: An Evaluation Study*, Swedish Council, Stockholm.

Jovanovic, B. (1982), 'Selection and the Evaluation of Industry', *Econometrica*, Vol. 50, No. 3.

Judd, C. M., Smith, E. L. and Kidder, L. H. (1991), *Research Methods in Social Relations*, 6th Ed., Holt Rinehart and Winston.

Judeh, Q. (1992), 'Prospects for the Exploitation of Local Primary Raw Materials in Industrialisation', *Shu'un Tanmawiyyeh: A Quarterly Journal on Development in the West Bank and Gaza Strip*, Vol. 2, No. 4, pp. 20-27.

June, M. L. P., Ariffin, H. and Ainuddin, R. O. (1990), 'A Comparative Analysis of the Management Characteristics and Practices of American and British Subsidiaries in Malaysia', *Malaysian Management Review*, Vol. 25, No. 1, pp. 3-8.

Kaiser, H. F. (1974), 'Little Jiffy Mark IV', *Educational and Psychology Measurements*, Vol. 34, pp. 111-117.

Kakabadse, A. (1983), *The Politics of Management*, Gower, England.

Kakabadse, A. and Margerison, C. (1985), 'What Management Development Means for American CEOs', *Journal of Management Development*, Vol. 4, No. 5, pp. 3-15.

Kakabadse, A., Ludlow, R. and Vinnicombe, S. (1987), 'Working in Organisations', in Kakabadse, A., Ludlow, R. and Vinnicombe, S. (eds), *Working in Organisations*, Penguin.

Kanan, O. (1998), 'Investment in the West Bank and the Gaza Strip', *Finance and Development Journal*, Vol. June, pp. 30-33.

Karami, A. and Analoui, F. (2001), *Strategy, Mission Statement and Firm Performance in Small and Medium Sized Enterprises*, Conference on Small Business and Enterprises Development, University of Leicester, UK, 29-30 March.

Katz, R. L. (1974), 'Skills of an Effective Administrator', *Harvard Business Review*, Vol. 52, September-October, pp. 90-102.

Kaynak, E. (1986), *International Business in the Middle East*, Walter de Gruyter, Berlin.

Kennedy, J., Loutzenhiser, J. and Chaney, J. (1979), 'Problems of Small Business Firms: An Analysis of the SBI Consulting Programme', *Journal of Small Business Management*, Vol. 17, January, USA.

Kenney, J. and Reid, M. (1986), *Training Interventions*, Institute of Personnel Management, London.

Kerrigan, J. E. and Luke, J. S. (1987), *Management Training Strategies for Developing Countries*, Lynne Reinner, London.

Kiesner, W. F. (1984), *Higher Education and the Small Business Person: A Study of the Training and Educational Needs, Uses and Desires of the Small Business Practitioner*, Ph.D. Thesis, Claremont Graduate School, UK.

Kim, J. and Mueller, C. (1978), *Factor Analysis: Statistical Methods and Practical Issues*, Sage, London.

King, D. (1964), *Training Within the Organisation*, Tavistock, London.

Kirkpatrick, D. (1994), *Evaluating Training Programmes*, Berrett-Koehler, San Francisco, California.

Kirkpatrick, D. L. (1976), 'Evaluation of Training', in Craig, R. L. (ed.), *Training and Development Handbook*, 2nd Ed., Paper 18. McGraw-Hill, New York.

Kolb, D. A., Rubin, I. M. and McIntyre, J. M. (1984), *Organisational Psychology: An Experimental Approach to Organisational Behaviour*, Prentice-Hall, UK.

Koontz, H. and O'Donnell, C. (1955), *Principles of Management*, McGraw-Hill, UK.

Koontz, H. and O'Donnell, C. (1980), *Management: A System and Contingency Analysis of Managerial Functions*, McGraw-Hill, UK.

Kotter, J. P. (1982), *The General Managers*, Free Press, UK.

Kreiken, J. (1975), 'Top Management Roles in Management Development', in Krein, J. T. and Weldon, C. K. (eds) (1994), 'Making a Play for Training Evaluation', *Training and Development*, Vol. 48, pp. 62-67.

Krentzman, H. C. and Samaras, J. N. (1960), 'Can Small Businesses Use Consultants?', *Harvard Business Review*, Vol. 38, May/June, pp. 126-136.

Kubr, M. and Prokopenko, J. (1989*), Diagnosing Management Training and Development Needs*, International Labour Organisation, Geneva.

Labbaf, H. (1996), *Managerial Effectiveness and Required Skills: A Study of the Senior Managers in Iran's Steel Industry*, Ph.D. Thesis, University of Bradford, UK.

Laird, D. (1978), *Approaches to Training and Development*, 2nd Ed., Addison-Wesley, Reading, Massachusetts.

Landheer, B. (1952), *Mind and Society: Epistemological Essays on Sociology*, Martinus Nijhoff, Netherlands.

Latham, G. P. and Crandall, S. (1991), 'Organizational and Social Factors', in Morrison, J. (ed.), *Training for Performance: Principles of Applied Hhuman Learning*, John Wiley, Chichester.

Latham, G. P. (1988), 'Human Resource Training and Development', *Annual Review of Psychology*, Vol. 39, pp. 545-582.

Lau, A. E. W., Newman, A. R. and Broedling, L. A. (1980), 'The Nature of Managerial Work in the Public Sector', *Public Administration Review*, No. 40, September/October, pp. 513-520.

Lee, C. (1991), 'Who gets Trained in What', *Training Journal*, October, pp. 47-59.

Lewis, M. and Kelly, G. (1989), *20 Activities for Developing Managerial Effectiveness*, Gower, UK.

Lewis-Back, M. (1995), *Data Analysis: An Introduction*, Sage, London, California.

Liao, T. F. (1994), *Interpreting Probability Models Logit, Probit, and Other Generalized Linear Models: Quantitative Application in the Social Science*, University of Illinois, Urbana-Champaign, Sage, Thousand Oaks, London, New Delhi.

Liedholm, C. and Mead, D. (1999), *Small Enterprise and Economic Development: The Dynamics of Micro and Small Enterprise*, Routledge, London and New York.

Liedholm, C. and Parker, J. (1989), *Small Scale Manufacturing Growth in Africa: Initial Evidence*, MSU International Development Working Paper, No. 33, Department of Agriculture Economics, Michigan State University, USA.

Likert, R. (1967), *The Human Organisation*, McGraw-Hill, New York.

Livingston, J. S. (1971), 'Myth of the Well-Educated Manager', *Harvard Business Review*, January-February, pp. 79-93.

Long, R. F. (1991), *Training: The Fourth Dimension of the Business*, Training Officer, November, 272-276.

Luthans, F. and Davis, T. R. V. (1979), 'Behavioural Self-Management: The Missing Link in Managerial Effectiveness', *Organisational Dynamics*, Vol. 8, No. 1, pp. 42-60.

Luthans, F., Rosenkrantz, S. A. and Hennessey, H. W. (1985), 'What Do Successful Managers Really Do? An Observational Study of Managerial Behaviors', *Journal of Applied Behavioral Science*, Vol. 21, pp. 255-70.

Lynton, R. and Pareck, U. (1967), *Training for Development*, Richard D. Irwin, Homewood, Illinois.

MA'AN (2000), *MA'AN Development Centre*, Report from MA'AN to Researcher, (in Arabic), Gaza, Palestine.

Maccoby, E. E. and Maccoby, N. (1954), 'The Interview: A Tool of Social Science', in Lindzey, G. (ed.), *Handbook of Social Psychology*, Wesley, Cambridge.

MacLean, D., Paton, R. and Vries, E. (1996), 'Personal Competencies and Outdoor Development for Managers', *Journal of Career Development International*, Vol. 1, No. 1, pp. 23-26.

MacMahon, J. and Murphy, E. (1999), 'Managerial Effectiveness in Small Enterprises: Implication for Human Resource Development', *Journal of European Industrial Training*, Vol. 23, No. 1.

Madge, J. (1962), 'The Origins of Scientific Sociology', in Young, P. V. (ed., 1966), *Scientific Social Surveys and Research*, 4th Ed., Prentice-Hall, UK.

Mak, W. (1999), 'Developing Enterprise Managers in China', *Journal of Education and Training*, Vol. 41, No. 6/7, pp. 319-324.

Mann, F. C. (1965), 'Towards an Understanding of the Leadership Role in the Formal Organisation', in Dubin, G. C., Hommans, F. C. and Miller D. C. (eds), *Leadership and Productivity*, Chandler, San Francisco.

Manpower Services Commission (1981), *A New Training Initiative*, Manpower Services Commission, Sheffield, UK.

Manz, C. C. and Sims, H. P. J. (1980), 'Self-Management as a Substitute for Leadership', *Academy of Management Review*, Vol. 5, No. 3, pp. 361-7.

Margerison, C. J. (1984), 'Chief Executives' Perception of Managerial Success Factors', *Journal of Management Development*, Vol. 3, No. 4, pp. 47-60.

Margerison, C. J. (1985), 'Achieving the Capacity and Competence to Manage', *Journal of Management Development*, Vol. 4, No. 3, pp. 42-55.

Martin, S. (1984), *International Trainer and Management Consultant*, Interview with Co-Author, University of California, Los Angeles, USA.

MAS. (1998), 'The Economic Policy', *Al-yyam* newspaper, April, Rammallah, Palestine.

Maslow, A. (1943), 'A Theory of Human Motivation', *Psychological Review*, Vol. 50.

Mathiassen, L., Borum, F. and Pedersen, J. S. (1999), 'Developing Managerial Skills in IT Organizations: A Case Study Based on Action Learning', *Journal of Strategic Information Systems*, Vol. 8, pp. 209-225.

McClelland, D. C. (1961), *The Achieving Society*, D. Van Nostrand, Princeton, N.J.

McCormick, D. and Pedersen, P. O. (1996), *Small Enterprises: Flexibility and Networking in an African Context*, Nairobi, Longhorn, Kenya.

McDonald, G. (1989), 'Personnel Management in Action: Manager Attitude to Training', *Asia Pacific Human Resource Management*, November, pp. 63-68.

McFarland, D. E. (1968), *Personnel Management Theory and Practice*, Macmillan, New York and London.

Mehesen, T. (1997), *The Decision to Establish a Training Course: A Case Study*, Third Workshop for Training in the Gaza Strip, Women's Affairs and Agricultural Relief Committees, Gaza Strip, Palestine.

Menard, S. (1995), *Applied Logistic Regression Analysis*, Sage, Thousand Oaks, London and New Delhi.

Mendonca, M. and Kanungo, R. B. (1994), *Conclusion: The Issue of Cultural Fit Models for Developing Countries*, Sage, New Delhi.

Mercer, D. (1996), *Marketing*, 2nd Ed., Blackwell, Oxford.

Merton, R. K. (1966), 'Mass Persuasion', in Young, P. V. (ed.), *Scientific Social Surveys and Research*, 4th Ed., Prentice Hall, UK.

Michael, S. and Beck, L. (1995), *Data Analysis: An Introduction*, Sage, London.

Middle East Economic Strategy Group (1998), *Recommendations on the Palestinian Economy*, http:// www.palecon.org. [Accessed 04-02-2000].

Migdad, M. (1999), *Performance Analysis of Small-scale Industries: Industrial Sectors in the Gaza Strip as a Part of the New Palestine Entity*, Ph.D. Thesis, DPPC, University of Bradford.

Migdad, M., Weiss, J. and Jalilian, H. (2001), 'Small-scale Industry in the Gaza Strip', in Morrissey, O. and Tribe, M. (eds), *Economic Policy and Manufacturing Performance in Developing Countries*, Elgar Publishing, UK and USA.

Miles, M. B. and Huberman, M. (1994), *Qualitative Data Analysis*, 2nd Ed., Thousand Oaks and Sage, London and New Delhi.

Miller, D. C. (1991), *Handbook of Research Design and Social Measurement*, 5th Ed., Sage, London.

Mintzberg, H. (1973), *The Nature of Managerial Work*, Harper and Row, New York.

Mintzberg, H. (1975), 'The Manager's Job: Folklore and Fact', *Harvard Business Review*, July-August, pp. 49-61.

Mitchell, G. (1993), *The Trainer's Handbook: The AMA Guide to Effective Training*, 2nd Ed., American Management Association, New York, USA.

Mol, A. J. and Vermeulen, L. P. (1988), 'Is Management Development Worth the Effort?' *Human Resource Management*, August, pp.18-29, Australia.

MOPIC (Ministry of Planning and International Cooperation) (1995), *Development Strategy in Palestine*, Public Management Conference, Al-Shawa Centre, Gaza, Palestine.

MOPIC (Ministry of Planning and International Co-operation) (1997), *Local, Private, and Governmental Programmes in the West Bank and Gaza*, MOPIC, Women Planning and Development Department, Palestine.

MOPIC (Ministry of Planning and International Co-operation) (1997), *The Palestinian Development Plan (1998-2000)*, MOPIC, Gaza, Palestine.

MOPIC (Ministry of Planning and International Co-operation) (1998), *Palestine, Poverty Report 1998*, National Commission for Poverty Alleviation, Palestinian National Authority, Palestine.

MOPIC (Ministry of Planning and International Co-operation) (1999), *First and Second Quarterly Monitoring Report on Donor's Assistance*, http://www.PA.net/reports/ aid_reports [Accessed 02-03-2000], Palestinian National Authority, Palestine.

MOPIC (Ministry of Planning and International Co-operation) (1999), *Third Quarterly Monitoring Report on Donor's Assistance*, [Online] http:// www.PA.net/building_state/ third_quarter.htm [Accessed 16-05-2000].

Morris, J. (1975), 'Developing Resourceful Managers', in Taylor, B. and Lippitt, G. (eds), *Management Development and Training Handbook*, McGraw-Hill, Great Britain.

Morrison, A. M. and McCall, J. V. (1978), *Feedback to Managers: A Comprehensive Review of Twenty-Four Instruments*, Center for Creative Leadership, Greensboro, North Carolina, USA.

Morse, N. C. and Weiss, R. S. (1955), 'The Function and the Meaning of the Work and Jobs', *American Sociology Review*, No. 20, pp. 191-198.

Morvaridi, B. (1998), *Interviewing: Module Two*, Graduate School, Faculty of Social Sciences and Humanities, University of Bradford, UK.

Mosawdy, T. (1999), 'Evaluate the Final Results of the First Palestinian Census', *Palestine Almoslema Magazine*, Year 17, Vol. 4, April, London.

Motthew, B., Miles, A. and Huberman, M. (1994), *Qualitative Data Analysis*, 2nd Ed., Sage, London.

Mullins, L. J. (1993), *Management and Organisation Behaviour*, 3rd Ed., Pitman, London.

Mumford, A (1975), 'The Role of the External Consultant', in Taylor, B. and Lippitt, G. (eds), *Management Development and Training Handbook*, McGraw-Hill, UK.

Mumford, A. (1986), 'Effectiveness in Management Development', in Mumford, A. (ed.), *Handbook of Management Development*, 2nd Ed., Gower, Hunts, Vermont.

Mumford, A. (1991), 'Developing the Top Team to Meet Organisational Objectives', *Journal of Management Development*, Vol. 10, No. 5, pp. 5-14.

Mumford, M. D. and Connelly, M. S. (1991), 'Leaders as Creators: Leader Performance and Problem Solving in Ill-Defined Domains', *Leadership Quarterly*, Vol.2, pp. 289-315.

Muna, F. (1980), *The Arab Executive*, Macmillan, London.

Muna, F. (1987), 'Manpower Training and Development: The Qatari Experience', *Journal of Management Development*, Vol. 6, No. 3, pp. 55-64.

Muna, F. and Bank, J. (1993), *The Making of the Gulf Managers*, Conference on Arab Management, University of Bradford, Bradford, UK, 6-8 July.

Murrell, K. L. (1984), 'Training and Development for Developing Countries', *Journal of European Industrial Training*, Vol. 8, No. 4, pp. 25-32.

Nachmias, C. and Nachmias, D. (1996), *Research Methods in the Social Sciences*, 5th Ed., Arnold, London.

Nadler, L. (1975), 'Developing Managerial Understanding of the Younger Generation', in Taylor, B. and Lippitt, G. (eds), *Management Development and Training Handbook*, McGraw-Hill, UK.

Naser, Y. (1999), *Palestine Small Business Enterprise: The Nature and Causes of Success*, PRIP and MAS, Jerusalem, Palestine.

Neck, P. A. (1977), *Enterprise Development, Policies and Programmes*, International Labour Office, Geneva.

NORAD (1993), *Evaluation of Development Assistance: Handbook for Evaluators and Managers*, NORAD, Oslo.

Norusis, M. (1993), *SPSS for Windows, Professional Statistics Release 6*, SPSS Inc, USA.

Nunnally, J. and Bernstein, I. H. (1994), *Psychometric Theory*, 3rd Ed., McGraw Hill, London.

Nunnally, J. C. (1978), *Psychometric Theory*, 2nd Ed., McGraw-Hill, New York.

Okasha, M. and Abu Zarifa, S. (1992), *Industrialisation in the Gaza Strip*, Arab Thought Forum, Jerusalem, Palestine.

Olsen, W. (1992), 'Random Sampling and Repeat Surveys in South India', in Devereux, S. and Hoddinott, J (eds), *Fieldwork in Development Countries*, Harvester Wheatsheaf, Hertfordshire.

Oppenheim, A. N. (1992), *Questionnaire Design, Interviewing and Attitude Measurement*, Pinter, London.

Pakes, A. and Ericson, R. (1987), *Empirical Implications of Alternative Models of Firm Dynamics*, Social Science Systems Research Institute, University of Wisconsin.

Palestinian Information Centre (1999), *News page*, [Online] http://www.palestine.inf.org [Accessed April 1999].

Palestinian Information Centre (2000), *News page*, [online] http://www.palestine.inf.org [Accessed, April 2000].

Palmon, R. (2000), 'Development of Leadership skills: Experience and timing', *Leadership Quarterly*, Vol. 11, pp. 87-114.

Palnet (2000), *Private Sector*, [Online] http://www.palnet.com/inv/private.htm [Accessed, February 2000].

Patton, M. (1990), *Qualitative Evaluation and Research Methods*, 2nd Ed., Sage, London.

PCBS (Palestinian Central Bureau of Statistics) (1995), *Economic Statistics in the West Bank and the Gaza Strip*, Current status report series, No. 2, Ramallah, Palestine.

PCBS (1996), *The Establishments Census*, Ramallah, Palestine.

PCBS (1998), *Labour Force Statistics in the Gaza Strip*, Gaza and Ramallah, Palestine.

PCBS (1999), *The Final Results of the First Palestinian Census*, [Online] http//www.pcbs.org/english/phc-97/popu.htm [Accessed, April 1999].

PCHR (1997), *The Israeli Policy of Closure, Legal, Political and Humanitarian Evaluation*, Series Study 6, Palestinian Centre for Human Rights, Affiliate of International Commission of Jurists, Geneva and Palestine.

Pedler, M., Burgoyne, J. and Boydell, T. (2001), *A Manager's Guide to Self-Development*, 4th Ed., McGraw-Hill, UK.

Peel, M. (1984), *Management Development and Training*, British Institute of Management, London.

Peters, T. J. and Waterman, R. H. (1982), *In Search of Excellence: Lessons from America's Best-Run Companies*, Harper and Row, New York.

Peterson, L. A. (1997), 'International Human Resource Development: What We Know and Don't Know', *Human Resource Development Quarterly*, Vol. 8, No. 1, pp. 63-77.

Pettigrew, A., Sparrow, P. and Hendry, C. (1988), 'The Forces That Trigger Training', *Personnel Management*, December, pp. 28-32.

Phillips, J. J. (1991), *Handbook of Training Evaluation and Measurement Methods*, 2nd Ed., Kogan Page, London.

Pickett, L. (1998), 'Competencies and Managerial Effectiveness: Putting Competencies to Work', *Personnel Management*, Vol. 27, No 1, pp. 103-115.

Pigors, P. and Pigors, F. (1987), 'Case Method', in Craig, R. L. (ed.), *Training and Development Handbook: A Guide to Human Resource Development*, pp. 414-429, Macmillan, New York.

Pomeranz, J. M. and Prestwich, L. W. (1962), *Meeting the Problem of Very Small Enterprises*, George Washington University, Washington.

Porter, L. W. (1983), 'Teaching Managerial Competencies: An Overview', *Organisation Behaviour Teaching Review*, Vol. 8, No. 2, pp.1-8.

Porter, L. W. and McKibbin, L. E. (1988), *Management Education and Development: Drift or Thrust into the 21st Century*, McGraw-Hill, New York.

Porter, L. W., Lawler, E. E. and Hackman, J. R. (1975), *Behavior in Organisations*, McGraw-Hill, New York.

Powers, E. A. (1983), 'The AMA Management Competency Programmes: A Development Process', *Organisation Behaviour Teaching Review*, Vol. 8, No. 2, pp.16-20.

Qudeh, W. (1999), 'Lending Institutions in Palestine-Field Study', *Palestinian Planning Centre*, March, Gaza, Palestine.

Quinn, R. E. (1988), *Beyond Rational Management*, Jossey-Bass, San Francisco, California, USA.

Rajab, M. (1997), *Obstacles Facing Palestinian Industry*, Paper presented at a Workshop on the Industrial Sector in Palestine, Ministry of Industry, Gaza, Palestine.

Read, C. and Kleiner, H. (1996), 'Which Training Methods are Effective?', *Journal of Management Development Review*, Vol. 9, No. 2, pp. 24- 29.

Reddin, W. J. (1970), *Managerial Effectiveness*, McGraw-Hill, New York.

Reddin, W. J. (1974), 'Managerial Effectiveness in the 1980s', *Management by Objectives*, Vol. 3, No. 3, pp. 6-12.

Reeves, M. (1996), *Evaluation of Training*, Peland UK Publications, Selangor.

Reichel, A. (1994), *Perceived Strengths and Weaknesses of Israeli Executives*, Working Paper No. 36, Department of Industrial Engineering and Management, Ben-Gurion University of the Negev, Israel.

Reichel, A. (1996), 'Management Development in Israel: Current and Future Challenges', *Journal of Management Development*, Vol. 15, No. 5, pp. 22-36.

Resnik, D. (1998), *The Ethics of Science*, Routledge, London.

Richards, G. (1984), *Opening Speech*, International Federation of Training and Development Organisations, Santa Monica, California.

Robinson, K. R. (1985), *A Handbook of Training Management*, 2nd Ed., Kogan Page, London.

Robson, C. (1993), *Real World Research: A Resource for Social Scientists and Practitioner-Researchers*, Blackwell, Oxford.

Root, M. (1998), *Philosophy of Social Science*, 4th Ed., Blackwell, Oxford.

Rosa, P., Scott, M.G. and Klandt, H. (1996), *Educating Entrepreneurs in Modernizing Economies*, Sterling Management Series, Aldershot and Brookfield, Avebury.

Rosow, J. M. and Zager, R. (1988), *Training: The Competitive Edge*, Jossey-Bass, San Francisco, USA.

Rosti J. R. and Shipper, F. (1998), 'A Study of the Impact of Training in a Management Development Program Based in 360 Feedback', *Journal of Managerial Psychology*, Vol. 31, No. 1/2, pp. 77- 89.

Rowntree, D. (1989), *The Manager's Book of Checklists: A Practical Guide to Improving Managerial Skills*, Gower, Aldershot.

Roy, D. A. (1977), 'Management Education and Training in the Arab World: A Review of Issues and Problems', *International Review of Administrative Sciences*, Vol. 43, No. 3, pp. 221-228.

Roy, S. (1995), *The Gaza Strip: The Political Economy De-development*, Institute for Palestine Studies, Washington.

Rummel, R. J. (1970), *Applied Factor Analysis*, North-western University Press, Evanston, Illinois.

Saari, L., Johnson, D., Mclaughlin, S. and Zimerle, D. (1988), 'A Survey of Management Training and Education Practices in U.S.A Companies', *Personnel Psychology*, Vol. 41, pp. 731-743.

Sadler, P. G., Kaz, U. and Jaber, H. (1984), *Survey of Manufacturing Industry in the West Bank and Gaza Strip*, UNIDO, 29 June, Palestine.

Safi, M. (1997), *Summary about the SMET Programme*, UNRWA, Department of Development and Planning, Gaza, Palestine.

Safi, M. (1998), *Developing Entrepreneurs in the Gaza Strip: Utilising Multidisciplinary Approaches to Strengthen Training for Business Start-up in the Gaza Strip*, MSc. Dissertation, Durham University, UK.

Saiyadain, M. S. and Ali, J. A. (1995), *Managerial Training and Development in Malaysia*, Malaysian Institute of Management, Kuala Lumpur, Malaysia.

Salman, H. (1997), *Woman Entrepreneurs: Microfinance and other initiatives for small-scale businesses in Palestine*, Conference on Arab Management, University of Bradford, Management Centre, UK.

Sapsford, R. and Jupp, V. (1996), *Data Collection and Analysis*, Open University, Sage, London.

Saunders, M., Lewis, P. and Thornhill, A. (2003), *Research Methods for Business Students*, 3rd Ed., Pearson Education, England.

Schamp, T. and Deschoolmeester, D. (1998), 'Strategic and Operational Planning Behaviour and the Survival and Growth Rate of Business Start-Ups: Management Training Matters', *International Journal of Entrepreneurial Behaviour and Research*, Vol. 4, No. 2, pp. 141-177.

Schein, E. H. (1994), *Organsational Culture and Leadership*, Jossey-Bass, San Francisco.

Schein, E. H. (1988), 'Management Education: Some Troublesome Realities and Possible Remedies', *Journal of Management Development*, Vol. 7, No. 2, pp. 5-15.

Scherer, W. T. (1978), 'How to Get Management's Commitment for Training', *Annual Review of Psychology*, Vol. 29, pp. 123-157.

Schermerhorm, J. R. (1984), *Management for Productivity*, John Wiley, New York.

Schmitz, H. (1995), 'Collective Efficiency: Growth Path for Small Scale Industry', *Journal of Development Studies*, Vol. 31, No. 4, pp. 529-566.

Schriesheim, C. A. and Kerr, S. (1977), 'Theories and Measurement of Leadership: A Critical Appraisal of Present and Future Directions', in Hunt, J. G. and Larson, L. L. (eds), *Leadership: The Cutting Edge*, Southern Illinois University Press, Carbondale, Illinois.

Sekaran, U. (1992), *Research Methods for Business: A Skill-Building Approach*, John Wiley, New York.

Sellitz, C. (1959), *Research Methods in the Social Relations*, Holt, NewYork.

Shaban, O. (1998), 'The Non-Success Reasons for the Training Programmes in Palestine', *Journal of Al-yyam*, Vol. 4, No. 1, pp. 14-18, Palestine.

Shaban, O. (1999), 'The SMET Programme Activities from 1995', *Journal of Al-yyam*, 9th June, Ramallah, Palestine.

Shaded, G. (1989), 'Israeli Policy for Development', in Gorge, E. (ed.), *The West Bank and the Gaza Strip: Development Challenges Under the Occupation*, Arab Unity Research Centre, Palestine.

Shaikh, F. (1988), *Management Leadership Style in the Private Sector in Jordan*, Ph.D. Thesis, University of Glasgow, Scotland.

Shath, A. (1998), 'Interview with Dr. Ali Shath', *Alrsala* newspaper, Gaza Strip, Palestine.

Sheldon, O. (1965), *The Philosophy of Management*, Pitman, London.

Simmons, D. (1975), 'The Case Method in Management Training', in Taylor, B. and Lippit, G. (eds), *Management Development and Training Handbook*, McGraw-Hill, London, UK.

Sinclair, J. and Collins, D. (1992), 'Viewpoint: Training and Development's Worst Enemies – You and Management', *Journal of European Industrial Training*, Vol. 16, No. 5, pp. 21-25.

Snell, S. A. and Wexley, K. N. (1985), 'Performance Diagnosis: Identifying the Causes of Poor Performance', *Personnel Administrator*, Vol. 30, No. 4, pp. 117-127.

Solomon, G. T. (1982), *The Relationship of Selected Characteristics of Small Business Owner-Managers to Their Businesses Probability of Success*, Ph.D. Thesis, School of Government and Business Administration, George Washington University, USA.

Spector, B. (1978), *The Economic Implication of a Middle East Peace Settlement: An Economic Development Model for the West Bank and Gaza Strip*, CACI-USAID, Washington.

Steers, R. (1977), *Organisational Effectiveness: A Behavioural View*, Goodyear, Santa Monica, California, USA.

Stephen, E., Mills, G.E., Pace, R.W. and Ralphs, L. (1988), 'Human Resource Development in the Fortune 500', *Training and Development Journal*, January, pp. 26-32.

Stewart, R. (1963), *The Reality of Management*, Heinemann, London.

Stewart, R. (1967), *Managers and their Jobs: A Study of the Similarities and Differences in the Way Managers Spend Their Time*, Macmillan, London.

Stewart, R. (1976), *Contrasts in Management*, McGraw-Hill, London.

Stogdill, R. M. and Coons, A. E. (1957), *Leader Behavior: Its Description and Measurement*, Bureau of Business Research, Ohio State University, Columbus.

Stoner, J., Freeman, R. and Gilbert, D. (1995), *Management*, 5th Ed., Prentice-Hall, USA and Canada.

Storey, D. J. (1986), *Enterpreneurship and the New Firm in the Survival of the Small Firm*, Gower, London.

Storey, D. J. (1994), *Understanding the Small Business Sector*, Routledge, London.

Sudman, S. (1976), *Applied Sampling*, Academic Press, New York.

Szilagyi, J. (1981), *Management and Performance*, Goodyear, UK.

Taha, H. (1994), *A Working Paper for the Food Industry in Palestine*, Office of President-Planning Centre, Gaza, Palestine.

Taylor, B. (1989), 'Training', in Molander, C. (ed.), *Human Resource Management*, Chartwell-Bratt, Bromley, Kent.

Taylor, B. and Lippit, G. (1975), *Management Development and Training Handbook*, McGraw-Hill, London, UK.

Taylor, N. (1966), *Selecting and Training the Training Officer*, I.P.M.

Temporal, P. (1990), 'Linking Management Development to the Corporate Future: The Role of the Professional', *Journal of Management Development*, Vol. 9, No. 5, pp. 7-15.

Thines, G. (1977), *Phenomenology and the Science of Behaviour: An Historical and Epistemological Approach*, George Allen and Unwin, London.

Thompson, N. (2002), *People Skills*, 2nd Ed., Palgrave Macmillan, New York.

Thornton, G. C. and Byham, W. C. (1982), *Assessment Centres and Managerial Performance*, Academic Press, New York.

Timmons, J. (1994), *New Venture Creation*, 4th Ed., Irwin, New York.

Torgal, V. (1998), *Rural Development Administration: A Sub-State Level Study*, Spellbound, Rohtak.

Trueloves, S. (1997), *Training in Practice*, Blackwell, Oxford.

UN (United Nations) (1996), *Private Sector – Putting Peace to Work*, United Nations, Gaza, Palestine.

UN (1998), *The UN and the Palestinian Development Plan*, Office of the Special Co-ordinator in the Occupied Territories, Gaza, Palestine.

UN (1997), *Economic and Social Conditions in the West Bank and Gaza Strip*, Office of the Special Co-ordinator in the Occupied Territories, Quarterly Report, April, Gaza, Palestine.

UN (1998-1999), *Program of Co-operation for the West Bank and the Gaza Strip*, Office of the Special Co-ordinator in the Occupied Territories, Gaza, Palestine.

UNIDO (1997), *UNIDO Support Programme to the Palestinian Industry (1998-1999)*, Programme framework, Unpublished, DRC, Gaza, Palestine.

UNRWA (1998), *Information about the International and Local Lending and Training Organisation in the Gaza Strip*, SMET Programme, Gaza, Palestine.

UNRWA (1998), *Project Proposal, Small and Micro-Enterprise Training*, Department of Development and Planning, Gaza, Palestine.

Urwick, L. F. (1952), *Notes on the Theory of Organizations*, American Management Association, New York.

Usis-Israel Organisation (1999), *The Occupied Territories,* [Online] http://www.usis-israel.org.il/publish/prcss/statc/archve/march/sd6_3-19.htm [Accessed 21-12-1999].

Van Clouse, G. H. (1990), 'A Controlled Experiment Relating Entrepreneurial Education to Students' Start-up Decisions', *Journal of Small Business Management*, Vol. 28, No. 2, pp. 45-53.

Van Dijk, Meine, P. and Rabellotti, R. (1997), *Enterprise Clusters and Networks in Developing Countries*, EADI Book Series 20, Frank Cass, London.

Vineall, T. (1994), 'Planning for Management Development', in Mumford, A. (ed.), *Handbook of Management Development*, 4th Ed., Gower, Hunts, and Vermont.

Vinterhav, E. (2000), *Industry in Palestine*, [Online] http://www.demesta.com [Accessed 05-06-2000].

Walker, J. and Guest, R. H. (1952), *The Man on the Assembly Line*, Harvard University Press, Cambridge.

Wall, R.G. (1963), 'Untangling the Snarls in Job Rotation Programme', *Personnel*, No. 42, pp. 59-65.

Warner, M. (1992), *How Chinese Managers Learn*, Macmillan, London.

Warr, P B., Bird, M. and Rackham, N. (1970), *Evaluation of Management Training*, Gower, Aldershot.

Warren, M. W. (1969), *Training for Results: A System Approach to the Development of Human Resources in Industry*, Addison-Wesley, Reading, Massachusetts.

WATC (2000), *The Training Programme*, [Online] http:// www.pal.watc.org [Accessed 04-02-2000].

Water, W. (1980), 'Managerial Skills Development', *Academy of Management Review*, Vol. 5, No. 3, pp. 449-453.

Water, W. (1993), *Total Quality Management Training*, MBA Dissertation, Management Centre, University of Bradford, UK.

Water, W., Adler, N. J, Poupart, R. and Hartwick, J. (1983), 'Assessing Managerial Skills through a Behavioural Exam', *Organisational Behavioural Teaching Journal*, Vol. 8, No. 2, pp. 37-44.

Wexley, K. N. and Latham, G. P. (1991), *Development and Training Human Resources in Organisation*, 2nd Ed., Harper Collins, New York.

Wexley, K. N. and Yukl, G. A. (1977), *Organisational Behaviour and Psychology*, 2nd Ed., Richard Irwin, Homewood.

Whetten, D. A. and Cameron, K. S. (1980), *An Assessment of Salient Management Skills*, Working Paper, University of Wisconsin, School of Business.

Whetten, D. A. and Cameron, K. S. (1995), *Developing Management Skills*, 3rd Ed., Harper Collins, New York.

Whyte, W. F. (1948), *Human Relationship in Restaurant Industry*, McGraw-Hill, New York.

Willcocks, S. G. (1998), 'Managerial Effectiveness in an NHS Hospital Trust', *International Journal of Public Sector Management*, Vol. 11, No. 2/3, pp. 130-138.

Wilson, C. L. and Shipper, F. (1992), *Task Cycle Management: A Competency-Based Course for Operating Managers*, Clark Wilson Group, Silver Spring, Maryland.

Wilson, J. (1999), *Human Resource Development*, Kogan Page, London.

Women's Affairs Center (2000), *Small Business Programme* (Report from Women's Affairs Center to Researcher, in Arabic), Gaza Strip, Palestine.

Woodall, J. and Winstanley, D. (1998), *Management Development Strategy and Practice*, Blackwell, Oxford, Massachusetts.

World Bank (1993), *Developing the Occupied Territories: An Investment in Peace*, Human Resources and Social Policy, The World Bank, Washington.

World Bank (1998), *West Bank and Gaza Update*, A Quarterly Publication of the West Bank and Gaza Resident Mission, Second Quarter.

World Bank and MAS (1997), *Development over Difficulties*, The Palestinian Economic Institution, Ramallah, Palestine.

World Bank Group (1998), *West Bank and Gaza Update*, A Quarterly Publication of the West Bank and Gaza, Resident Mission, Second Quarter, World Bank, Palestine.

Worth, R. (1998), *Organisation Skills*, Ferguson, USA.

Wusten, H. (1993), 'Political Geography for War and Peace in PT', in Taylor (ed.), *Political Geography of the Twentieth Century*, Belhaven Press, London.

Yaghy, A. (1996), 'The Needs for the Palestinian Development', *AlNahar Journal*, 11th April, Palestine.

Young, P. V. (1966), *Scientific Social Surveys and Research*, 4th Ed., Prentice Hall, USA.

Yukl, G. (2002), *Leadership in Organisations*, 5th Ed., Prentice Hall, USA.

Zahlan, A. (1997), 'The Institutional Fabric of Urban Development', in Zahlan, A. (ed.), *Reconstruction of Palestine: Urban and Rural Development*, Kegan Paul, London.

Zeisel, J. (1997), *Inquiry by Design: Tools for Environment-Behaviour Research*, Cambridge University Press, Cambridge.

Zikmund, W. G. (1997), *Business Research Methods*, 5th Ed., The Dryden Press, Orlando.

Index

technical 40, 42, 43–4, 99, 147
trainers 48, 160
training 13, 32–3, 34, 38–45, 51, 53, 148
women 77–8
Skinner, W. 31
small and micro enterprises (SMEs)
  contribution to development 2–4
  definitions of 1–2
  effectiveness 7–9
  establishment year 92–3, 151
  finance 98
  firm sectors 93–4, 151, 158
  investment 96–7, 116, 117–18, 151
  lending to 56–9, 71–4
  location of 91–2, 151, 158
  management training and development 59–61, 74–8
  management training programmes 67, 78–83, 91–104, 105, 129–44, 145–71
  managerial skills 107–27, 152–4
  managerial weaknesses 4–5, 67, 132–3, 137–44, 150, 155, 161
  Middle East 55–66
  nature of business 97–8
  obstacles and weaknesses facing training 129–44, 155
  ownership type 94–5
  profit 95–6, 116, 119, 151
  success of 95, 103, 116, 118, 141, 143
SMET Programme 80–1, 92, 96–7, 98, 100–1, 151–2
Steers, R. 28–9
Stewart, R. 25, 44
Stoner, J. 7, 15, 16, 17
strategic planning 38, 41, 154
stress 111, 112, 121–2
subcontracting 97–8
supervision 89–91
sustainable development 69, 81
SWOT analysis 76, 77
systems approach 14, 49–53, 156–7
Szilagyi, J. 18

Taylor, D. 60, 65
team work 112, 113, 123
Temporal, P. 46–7

time management 111, 112, 115–16, 118, 121–2, 154
TNA *see* training needs assessment
top management
  management development 27, 47, 157
  managerial hierarchy 19
  managerial skills 39, 40, 41, 42, 43, 44, 45
  roles 22–4
  training and development 32, 47–8, 53, 66
trainers 48–9, 55–6, 62, 70
  development of 37, 159–60
  SMET Programme 80
  weaknesses 130, 132–4, 135–7, 138–44, 155, 159
training 5–7, 9, 13, 31–7
  aims of 33–5
  Arab countries 59–66, 74
  definitions of 32–3
  evaluation of 51–3, 157, 163, 170
  future research 171
  lending programmes 57–8, 72–3, 80
  methods 35–7, 102, 160
  models of skills training 38–45
  obstacles and weaknesses 129–44, 150, 155
  on-the-job 6, 32, 35, 36, 99, 158
  skill-based education 26
  SMEs in Palestine 55–6, 67, 70, 74–83, 91–104, 105, 147–9
  systems approach 49–53
  transfer of 111, 112, 121–2, 171
  see also management training; management training and development; management training programmes
training needs assessment (TNA) 49, 59, 156, 167
Training Services Agency 28
transfer of training 111, 112, 121–2, 171
trust 163

United Nations (UN) 37, 100
United Nations Relief and Work Agency (UNRWA) 67, 68, 75, 104, 147, 150
  lending programmes 56, 57, 71, 73
  training programmes 80, 92, 94–5, 97, 101

For Product Safety Concerns and Information please contact our
EU representative GPSR@taylorandfrancis.com Taylor & Francis
Verlag GmbH, Kaufingerstraße 24, 80331 München, Germany